NAUM GABO

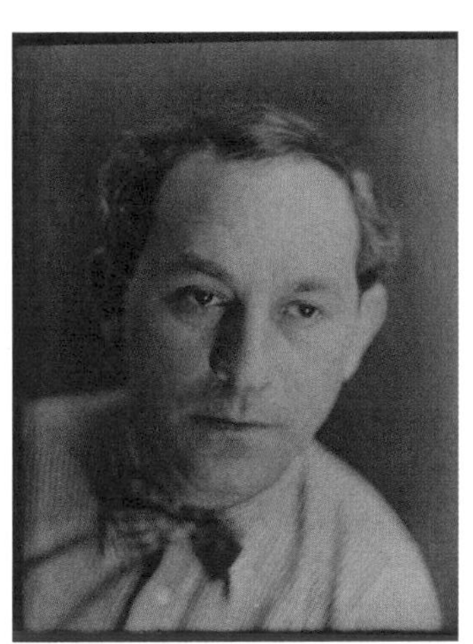

Photograph of Gabo in his studio with
Torsion: Project for a Fountain 1970–3

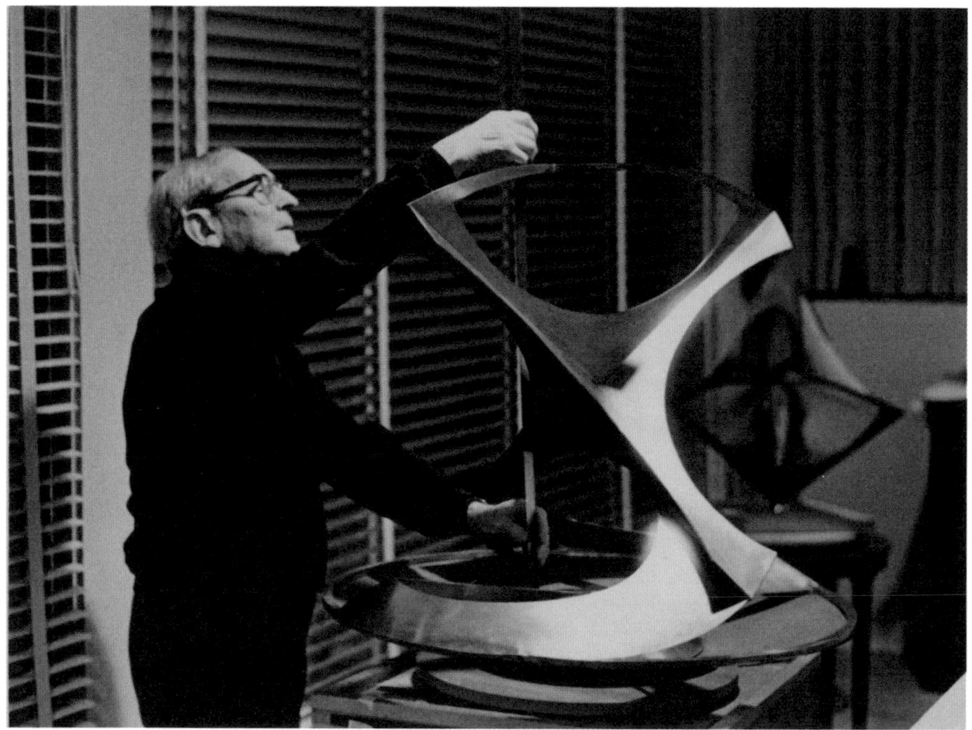

Natalia Sidlina

NAUM GABO

Translated by Sarah Cabrol-Douat and Natalia Sidlina

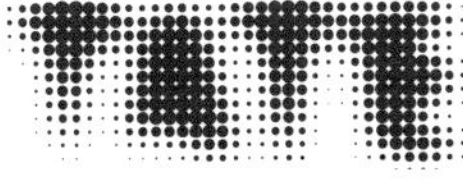

First published in Russian by Sergei Gordeev's
Publishing Project 'Russian Avant-Garde',
© S. Gordeev and ABCdesign 2011

First published in English 2012 by order
of the Tate Trustees
by Tate Publishing, a division
of Tate Enterprises Ltd,
Millbank, London SW1P 4RG
www.tate.org.uk/publishing

English language edition © Tate 2012
Reprinted 2020

A catalogue record for this book is available
from the British Library

ISBN 978 1 84976 066 9

Distributed in the United States and Canada
by ABRAMS, New York

Library of Congress Control Number:
2012931250

Designed by ABCdesign
Page layout of this edition by Maria Spann
Colour reproduction by Evergreen, China
Printed in UK by Cambrian Printers

Cover: (left to right, top to bottom) details of
works illustrated on (front) pp.127, 49, 62,
87, 59, 150, 157, 188; (back) pp.37, 154,
129, 175, 54, 167

Measurements of artworks are given in
centimetres, height before width and depth

ACKNOWLEDGEMENTS

I would like to express my gratitude to Naum Gabo's daughter Nina Williams and his son-in-law Graham Williams for their unfailing encouragement and support. Without their generosity and that of David Juda of Annely Juda Fine Art and Valery Novikov of Clear Gallery this publication would not have become a reality. I would like to thank Christina Lodder and Martin Hammer for the inspiring quality of their highly detailed and extensive publications on the art and career of Gabo, and Professor Lodder in particular for her valuable advice and help in preparing this book for publication. I am grateful to Sarah Cabrol-Douat and Professor Donald Rayfield for their part in translating and editing the text, to Adrian Glew and his colleagues at the Tate Library and Archive, to Liubov Pchelkina at the State Tretyakov Gallery, and to my family for all their help and support.

INTRODUCTION

Naum Gabo (1890–1977) is considered to be one of the most inventive figures in the history of the Russian avant-garde. Born on the border of Russian and Belarusian lands of the Russian Empire, he spent his life roaming the world, from Munich to Oslo, Moscow to Berlin, Paris to London, and finally settling in the New World. Gabo became renowned internationally as one of the leading figures of Russian constructivism and his works are held in the collections of the world's most respected museums. Yet he is all but unknown to his compatriots; specialists in his homeland have regarded him as a leader of Western geometric abstraction in sculpture. Hardly any of his works remain in Russian state or private collections; his personal archive was taken to Europe and the USA in the 1920s and 1960s. It is now housed in London's Tate, the Beinecke Library of Yale University, and in the Berlinische Galerie.[1] ■ Gabo's life and work has been researched thoroughly by leading British scholars Christina Lodder and Martin Hammer, who published the first detailed study, *Constructing Modernity: The Art and Career of Naum Gabo*, in 2000.[2] My present text has been influenced strongly by their pioneering monograph, as well as by the various catalogues published in connection with exhibitions organised by the former director of the Berlinische Galerie, Dr Jörn Merkert.[3] I have also been able to

[1] TGA784, TGA798, TGA7711, TGA801, TGA8117, TGA9313, TGA9314, TGA200734, Tate Archive, London; Naum Gabo Papers, Yale Collection of American Literature, Beinecke Rare Book and Manuscript Library, Yale University, Yale, CT; BG-Ar 3/97, Künstler-Archive, Berlinische Galerie, Berlin.

[2] *Constructing Modernity* 2000.

[3] Jörn Merkert (ed.), *Naum Gabo: Ein russischer Konstruktivist in Berlin 1922–1932*, exh. cat., Berlinische Galerie, Berlin 1989.

Self-Portrait 1912
Oil on canvas, 56 x 47.5

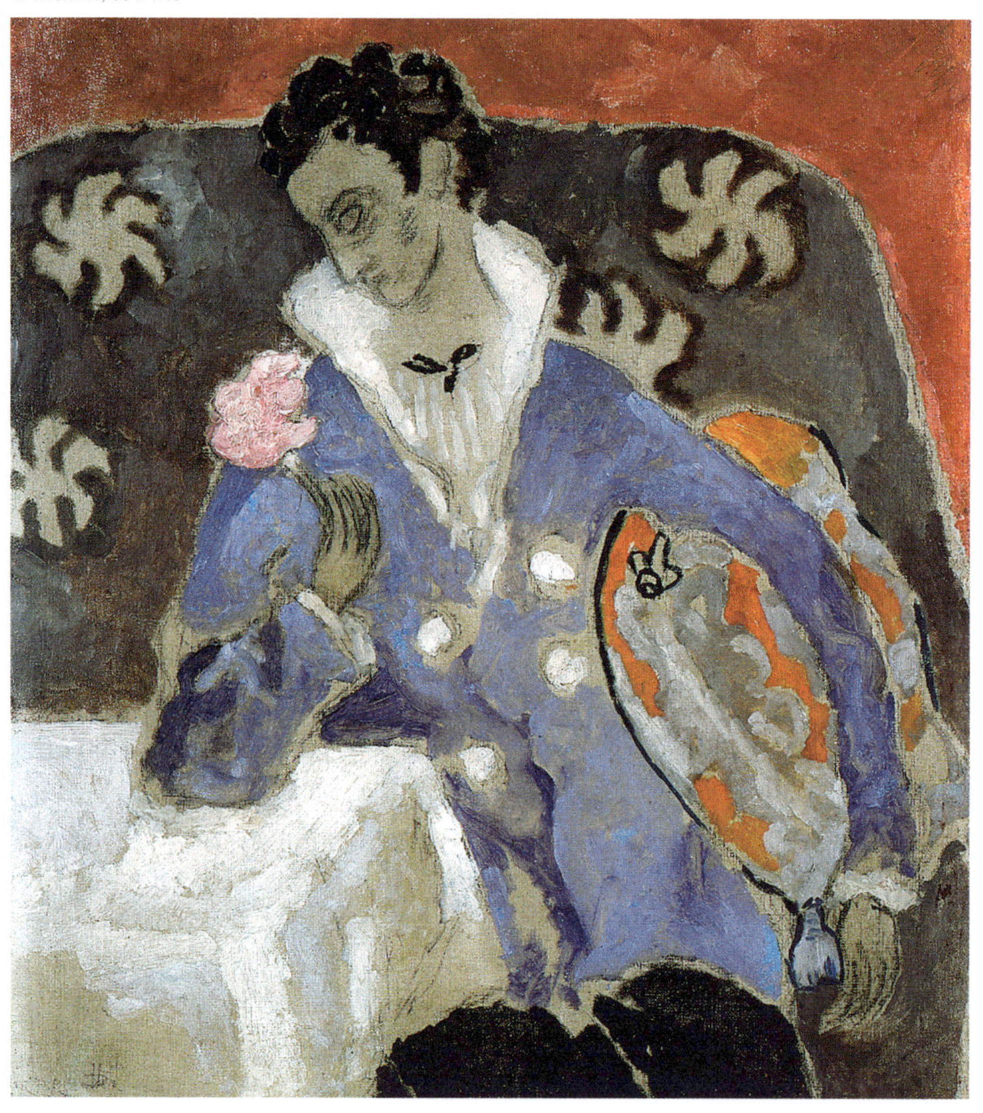

study at first hand the material from Gabo's archive (manuscripts, drawings and models), which is now at Tate and from 2007 to 2010 was the subject of an extensive programme of cataloguing and research. Despite this, Gabo's life is still shrouded in mystery. Like many modernist artists of his generation, Gabo deliberately mystified certain aspects of his life and work. His whole biography is steeped in uncertainty – the precise place and date of his birth, the exact circumstances behind the creation of his first sculptures and the location of a number of his works. Having lived most of his life on the other side of the 'Iron Curtain', Gabo actively built up a reputation as a pioneer of Russian constructivism, presenting European and American experts with his own views on the onset and development of the Russian avant-garde. Gabo also showed himself to have sharp analytical skills, being one of the first interpreters of Russian abstract art to value the impact of Mikhail Vrubel's oeuvre and of the sacral art of icon painting on the younger generation of artist-innovators in early twentieth-century Russia.[4] ■ Gabo created fewer than a hundred distinctive sculptural forms in the sixty years of his artistic career.[5] Many of his constructions exist in several versions; others are unique. He tended to work in series, creating a number of works to explore the formal language and expressive means of a particular shape or method of creation. Such an approach explains Gabo's particular system of dating his works. It was not the process of construction of the actual sculpture but the mental image that he considered to be the genesis of the work. A sculpture was dated not by the year of its physical realisation but according to when its

[4] Naum Gabo, 'The Concepts of Russian Art', *World Review*, London, June 1942, pp.48–53.

[5] Catalogue Raisonné 1985, pp.193–272.

form had crystallised in Gabo's mind. He always strove to find the materials that most suited the forms brought into being by his unique spatial imagination. ■ Within a broadly chronological framework, this book looks at Gabo's artistic career in terms of his development of new methods of making sculpture, demonstrated in a series of works that he called 'themes'. The initial research was conducted for the earlier Russian edition of this monograph, published in the series 'Masters of the Russian Avant-Garde' (Sergei Gordeev Publishing Project, 2011). As the first comprehensive publication on Gabo's creative career in the Russian language, it aimed to acquaint a wide spectrum of Russian readers with Gabo's works, placing him among the other leading figures of the revolutionary artistic developments of the early twentieth century. Various resources were used in preparing this publication, but by far the most important materials, including original works of art, archival papers and objects, documents and illustrations, came from the Tate Collection, Library and Archive.

CHILDHOOD AND STUDENT YEARS (1890–1914)

Two talented artists were born to the family of Abraham Boris Pevsner and Fanny Ozersky – the painter and sculptor Natan, later known as Antoine, and Naum Nehemia Pevsner, who later made his name as Naum Gabo.[6] When in 1915 he chose to pursue an artistic career, Naum Pevsner adopted the pseudonym Naum Gabo so as to avoid confusion with his brother. Alexei Pevsner, the artists' younger brother, believed that Gabo chose this pseudonym for its ancient Hebrew meaning of 'future', although this assumption has proven to be incorrect.[7] At home, Naum was called Nekhem; he and Natan used nicknames for one another – 'Ibragim' for Naum and 'Taras' for Natan. ■ The precise date and place of the sculptor's birth are unknown. Gabo's parents registered their fourth son as born on 5 August 1890 according to the old Julian calendar, which corresponds to 17 August 1890 of our modern Gregorian calendar. It is highly likely that this information was incorrect and that his year of birth was altered on registration in order to avoid military conscription in the future.[8] Such a practice was often employed by Jewish families in the Russian Empire; Marc Chagall, for instance, never knew the precise date of his birth.[9] The majority of biographies state the

6 For information on Gabo's and Pevsner's names see *Constructing Modernity* 2000, pp.11–12 and J.-C. Marcadé, *Pevsner (1884–1962): Colloque international Antoine Pevsner tenu au Musée Rodin en décembre 1992*, Art Édition et Les Amis d'Antoine Pevsner, Paris 1995, pp.243–56.

7 A.B. Pevsner, *Doroga po obochine …*, MP 'Izmailovo', Moscow 1992, p.32.

8 *Constructing Modernity* 2000, p.12.

9 Bella Chagall, *Lumières allumées*, Gallimard, Paris 1973, p.253.

town of Bryansk as the sculptor's birthplace, although Gabo himself gave the town of Klimovichi in the district of Mogilev (in Belarus) as his native town, as did his elder brother Antoine. ■ Gabo grew up in a large, wealthy Jewish family who settled in Bryansk when Naum was about seven years old. The Pevsner family home was situated in the so-called Railway Station suburb, which built up around the new Bryansk–Orlovsky hub station on the Riga–Oriol Railway. The suburb was a borough of Bryansk, situated several miles from the city centre. 'On the left bank of river Desna at Bryansk's Railway Station suburb my father established a special metal works producing low-friction alloys. It supplied the railways throughout Russia with Babbitt alloy.'[10] ■ The Oriol District Statistic Committee ledgers for 1897 show no evidence that such a business or factory existed. The 1906 map of Bryansk showing the Railway Station suburb is similarly devoid of any such metal works. It is possible that the family business, run by Boris and his elder sons Mark and Eremei, was contracted to the Rail-Rolling and Ironworks Factory of the Maltsov Corporation, the largest business in the region at the time. ■ The Pevsner family was quite liberal in its religious practice and beliefs: 'My father was a non-practising Jew. He did not believe in the Talmud but only in God. He told me of God, The One of all religions.'[11] The children were brought up by a Russian nanny called Praskovia. She hung Orthodox icons on the nursery walls, so Gabo was familiar with the ritual art of icon painting from a very early age. As a teenager, he often visited the nearby Belye Berega (White Banks) monastery. In Alexei's biographical essay on his brothers, he refers to certain members

10 Naum Gabo, *Kak ya stal revolutsionerom, kniga 2*, [1970s], p.3, TGA.

11 Naum Gabo, *Pro Mayakovskogo na oborote*, p.23, TGA.

Antoine Pevsner 1884–1962
Portrait of Mother 1911
Oil on canvas, 38 x 36 (oval)

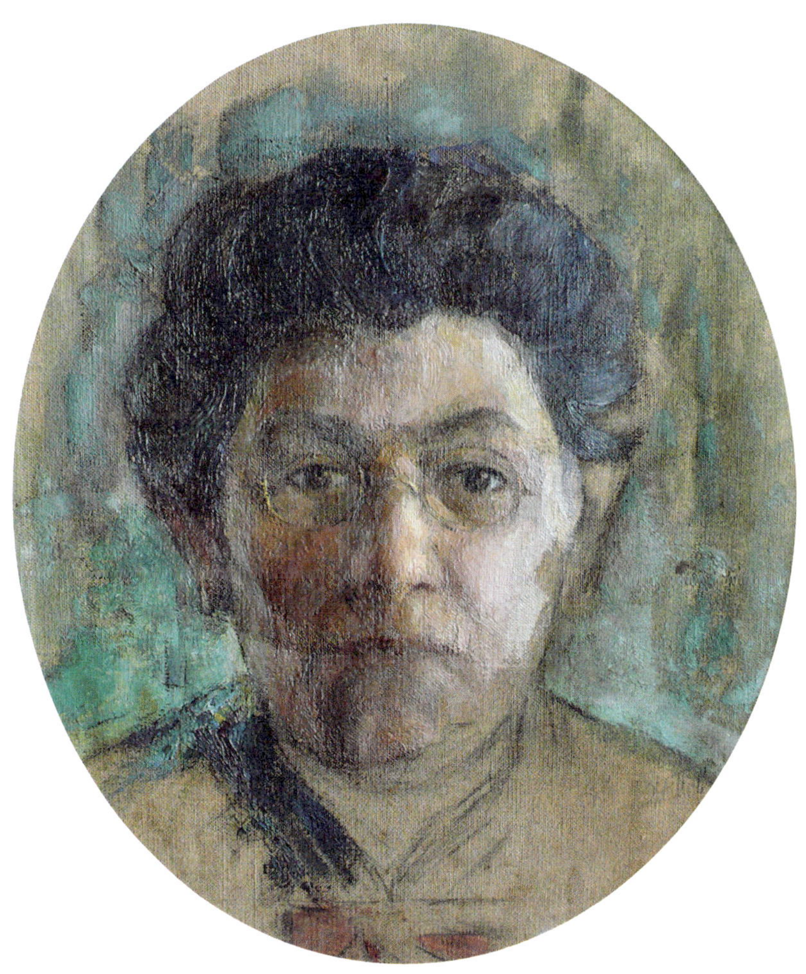

$\rightarrow$

View of Railway Station suburb, town
of Bryansk, 1900s
Postcard

Photograph of Boris Pevsner, c.1912

Map of town of Bryansk with Railway Station
suburb, 1906 (detail)

Photograph of Naum Gabo aged about
fourteen, c.1905

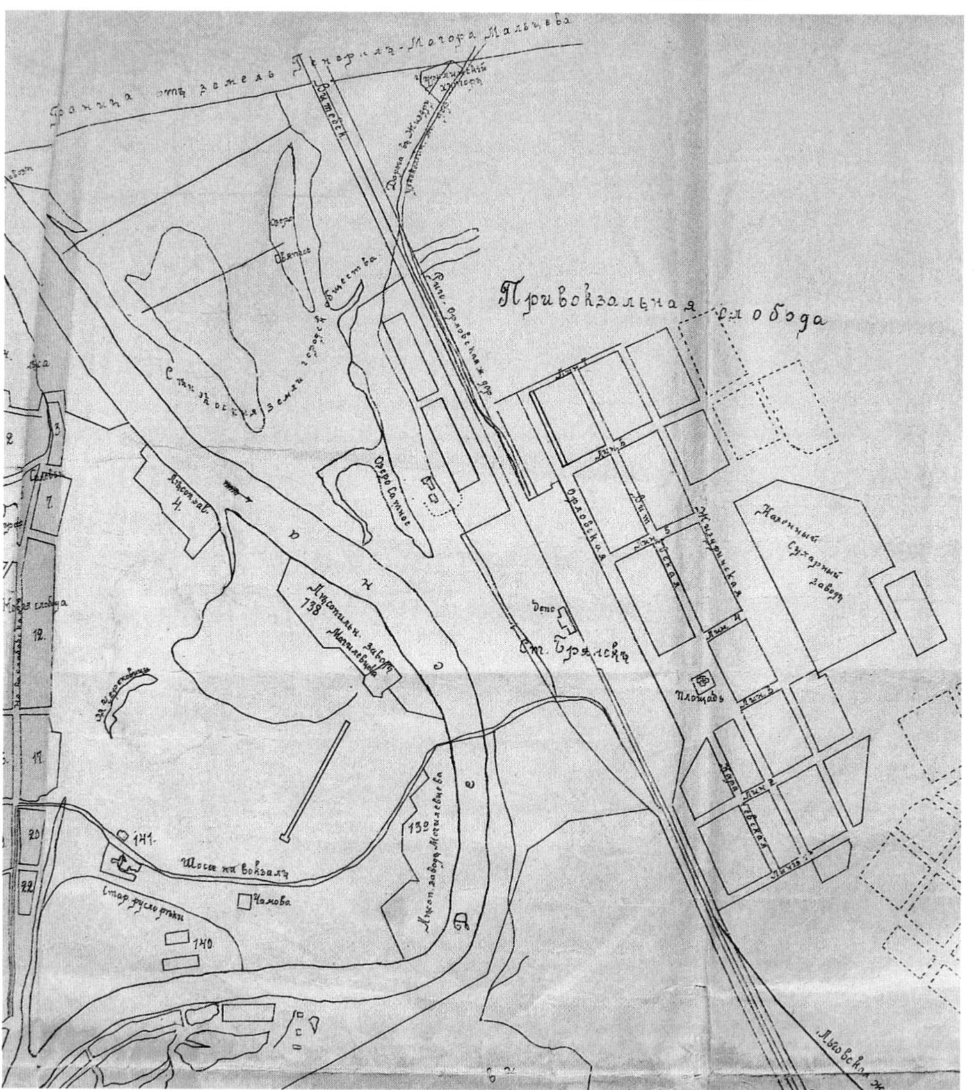

№ 27. г. Брянскъ. Видъ на привокзальную слободу съ моста.

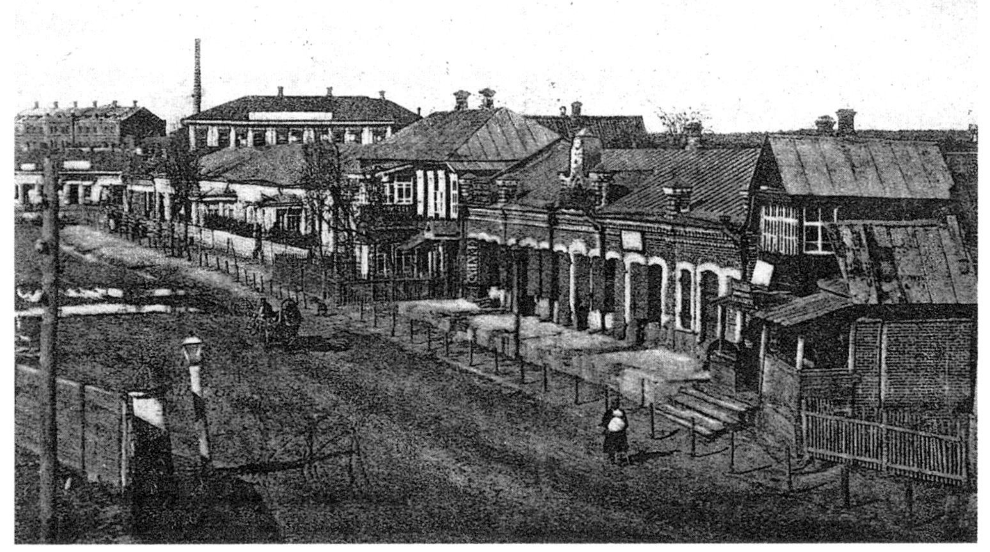

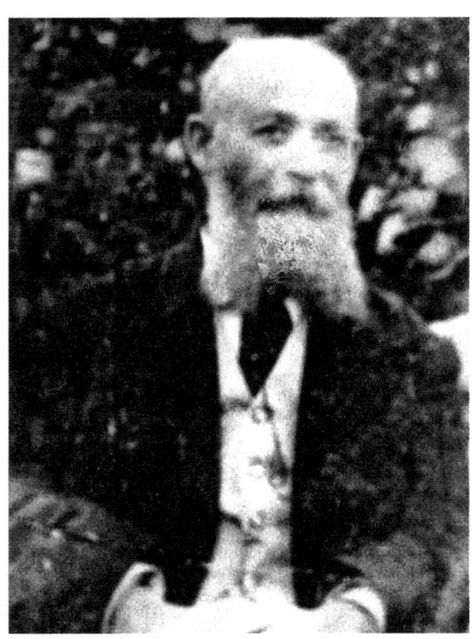

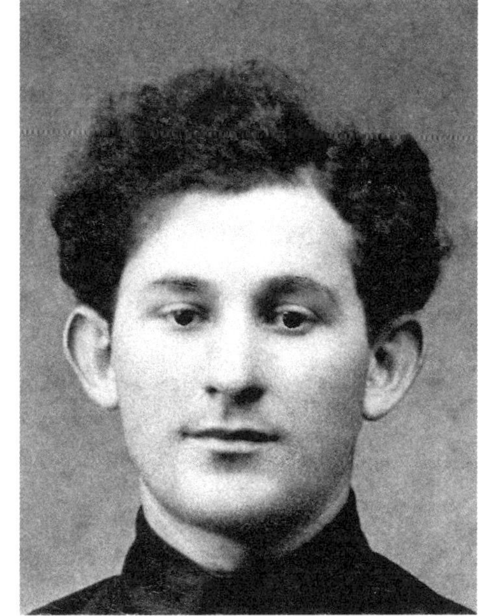

of the family being religious,[12] and Gabo himself as a high school student in Kursk went through a 'year of religious searching' and became interested in Orthodox Christianity. ■ Gabo professed, 'Art was something which always played a great role in my life – I never lived without it.'[13] His brother Antoine was the first in the family to choose to be an artist. Gabo remembered Antoine bringing a friend from the Kiev Art School home for the summer holidays. The students took Naum along for their studies *en plein air*. Gabo also took up drawing, although he considered 'drawing something which is visible cannot be so difficult, but trying to convey an unseen image from one's head is what is really challenging'.[14] Through Antoine, Gabo became acquainted with the paintings of Mikhail Vrubel, which deeply moved him. In Gabo's publications of later years, he maintained that Vrubel's influence on the development of visual perception of artists of Gabo's generation was no less significant than that of Paul Cézanne.[15] ■ In 1904, after Naum was expelled from the Bryansk school for a disrespectful poem, his elder brother Mark took him to Tomsk, 3,700 km away from home. The intention was to prepare Gabo for entry to a secondary school or a college while keeping him under the close supervision of Mark who was completing his studies in engineering there. Naum, who at the time considered himself a poet, spent his time writing verse. His tutors were university students who paid no heed to his indifference to study and who introduced him to the town's flourishing revolutionary activity. Throughout his life, Gabo was taken up with the 1905 and 1917 revolutions, their objectives, their outcome and their impact on art.

[12] *Biographical Sketch* 1964, p.31.

[13] Naum Gabo, *K portretam*, p.165, TGA.

[14] Ibid., p.167, TGA.

[15] *Of Divers Arts* 1962, p.155.

Photograph of Mark and Eremei Pevsner
on horseback, 1920–30

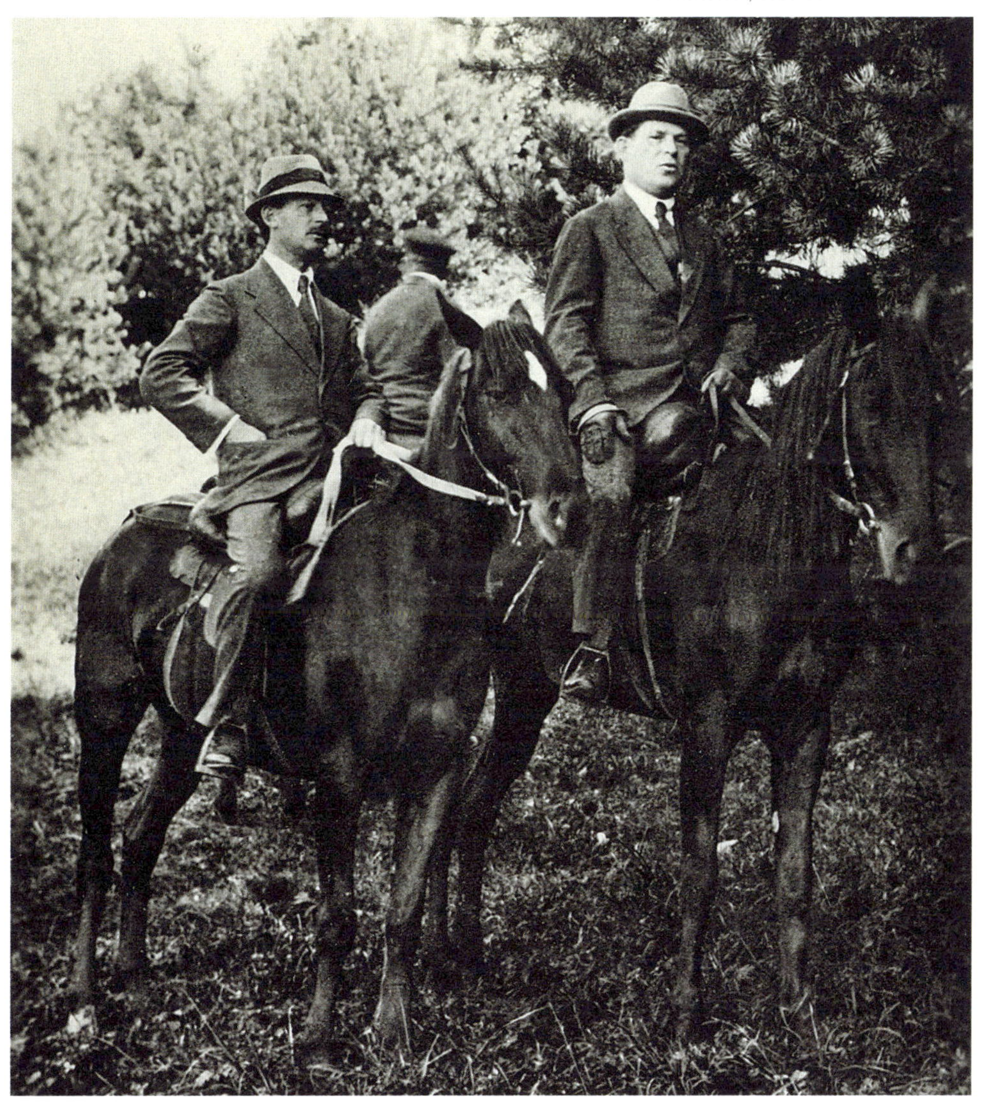

His autobiographical notes record the artist's personal involvement in the events of this turbulent period.[16] Gabo's verse is a spirited account of the ultra-nationalist Black Hundreds' bloody attack on a revolutionary meeting at the Tomsk theatre in 1905: ■ 'I recall everything, ■ My rage and my suppression. ■ The glow of the fire, ■ The cries of the dying on the Tomsk theatre roof. ■ The whooping of Cossacks and ■ The laughter of Black Hundreds. ■ I recall brightness of the church banners, ■ The bullets went through it. ■ I remember a deadly hail ■ Of a chattering machine gun ■ As it cut in half ■ A blue uniform body ■ Of a student, crucified against the wall.'[17] ■ When Gabo, who nearly perished himself during the attack, recovered from his state of shock, he was sent back home immediately and later enrolled at the gymnasium in the nearby town of Kursk. Many years later, Gabo revealed that he considered his art to belong to the kind of truly revolutionary activity to which he was initiated in the 1900s by members of the Bryansk and Tomsk youth underground movement. Gabo believed art could play a decisive role in society and he propagated the utopian idea of social improvement through the radical transformation of man's environment by art. He conceived the majority of his constructions as projects for monuments for the cities of the future. ■ His studies at the Kursk gymnasium were similarly ineffective in instilling in him the importance of scholarship. Gabo failed his 1909 spring exams: 'I then left Kursk, bypassing my parents' home in Bryansk to go to the Belye Berega monastery I had frequently visited in previous summers. As a result, I was obliged to leave Kursk and take my high school certificate the following

16 Naum Gabo, *Kak ya stal revolutsionerom*, TGA.

17 Naum Gabo, *K portretam*, p.90, TGA.

year as an external student'.[18] ■ 'When the [school] director asked "Where exactly do you intend to continue your education?" I, without hesitating or even thinking, so surprised was I by the question, replied: "I want to enrol in the architectural faculty of the Academy of Arts."'[19] Gabo surprised himself by giving such an answer, as at the time he saw his future as lying in poetry.

AT THE CROSSROADS, OR BETWEEN SCIENCE AND ART Gabo's student years were of great consequence in deciding his future as an artist. The choices that presented themselves to him at the time were three: to fulfil his mother's dream by becoming a doctor; to follow the family tradition and become an engineer like his father and two eldest brothers; or to fulfil his own ambition of becoming a poet. As we know, none of these paths came to fruition, but the training Gabo received in science was influential in his gaining the reputation of an artist-engineer, a scientific sculptor who calculated his constructions like mathematical formulas. ■ In the summer of 1910, at his parents' insistence, Naum entered Munich University, signing up for courses in the medical and natural sciences. After two years of trying to comply with his parents' wishes, he abandoned medicine, evidently having no inclination for the profession. In 1912, he was attending engineering courses at the Technische Hochschule. Gabo later wrote that he was greatly interested in physics and that he chose to study in Bavaria for the opportunity to attend the lectures of such renowned professors as Alfred Bauer and Wilhelm Röntgen. Gabo recalled with awe attending seminars in which students and professors discussed the ideas of Albert Einstein. ■ 'It was the epoch of

[18] Naum Gabo, *K portretam*, p.160, TGA.

[19] Naum Gabo, Undated notebook 9313/2/7/29, pp.1–2, TGA.

→

Photograph of Naum Gabo in front
of Munich University, c.1913

Photograph of Pevsner family picnic
in Russia, c.1910

revolutions and the real revolution in the [aftermath] of which we are still living, was started by artists and by scientists … Nobody believed that the Theory of Einstein, for instance, or an abstract painting could be true … People were shouting, people were offended, but their mentality was shaken, because without even wanting it, without knowing it, the work [of artists and scientists] made an impression on their minds.'[20] ■ From 1912–14, Gabo began to take courses in philosophy and was particularly interested in the teachings of Immanuel Kant. The sculptor himself admitted that philosophy was a 'sin' that he could not resist. Kant's influence on Gabo was such that, throughout his life, the sculptor expressed, expounded and promoted his aesthetic ideas through lectures, publications and other media. According to Kant's teachings, the talent of genius is manifested through 'aesthetic ideas'. The origination of such ideas gives art its significance on the scale of human values. These ideas are generated in a genius's imagination – an inborn mental predisposition of mind through which nature is mastered.[21] ■ During the same period, Gabo attended various lectures in art history. It was the impact made by the teachings of Professor Heinrich Wölfflin, who instigated a formal-comparative approach to aesthetic analysis, that sealed his fate. Following Wölfflin's advice, in June 1913 Gabo set off to explore Italy. His impressions after contemplating the masters of Renaissance art in their original surroundings were heightened by Wölfflin's teachings on the autonomous, self-contained qualities of art forms. Familiar with the most recent trends of European modernism, Gabo

[20] Post production script for *The New Masters, Programme 9: Naum Gabo – Construction in Space*, BBC2, broadcast on 8 August 1972, p.9, TGA.

[21] A.T. Winterbourne, 'Art and Mathematics in Kant's Critical philosophy', *British Journal of Aesthetics*, vol.28, no.3, 1988, pp.269, 277.

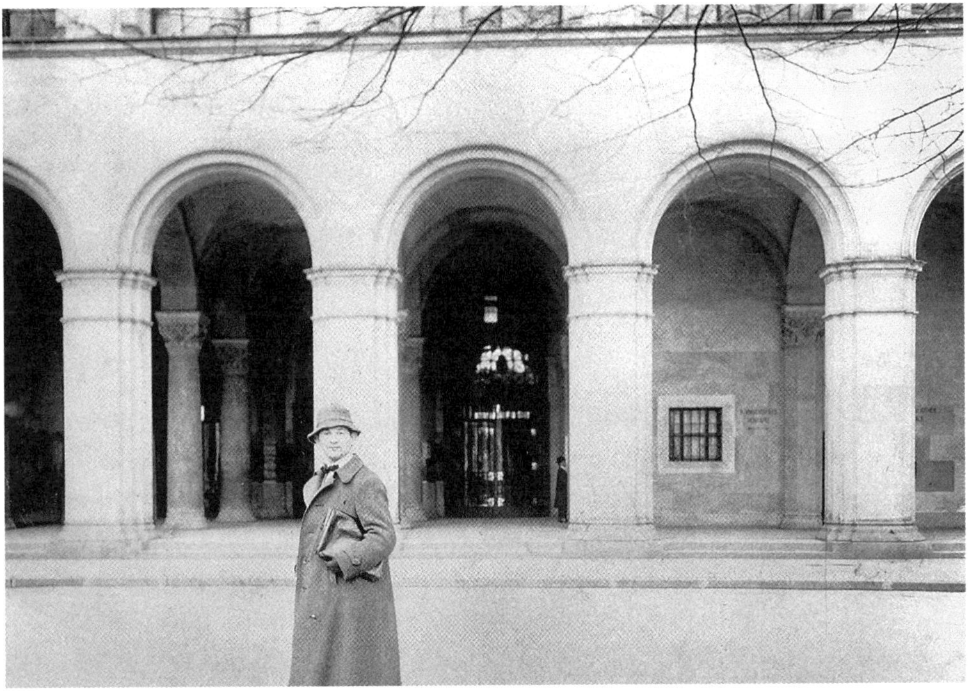

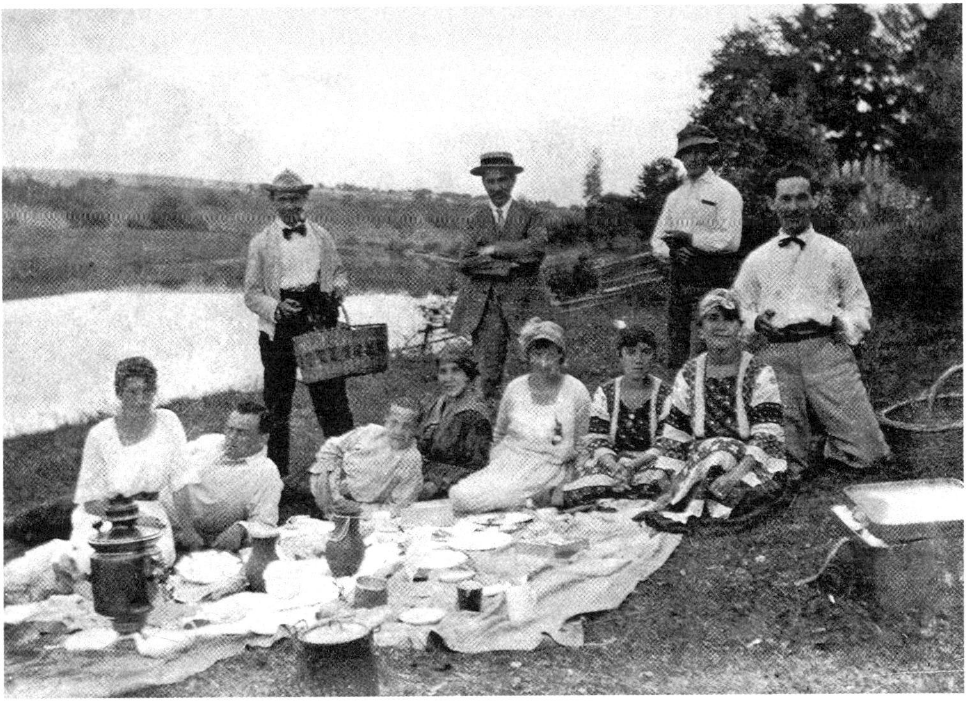

devoted himself to the idea of creating a new pictorial language that would correspond to the spirit of change at the turn of the century. In 1912–13, Gabo visited his elder brother Antoine in Paris. Having failed to enter the Imperial Academy of Art in St Petersburg, Antoine spent two years in Bryansk before deciding to pursue his artistic career in Europe, where the general attitude towards Jewish artists was far more congenial than in Russia. In September 1911, he had accompanied Gabo on his return to Munich from summer vacations in Bryansk and continued his journey west, settling in Paris.[22] He soon became involved with the vibrant circles of émigré artists, establishing close friendships with Alexander Archipenko and Amedeo Modigliani. His paintings of the time show a particular interest in fauve art and cubism. ■ Munich, where Gabo was to spend four years as a student, was considered the second art capital of Europe at the turn of the century and a city of 'philosophical art'. Here Gabo had wide opportunities to become acquainted both with the finest works of the Old Masters and the latest trends in contemporary art. Munich attracted Russian artists like Wassily Kandinsky and Alexej von Jawlensky, who studied drawing at the renowned Anton Ažbe school of art. Marianne von Werefkin's salon was a centre of creative exchange among artists, poets and actors. The city saw the launch of a new era of abstraction in art, with Kandinsky's painterly 'impressions' and 'compositions'. ■ According to the recollections of Alexei, the youngest of the Pevsner brothers, Gabo, when on holiday in Bryansk, took to drawing, watercolour and oil painting: 'His drawings were done swiftly and impetuously and were fascinatingly imaginative, expressive and

Christmas c.1912
Pastel on paper, 36.3 x 45

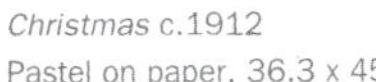

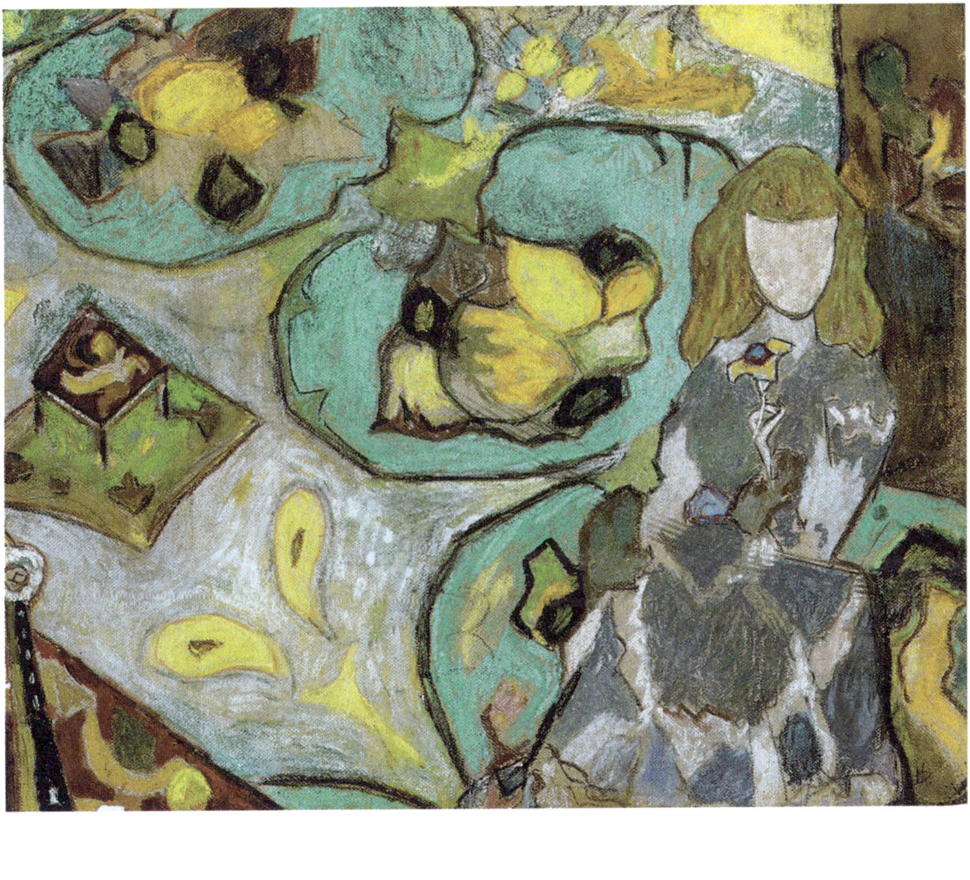

О БРАТЬЯХ НАУМЕ ГАБО и АНТУАНЕ ПЕВЗНЕРЕ

БИОГРАФИЧЕСКИЙ ОЧЕРК

Алексея Певзнера

После многолетней разлуки с моими братьями Наумом Габо и Антуаном Певзнером я получил возможность лучше ознакомиться с их произведениями, которые они выполнили в период с 1923 по 1959 г.г. и, лично зная их работы до этого периода, я намерен в настоящем биографическом очерке поделиться с теми, кого это может интересовать о том, как росли и развивались мои братья, и как выкристаллизовывалось их творчество.

1

Наум Габо /по рождению - Наум Неемия Певзнер/ родился в 1890 году. Детство его прошло в тиши захолустья, в маленьком городке, окруженном полями, лугами и лесами, когда в мире уже сверкали зарницы грозного XX века.

Дом наших родителей находился на окраине города, на стреле двух дорог. Одна дорога мощеная булыжником уходила в "будущее", туда - где железная дорога, чтобы уезжать в большие города. Мы не любили эту дорогу. Она была пыльная. По ее обочинам не росли цветы, а гудели телеграфные провода, протянутые на голых столбах. Другая дорога уходила в "прошлое". Это был шлях, поросший травой, по сторонам которого стояли вековые березы. По этой дороге проезжала когда-то царица Екатерина и в ее честь были высажены березки. Так и назывался этот шлях "Берез-

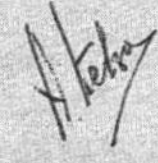

First page of the manuscript 'Concerning my
Brothers Naum Gabo and Antoine Pevsner.
Biographical Sketch of Alexei Pevsner', 1960

romantic.'[23] The Russian painter Vrubel seems to have been the only authority respected by Gabo. Not fond of life studies, he preferred to give a painterly expression to imaginary forms. Judging by the few surviving examples of Gabo's early paintings, one would probably not consider him an exceptionally gifted painter. Nevertheless, by the time the First World War began, Gabo was adamant about not pursuing a career in engineering. He was far more attracted by the art world than by science. 'It was the fourth year of my studies [in Munich] and I had another six months to finish my thesis, you know, but I have decided, I knew, that I was not going to be an engineer. I already had certain ideas in mind … In August 1914 I was already prepared to make sculptures in a new way'.[24] ■ Without a doubt, Gabo's scientific training was a great stimulus in his development as an artist and creative thinker. However, it must not be forgotten that Gabo was by no means a scientist. He did not specialise in any particular area of science, nor did he show great talent in science during his sporadic and uncompleted period of studies. Science played a much lesser role in his career than is commonly assumed. ■ The outbreak of the First World War marked a critical change in Gabo's creative development. A university student influenced by the latest trends in European art and encouraged by the futuristic vision of the recent scientific discoveries, he would soon launch his own creative experiments with three-dimensional forms in sculpture.

23 *Biographical Sketch* 1964, p.6.

24 *Three-hour interview with Gabo by John Read, 1973.* AV record, TGA.

GABO'S CONSTRUCTIONS AND RUSSIAN CONSTRUCTIVISM (1914–22)

GABO'S FIRST FIGURATIVE CONSTRUCTIONS AND HIS STEREOMETRIC METHOD With the outbreak of the First World War in August 1914, Gabo became an enemy alien in Germany and was forced to interrupt his studies in engineering, philosophy and art history, and to flee to the safety of neutral Norway. He was accompanied by his brother Alexei and later joined by Antoine in 1915. By taking refuge in a neutral country, the brothers avoided the threat of being conscripted into the Tsarist army. Alexei later wrote in detail of his brothers' artistic progress, witnessed by him during this period, in his *A Biographical Sketch of my Brothers, Naum Gabo and Antoine Pevsner.*[25] The brothers settled in the capital, Christiania (now Oslo), spending their time travelling and practising winter sports while Alexei enrolled at the university to study physics. With financial support from their parents, Naum and Antoine were able to devote their time to artistic experiments, resulting in the appearance of Gabo's first sculptures created using an original and revolutionary technique. Their rather sudden appearance is still baffling to art historians. ■ The first group of works, conceived between

[25] First published in English in Amsterdam by Augustin and Schoonman in 1964.

1915 and 1917, was a series of four figurative sculptures including two heads, a bust and a torso. They were assembled, like a house of cards, from carefully cut out cardboard planes. The honeycomb-like pockets of air of which the paper and card structure was comprised replaced the volume and mass of traditional stone and bronze sculpture. Gabo called his new method of creating open planar constructions 'stereometric'. Alexei described Gabo's first sculptures in his memoirs: ■ 'Those ideas, I believe, were evoked in him by the depth that he saw around him in the Norwegian fjords. He endeavoured to represent this depth in the things around us and frequently had recourse to effects obtained by applying the methods of reverse perspective, such as the ancient Byzantines used to render depth and movement. He spoke to me much about the meaning of line in sculpture, and that its function was not to delimit the boundaries of things but to show the trends of hidden rhythms and forces in them. ■ Space and time, the infinity of the universe, the entire starry cosmos that surrounds us – those were the things that constantly exited [sic] him. ■ In order to embody all those ideas in real forms Gabo began in the winter of 1915–16 to construct various figurative models and heads, which he made out of pieces of thin coloured cardboard pasted together in joined planes. He found it extremely difficult to determine right away the necessary outline of each plane, and he often had to stick things to them or cut them down to get the necessary size but in the end he would produce something remarkable for its expressiveness and vividness. In his sculptures an outline appeared, lines of directions were defined, and depth was revealed; it was possible for each sculpture to expand in any dimensions one chose, merely by expanding each joined plane with the aid of a planimeter …'[26] ■ It is hard to believe that it was possible for a young amateur artist who had received no professional training and had no close connections with artistic circles to conceive and develop a new sculptural method and then, moreover, to apply it to creating extraordinarily novel and artistically expressive forms.[27] The phenomenon was the result of a whole complex of influences, observations and experiments. Gabo had always been impressed by the art of the Russian orthodox icon, with its symbolic language of colours and the precise rhythmic arrangement of one-dimensional painted planes. He had similarly studied the cubists' exploration of form and its deconstruction into basic shapes, just as he had admired the original crystal-like texture of the brushstrokes on Vrubel's canvases. The artist's early pencil studies of the Norwegian period reflect his creative development from figurative compositions such as *Studies of Mother and Child* 1916–17 or *Kneeling Figure* c.1916 to minimal cubist forms. In his later works, Gabo rarely used drawings as preliminary studies for his three-dimensional constructions, but rather as a simultaneous interpretation of an already developed spatial form on a planar surface. In this sense, the drawings in which Gabo laid the foundations for further developing his stereometric method are unique. ■ Gabo achieved an impressive articulation of form in his first series of works, adopting a hands-on approach and manually cutting and reshaping each piece of coloured card, the only material widely available to a novice sculptor during the First World War. Later, in order to demonstrate his stereometric method, Gabo

26 *Biographical Sketch* 1964, p.14.

27 Discussed in *Constructing Modernity* 2000, pp.31–52.

Красивые горы. Электричкой доехали до *Slemdal'а* . Пошли, -
по дороге тихо, человека не видать и спросить не у кого,
где этот *Fossheim Hotel...?*   Вот это самая настоящая
прелесть, сказал брат.... И вот поселились мы надолго в
этом *Hotel'е*   . Близко от Гольмен Коллен.

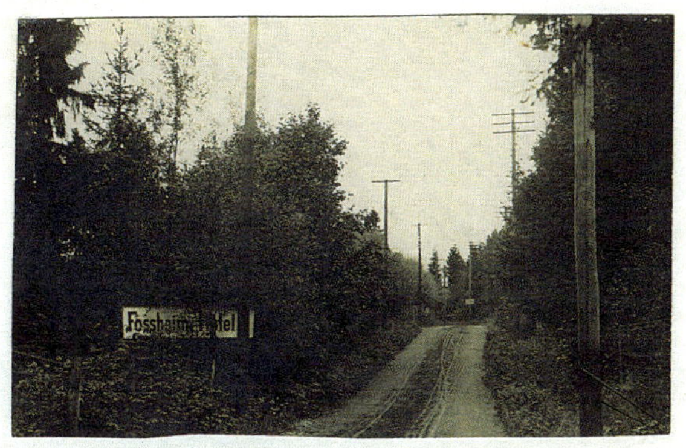

фиг II

Скоро и зима наступила 1914-1915 года... Снега насыпало
горы... И стало нам вдвоем хорошо и спокойно на душе,
совсем как в детские годы...

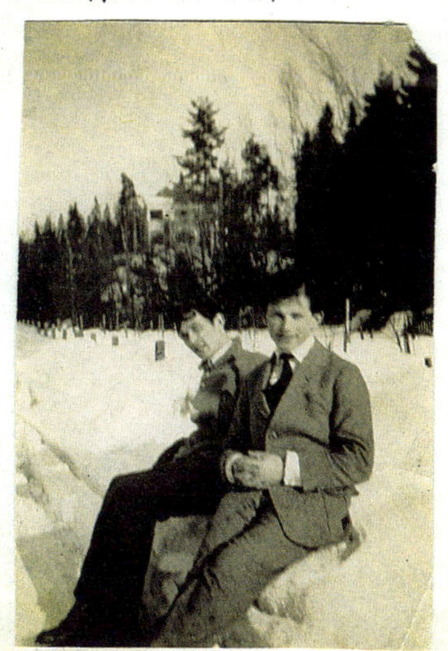

фиг 12

produced two cubes that 'illustrate the main differences between two representations of the same object, one corresponding to a carving and the other to a construction. The main distinctions are in the different methods of execution and the different centres of interest. The first represents a volume of mass; the second represents the space in which the existing mass is made visible. Volume of mass and volume of space are, sculpturally speaking, not the same thing. Indeed, they are two different materials.'[28] ■ Spatial mathematical models were widely used in universities at the end of the nineteenth and in the early twentieth centuries to demonstrate complex mathematical ideas, and Gabo was familiar with a number of them, including those of Alexander von Brill. The honeycomb-like, colourful models of the Munich-based German mathematician von Brill were assembled from intersecting cardboard planes. The method of constructing spatial structures from flat card templates was of far more interest to Gabo than the mathematical principle itself, thus the influence of these models was not through their purely scientific concept but through the way in which it was visually expressed. Gabo later stated: 'Asked whether science has made an impression, I mean, has had an influence on my work, I should say yes, just as on everybody else – you cannot avoid scientific ideas, because they do usually come in life … I can say that my first constructions, the heads, were based on a scientific principle.'[29] ■ Gabo applied his newly developed stereometric method to only four figurative sculptures: *Constructed Head No.1* c.1915, *Constructed Head No.2* c.1916, *Constructed Head No.3 (Head in a*

[28] Naum Gabo, 'Carving and Construction in Space', in *Circle* 1937, p.106.

[29] *Transcript of the Interview of J. Read with Naum Gabo in Arts Features, 8 November 1972, part I, p.5, Yale.*

Photograph of *Constructed Head No.1*
c.1915

*Two Cubes (Demonstrating the Stereometric
Method)* 1930
Painted plywood, two objects,
each 30.5 x 30.5 x 30.5

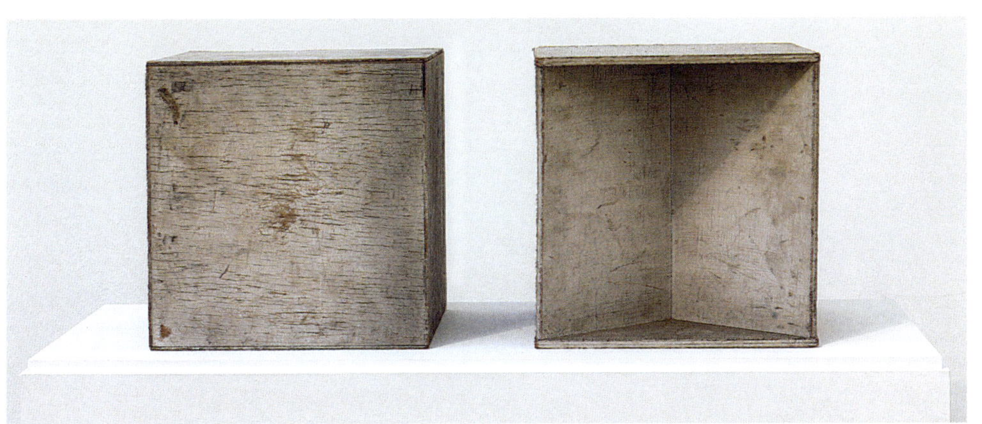

Studies of Mother and Child
c.1916–17
Pencil on card, 30 x 26

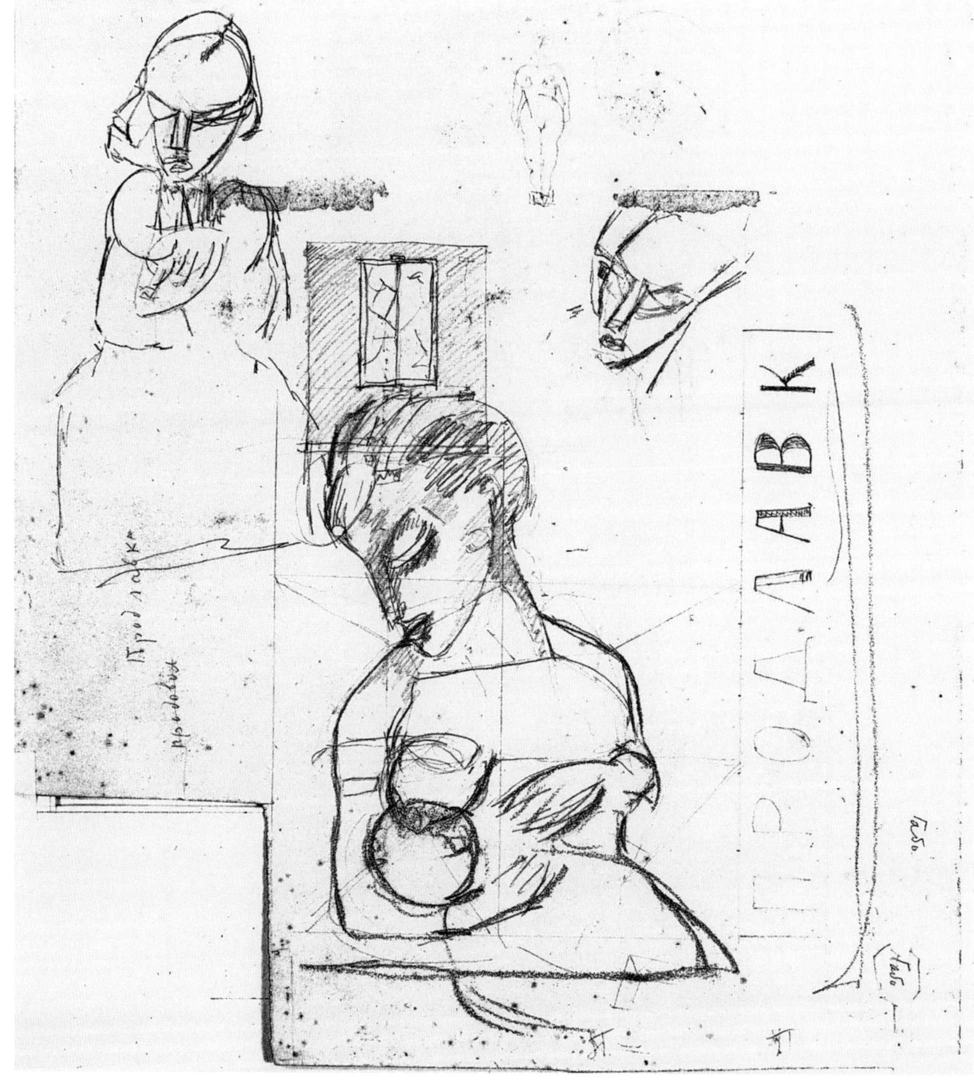

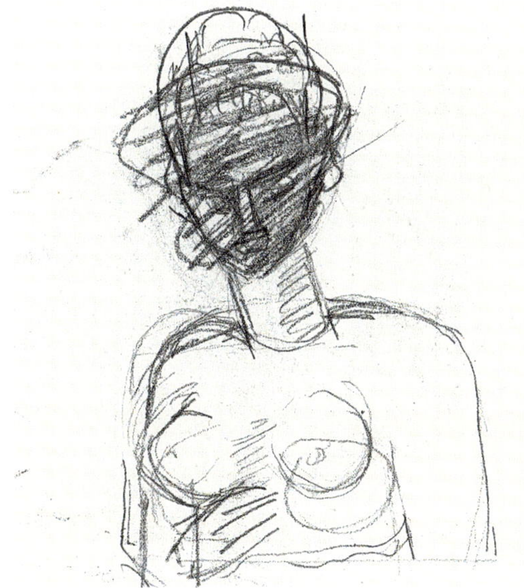

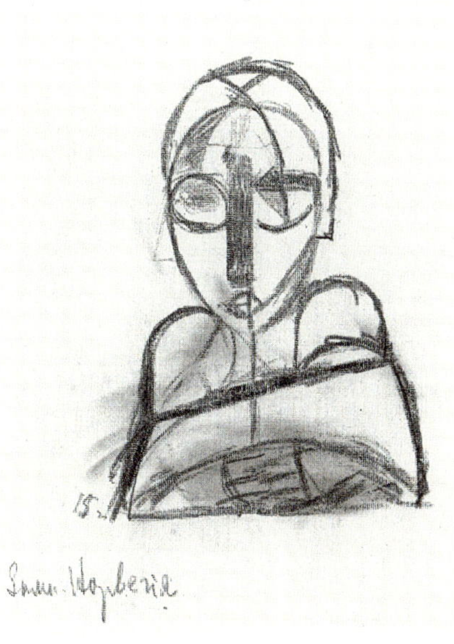

Study of Female Torso c.1916
Pencil on paper, 48 x 35

Study for Constructed Head No.2 c.1916
Blue pencil on paper, 18 x 11

Corner Niche) c.1916–17 and *Constructed Torso* c.1917. According to Alexei Pevsner, all four were conceived in Norway and created from card templates of various shapes and sizes. The pieces of card were pasted together in planes to form an intricate structure, which, opening outwards from its axis, drew the outside space into the very medium of the sculpture. The sculpture was shaped entirely by flat, intersecting planes rather than by the traditional technique of carving or modelling. Gabo later emphasised the significance of his technique: ■ 'I know of no artist in the years 1914–15 who applied the pure stereometrical principle of building a volume as a system to art. A haphazard use of criss-cross surfaces, which might be found in cubist painting or in a contra-relief of Tatlin's at that time, is a far

Model for Constructed Head No.3
(Head in a Corner Niche) 1916–17
Cardboard, 61 x 48.5 x 34.5

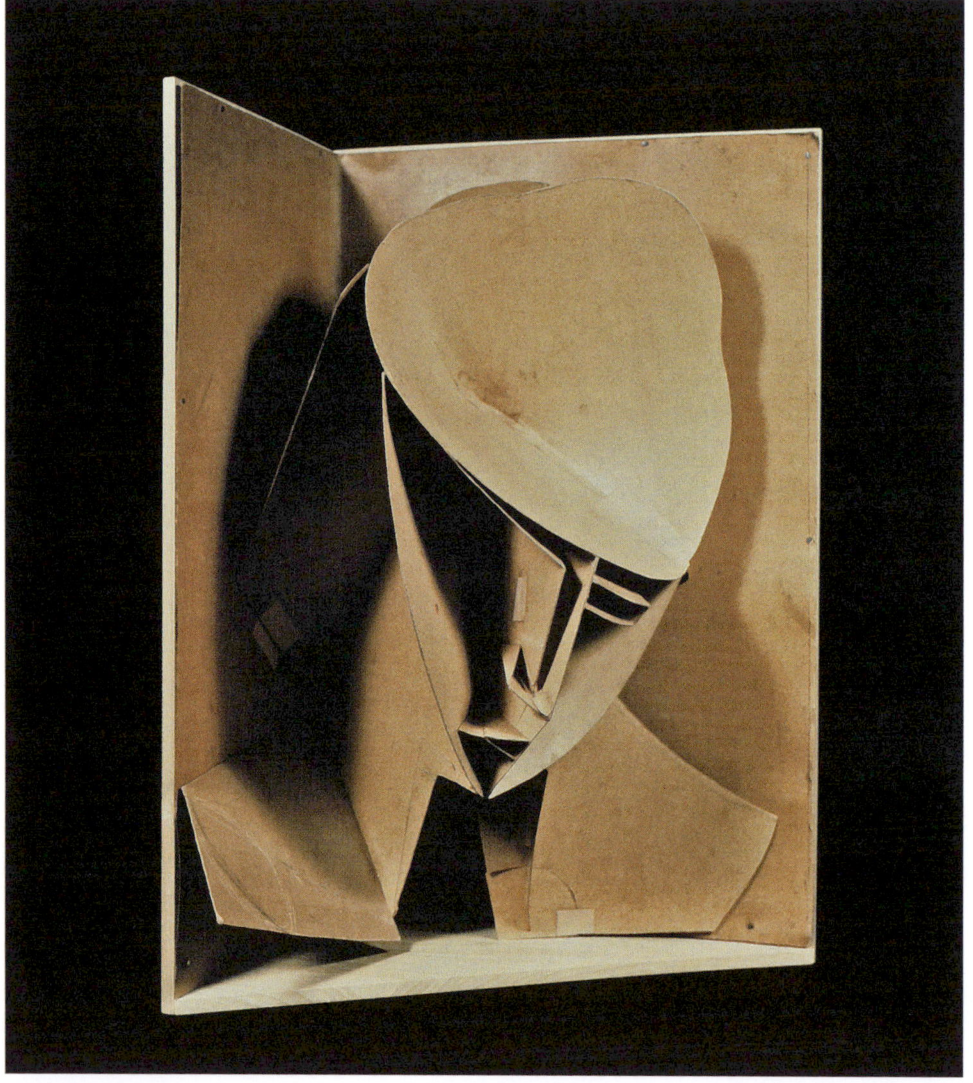

Constructed Head No.1 c.1915
Plywood, 53.5 high

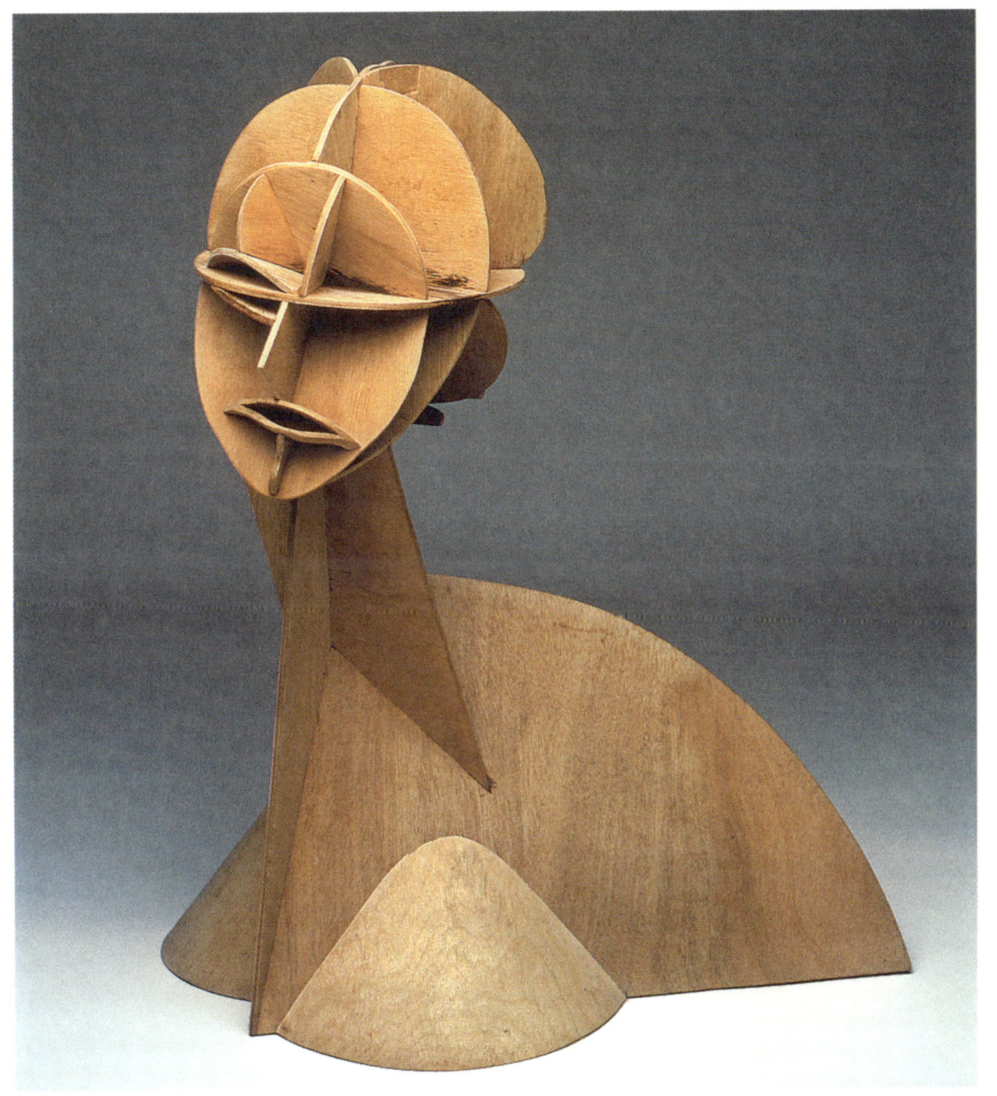

→
Photograph of *Constructed Head No.2*
c.1916, 1924

cry from the application of a well-defined stereometrical system to the building of a finite and limited volume such as my heads were. I consider that a great step forward in the development of structure in space, and this I pride myself on having done.'[30]

THE MADONNA OF THE TWENTIETH CENTURY *Constructed Head No.2* is undeniably the sculptor's most renowned work. Gabo's sentimental attachment to his creation is evident in his diary entry of 5 August 1966, where he refers to the sculpture as 'his child', raised by his hands from the tiny card model of 1916 to the two-metre high Corten steel construction of 1966. In celebrating his birthday that year, he also celebrated the fiftieth anniversary of the sculpture whose image he had carried with him through revolutions, wars and his wanderings around the world.[31] At the opening of the Gabo exhibition at the Tate Gallery in 1966, the director of the Royal College of Art, Dr Christopher Cornford, referred to the work as 'the Madonna of the Annunciation of the 20th century', which *'embodies in her very structure the most beautiful and profound discovery of 20th century art'.*[32] It was indeed a Madonna of the rapidly receding century, a symbol of the sculptural achievements of the last hundred years. The work is an interpretation of the human image, closely connected to the era of classical sculpture, and reinterpreted in the spirit of the modern age. ■ The history of the work is shrouded in mystery. The original version of *Constructed Head No.2* was executed from galvanised iron painted with yellow ochre. Gabo exhibited the work on two occasions in Moscow between 1917 and 1922, before it was included in the *First Russian Art Exhibition* and shown in

[30] *Constructing Modernity* 2000, pp.50–1.

[31] Naum Gabo, Diary, 5 August 1966, TGA.

[32] Christopher Cornford, *Thoughts at the Gabo retrospective: Tate Gallery 1966*, p.1, TGA.

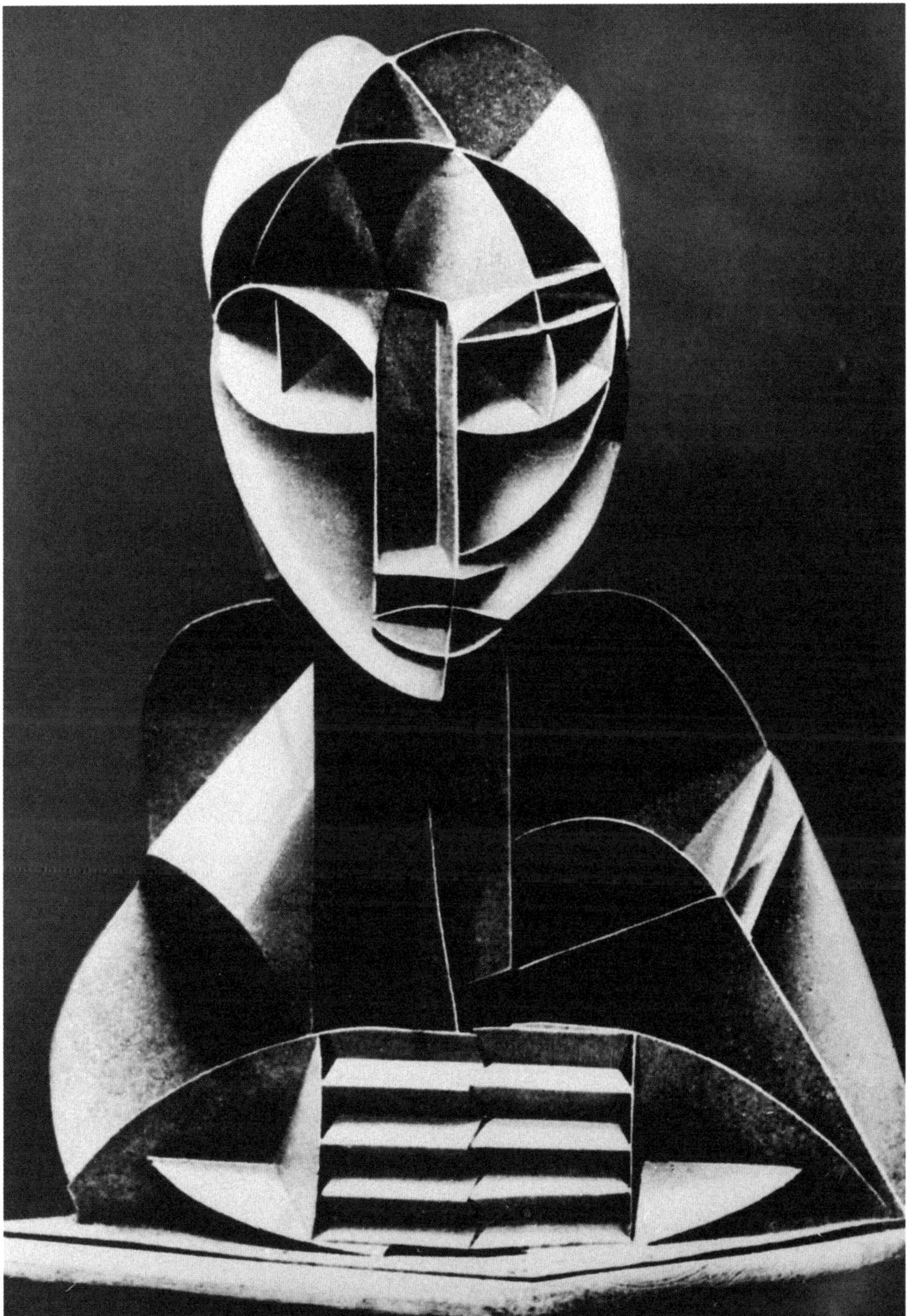

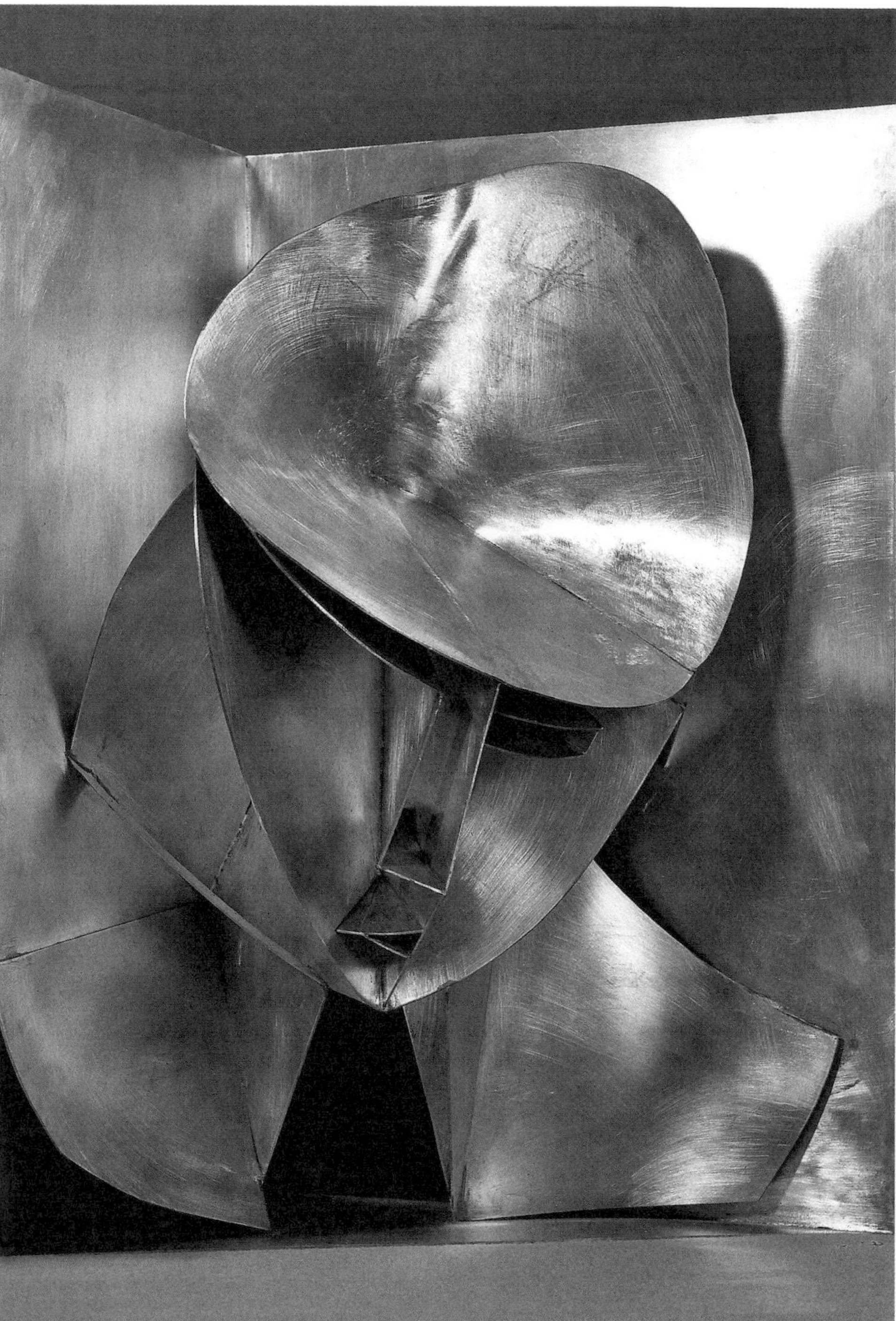

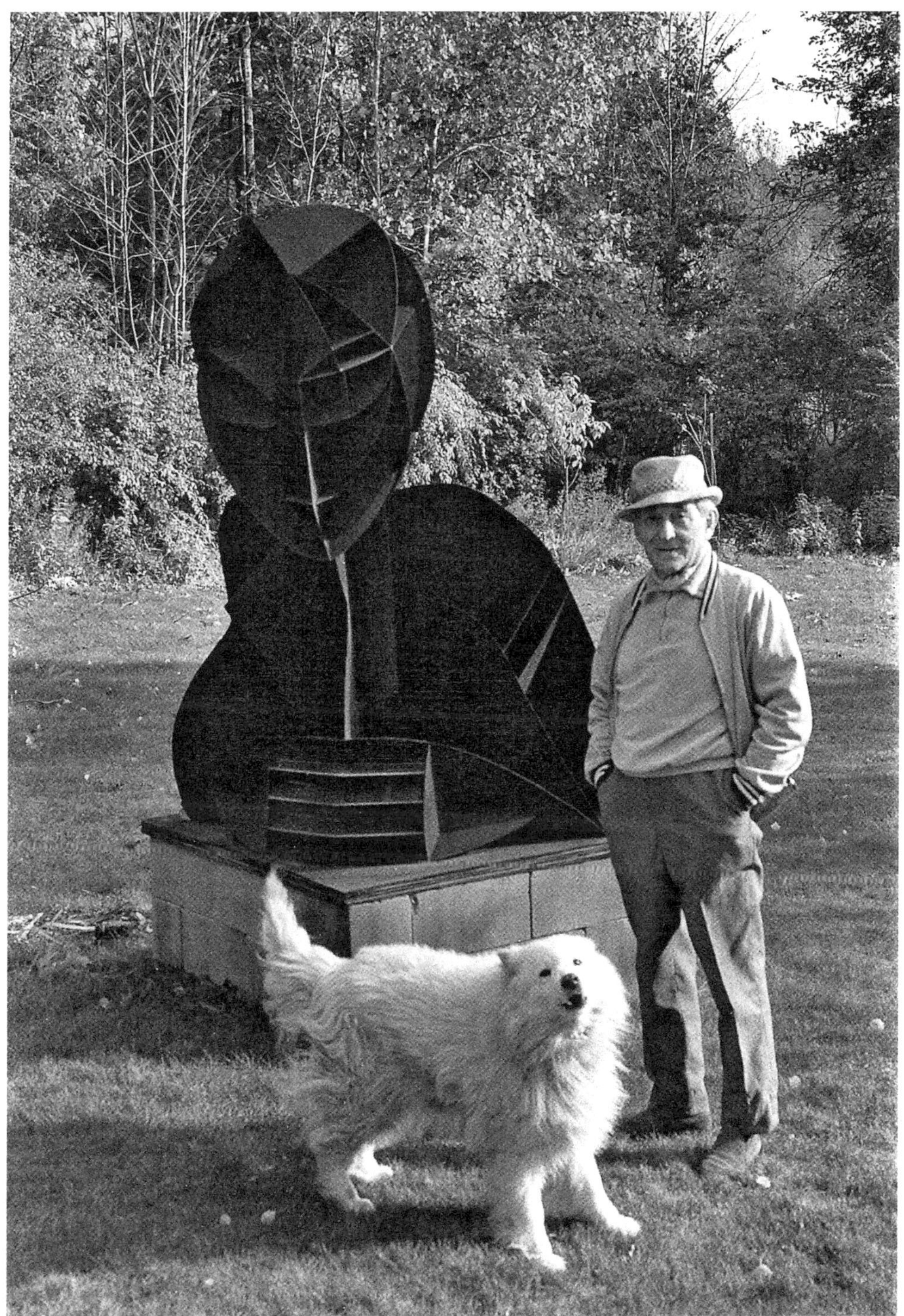

← (p.38)
Constructed Head No.3
(Head in a Corner Niche) 1964
Bronze, 62.2 x 70 x 35

← (p.39)
Photograph of Gabo and Snezhka
by *Constructed Head No.2* 1966,
Middlebury, Connecticut, 1967

Constructed Head No.2 c.1916
Galvanised iron, 45 x 43.2 x 43.2

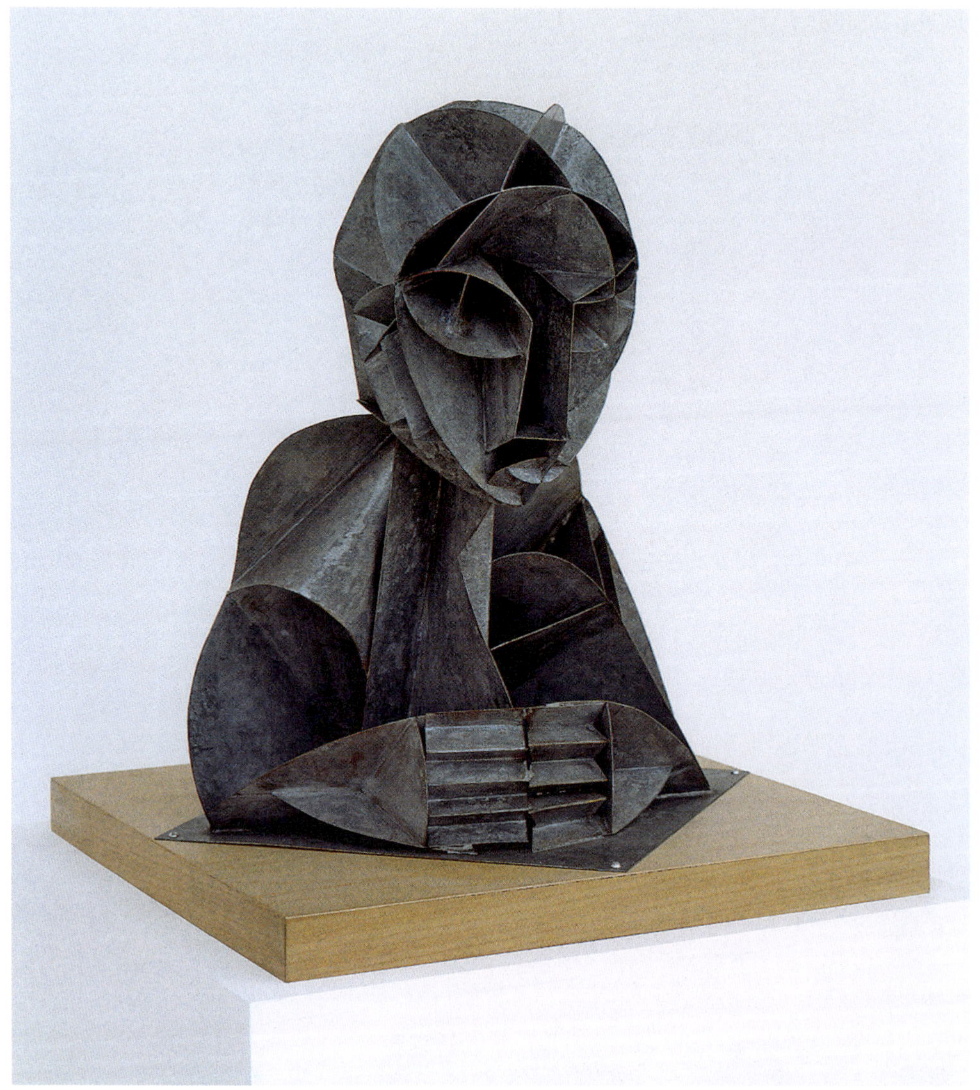

Berlin in 1922 and Amsterdam in 1923. The exhibition catalogue lists Gabo's contribution as nine sculptures and one work on paper. According to Gabo, *Constructed Head No.2* vanished after the end of the exhibition, presumably returned to Moscow. In the meantime, the artist himself had settled in Berlin where he continued exhibiting *Constructed Head No.2*, though a later version of it, constructed in 1923 from ivory-coloured opaque plastic. From 1925 to 1948, at the peak of Gabo's career, *Constructed Head No.2* was no longer exhibited, as was the case with his other figurative works. At some time towards the end of the 1950s, the original iron *Constructed Head No.2* mysteriously reappeared in Gabo's personal collection. Having restored it by removing the primary coat of paint, he began to exhibit it again in 1965. During the same period, he created several new versions of his *Heads* of varying sizes, including the two large-scale *Constructed Head No.2*, one of them mentioned in his diary entry of 5 August 1966. The question remains as to how the original sculpture came to be reunited with its creator; nor is it clear why the early figurative works were not exhibited between 1930 and 1950. However, perhaps the biggest mystery of all is why Gabo would suddenly, at the end of the 1950s, return to his first figurative constructions, which were so distant from the mature works of the renowned pioneer in abstract sculpture that he had become. ■ It would be difficult to provide an objective, factual response to such questions. The leading Gabo scholars Martin Hammer and Christina Lodder have proved that the work had, in fact, always been in the possession of the sculptor.[33] Most probably, Gabo sold *Constructed Head No.2* to [33] *Constructing Modernity* 2000, pp.456–7.

the Acquisitions Committee of the Museum Bureau within The People's Commissariat of Enlightenment (Narkompros) along with his final figurative work, *Constructed Torso* 1917. After the closure of the *First Russian Art Exhibition*, it was supposed to return to Russia, but Gabo preferred to keep the work himself and therefore refrained from exhibiting it as, strictly speaking, it did not belong to him. By 1965, when he re-exhibited the work, Gabo was perfectly aware of the historical importance of his oeuvre in the context of the development of modernist sculptural form. Although he was devoted to non-figurative art, his early experiments with three-dimensional structures were primary examples of a transitional art form – from the representative image to non-objective construction. ■ Upon Gabo's death, his studio revealed yet more works hitherto considered lost. Among those discovered were the dismounted *Constructed Head No.1* and two early card *Models for Constructed Torso*. In 1995, in a dramatic series of events, the *Models for Constructed Head No.2* and *Constructed Head No.3* also reappeared, having been hidden in 1968 by Gabo's assistant, Charles Wilson, on strict orders from the sculptor. Gabo had given Wilson a mysterious parcel soon after receiving a visit in America from his younger brother, Alexei. The brothers had been reunited by chance in 1959 after almost forty years of separation. Gabo confided to Wilson that Alexei had smuggled the models out of the USSR, where they had been kept in secret since Naum's departure in 1922. Gabo had warned Wilson that, should the Soviet authorities become aware of the smuggling, his family would be in great danger and that therefore no one, not even Gabo's wife and daughter, should ever know about the parcel.

Photograph of templates for *Constructed Head No.2* prior to conservation, 1995

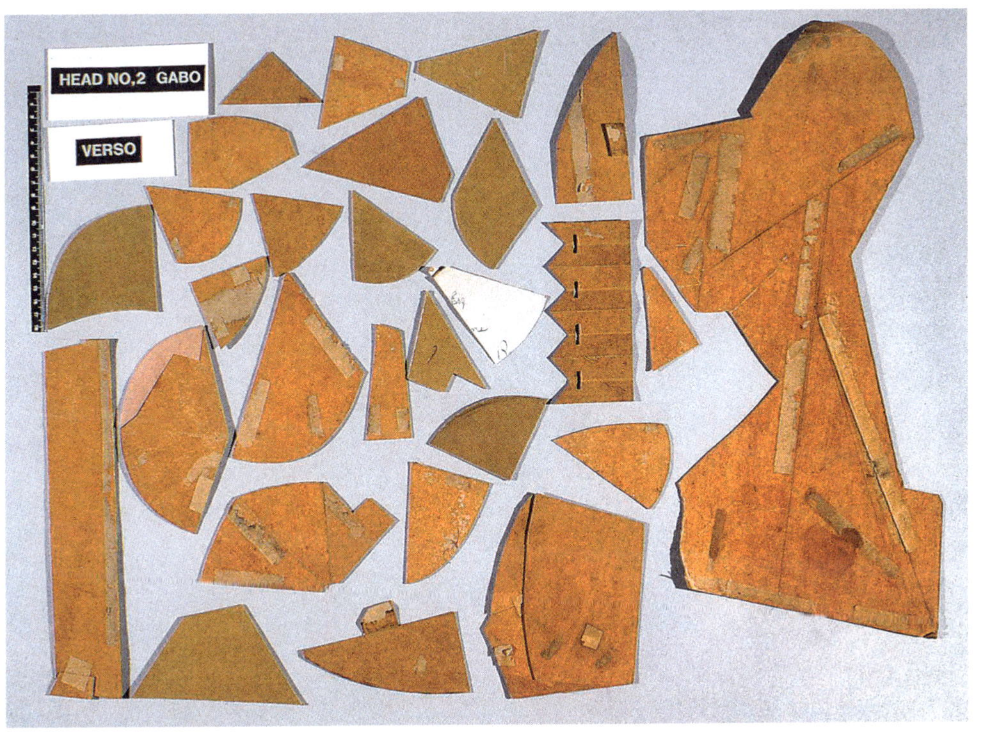

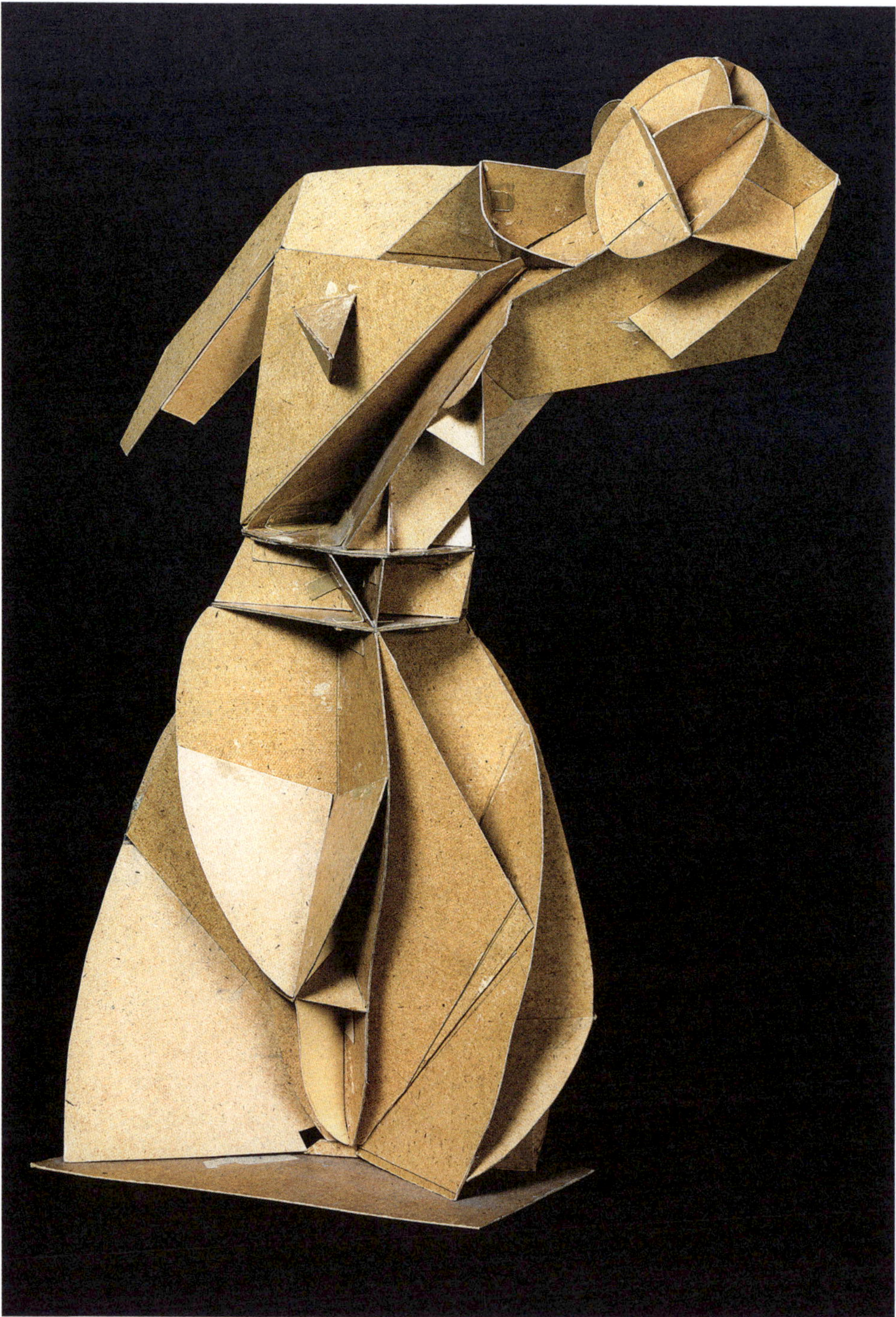

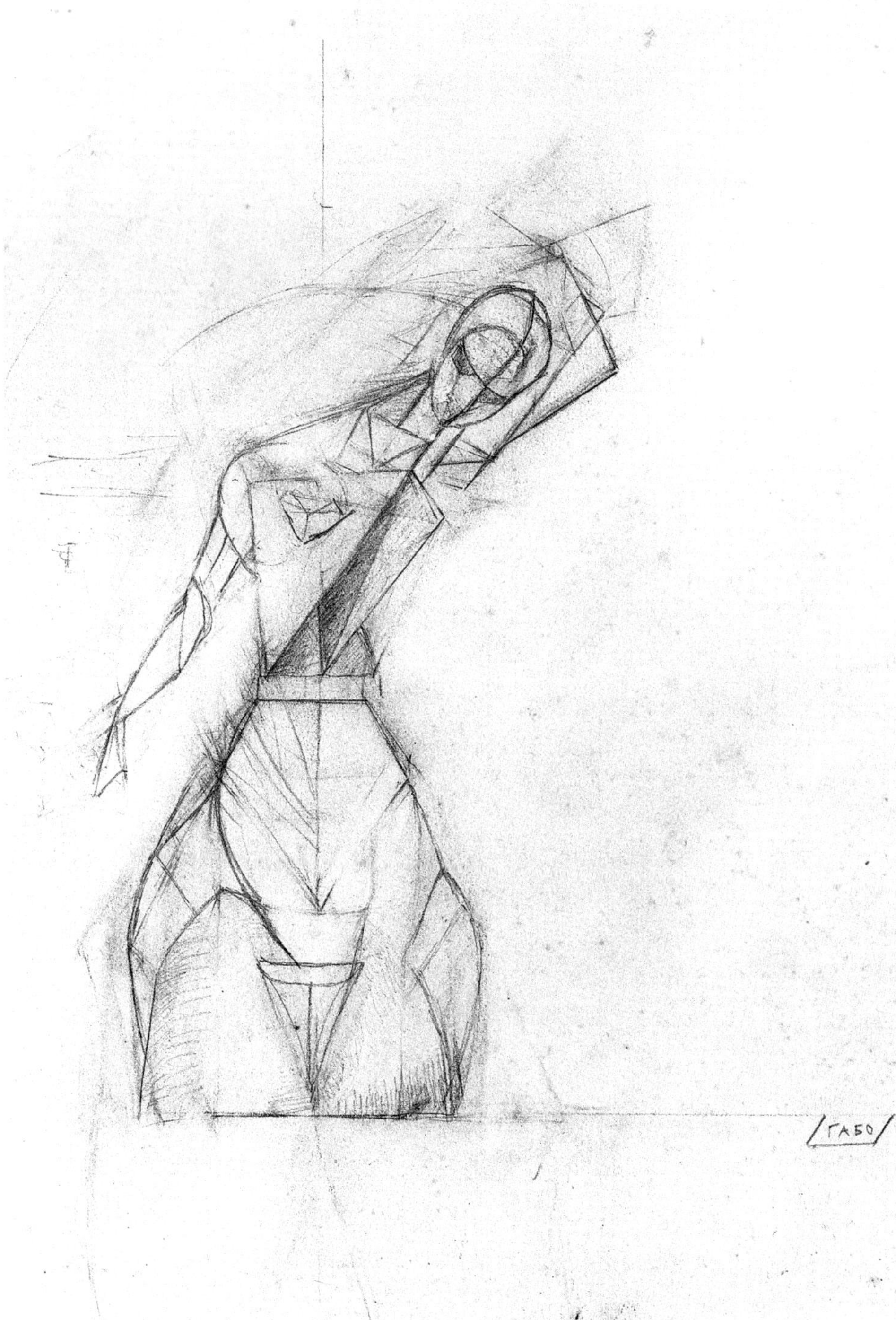

ГАБО

← (p. 44)
Model for Constructed Torso c.1917,
reassembled 1981
Cardboard, 39.5 x 29 x 16

← (p. 45)
Study for Constructed Torso 1916
Pencil on paper, 42.2 x 33

■ In 1993, after Gabo's widow, Miriam, had passed away, Wilson made the decision to reveal the secret to Gabo's only child, Nina Williams. She suggested that the Tate Gallery's Sculpture Conservation Department should handle and document the disassembled *Model for Constructed Head No.2* and *Model for Constructed Head No.3* along with templates for one other construction. The newly reassembled models were revealed to the public in 1999 at the Naum Gabo exhibition at Annely Juda Fine Art in London. The story of their rediscovery was published in the exhibition catalogue.[34] Gabo seems to have always kept the 1916–17 card models in his possession, as was the case with the original *Constructed Head No.2*. In the extensive correspondence between Gabo and Alexei, the brothers often discussed the photographs and early works by Gabo and Antoine that Alexei had kept with him in Moscow since 1922, all of which were shipped officially to Gabo, with permission from the Soviet cultural authorities. The models contained in the mysterious parcel were never mentioned. It is reasonable to presume that Gabo would almost certainly have needed the models in 1922 as templates in order to replace fragments in the unfortunate event of damage to the works during their shipment from the Soviet Union to Berlin. We can only speculate on Gabo's reasons to use Alexei's 1968 visit as an excuse to pass the card models to Wilson. It could be that he deliberately kept the models and the original work a secret in order to create a legend about the lost masterpieces of early constructive sculpture and to protect them from the sceptical eye of art critics. ■ The quantum leap taken by Gabo in the

[34] Graham Williams, 'The rediscovered Models for Nos. 2 and 3. 1916/17', in *Naum Gabo. Catalogue of the Exhibition, 29 April–26 June 1999*, Annely Juda Fine Art, London 1999, pp.[10–14].

initial development of non-representational sculpture technique remains to this day underestimated. The very simplicity of the idea behind Gabo's stereometric method and the fact that he, a young, autodidact artist, should have invented it overshadowed its ingenious originality. Even during Gabo's lifetime, the young generation of sculptors, active in the 1960–70s, overlooked the revolutionary step that Gabo had taken in his early works. William Tucker expressed his scepticism in his publication *The Language of Sculpture*: 'In the *Female Nude* of 1910 Picasso dispenses with the faceting of the background completely, and the figure reads so strongly as an illusioned construction that I imagine it would not be too difficult to make it physically with sheet steel or plywood (as Gabo was virtually to do in his constructed steel *Head* of 1916)'.[35] Cubism played an important part in Gabo's artistic development and later, in his scholarly publications, he highlighted the movement's major role in the emergence of modernism. It is clear that his own early creative experiments followed in the footsteps of Pablo Picasso and Georges Braque, although their result was no mere imitation. Gabo took a decisive and unprecedented step forward when he moved from the traditional sculptural practice of modelling and carving and adapted the assembly methods of Vladimir Tatlin's counter-reliefs to the new age method of construction.

MOSCOW EXPERIMENTS The Pevsner brothers made the decision to leave peaceful Norway on learning of the 1917 February Revolution in Russia. Gabo, who carried with him a folder of the dismounted models of his constructions, was already concerned about the reception of his works at

[35] William Tucker, *The Language of Sculpture*, Thames and Hudson, London 1974, p.65.

home: ■ 'I looked at my suitcase and a clumsy package of models and drawings of mine wrapped in bed linen and my brother's studies and paintings tightly packed and bound with cord by its side … Where am I taking my sculpture to? (I knew my works at first glance could arouse resistance and even disgust in people. I experienced this when showing my works to friends at my studio. I was friendly with many artists but could not recall a single sculptor in my entourage. They were very friendly and, not wanting to hurt me, kindly asked me to explain what my sculpture meant and if I really was convinced that it was indeed sculpture? I tried to explain as well as I could … What would happen to it at home? Would it be accepted and understood?)'[36]
■ Passing through Petrograd on the way home to Bryansk, Gabo and his brothers witnessed first-hand the changes brought about by the first socialist revolution in history. In his youth, Gabo was rather left-wing and the events in his homeland fascinated him. After a short stay at their parents' house in order to arrange new identification papers and settle the rather problematic issue of conscription, the brothers set off for Moscow. During the winter of 1918–19, they shared a loft studio in the Pertsov House by the Moscow River, across the road from the Cathedral of Christ the Saviour.[37] Pevsner was actively involved in the artistic life of the capital. In the immediate aftermath of the October Revolution, avant-garde artists were given unprecedented freedom of expression in their creative experiments. The brothers took a key part in the process – Pevsner was a committee member of the All-Russia Central Exhibitions Bureau and he lectured at the Svomas (The State Free Art Studios, which became the Vkhutemas, or The

36 Naum Gabo, *K portretam*, p.13, TGA.
37 Naum Gabo, Diary, 23 August 1940, TGA.

Naum Gabo's photographic identification
document, c.1917

Photograph of *Constructed Torso* 1917
at the *First Russian Art Exhibition*,
Berlin, 1922

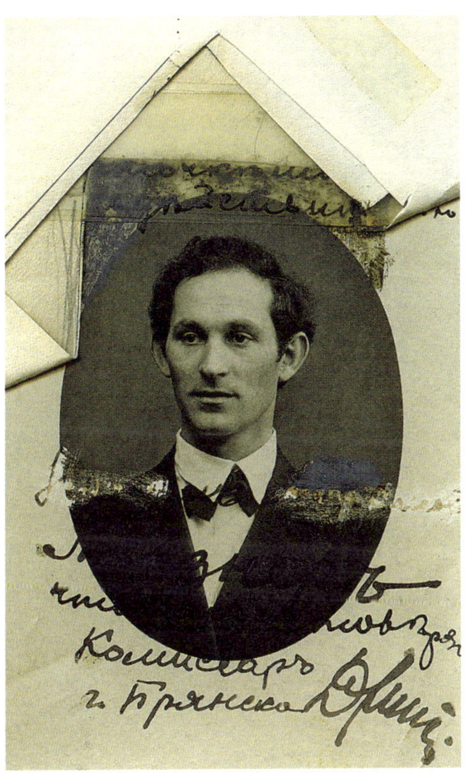

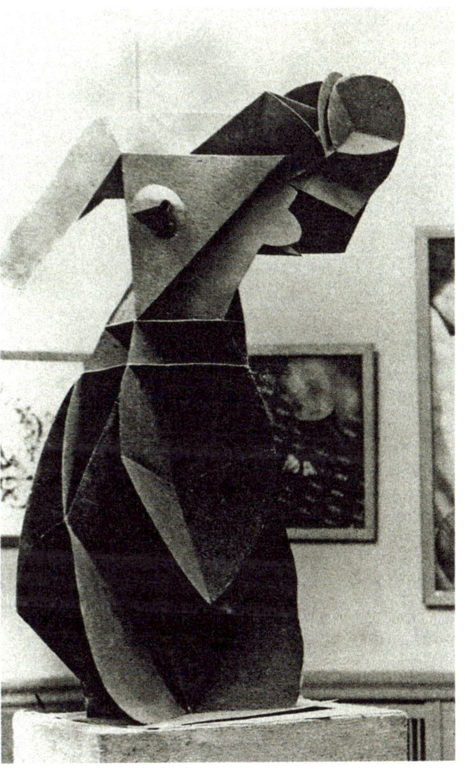

Higher Artistic and Technical Workshops, in 1920), having taken over the Painting Studio from Kazimir Malevich when he left for Vitebsk in autumn 1919. Pevsner also participated in group exhibitions of avant-garde art and became closely acquainted with Aleksandr Rodchenko, Varvara Stepanova, Nadezhda Udaltsova, Lyubov Popova, El Lissitzky and Natan Altman. His network of friends and colleagues enabled Gabo to frequent artistic circles where he actively participated in gatherings and debates while maintaining his independence of any particular group or school. ■ From 1917–20, Gabo evidently continued working on his *Heads*, testing new materials and perfecting his stereometric method of construction. The full-scale metal works, including *Constructed Torso*, the final piece in his figurative series, were most probably executed in 1917–18, after his departure from Norway. By that time, he had proved that the stereometric method could be applied even to classical subjects, such as a human bust or torso, allowing for a new interpretation of traditional form. Gabo was never to return to figurative sculpture. He later explained: ■ 'Dim and deceptive are the reflections of man's image, his physical appearance incompatible with his true traits if we perceive him as an outsider, a stranger. Only in ourselves, in our own consciousness of his and our own existence, may we find the essence of what makes him and us human. That is why, ladies and gentlemen, I have abandoned as futile my efforts to represent him in the vesture of his moral skin and flesh; that is why I have shattered the clay and stones of those graven images I used to make of him in my youth.'[38] ■ Gabo's stereometric method was never taken up by his contemporaries, but was adopted and revised by

[38] *Of Divers Arts* 1962, p.16.

Antoine Pevsner who, under Gabo's influence, shifted from painting to sculpture in 1923.

KINETIC CONSTRUCTION From 1918–20, Gabo embarked on a study of transparency in sculpture, pioneering the use of plastics and glass in his first non-objective constructions. The notion of transparency is related closely to Gabo's ideas of the inner dynamic qualities of artwork. This notion, in opposition to the traditional static nature of sculpture, he called 'kinetic rhythm'. In the winter of 1919–20, Gabo created an object known as *Kinetic Construction (Standing Wave)*, which illustrated the new artistic principle. According to Gabo, it was designed as a visual aid for art students. The primary importance he gave to kinetic rhythms in art was highlighted in his first publication, *The Realistic Manifesto* of 1920: 'We reject the thousand-year-old Egyptian delusion in art which held that static rhythms are the only elements of visual creativity. ■ We assert a new element in visual art, KINETIC RHYTHMS, as the basic forms of our perception of real time'.[39] ■ In the early 1920s, the idea of movement in art was closely associated with that of electricity, mechanics and industrial progress in general, futurist artists of the previous decade having paved the way for such a new mindset. In his 'Art and Pangeometry' article published in the 1925 *Europa-Almanach*, Lissitzky foretold the symbolic significance of dynamic construction: ■ 'Tatlin and the constructivists in Moscow represented movement by means of symbols. The individual bodies in the *Monument to the Third International* revolve each around its own axis at its own velocity: a year, a month, a day. In 1921 Puzakov constructed a mobile relief which, with a Dadaistic touch,

39 Naum Gabo, Noton Pevzner, 'The Realistic Manifesto (1920)', translated from Russian by Christina Lodder, in *Gabo on Gabo* 2000, p.33.

symbolized or caricatured a factory-committee in session. Gabo stylized a pendulum-movement of a metronome (*Russian Art Exhibition*, Berlin 1922)'.[40] ■ The 'pendulum-movement of a metronome' mentioned by Lissitzky was in fact the first motorised object of kinetic art in history. Although Gabo did not invent kinetic sculpture, he was indisputably a pioneer in introducing motion into art, as were his contemporaries Marcel Duchamp, Tatlin and Rodchenko. A number of avant-garde artists experimented with mobile objects, set in movement either by technical means or by incorporating movable parts. These experiments, allowing for the exploration of new mediums and the development of unconventional art forms, were a step forward in the search for a fourth dimension in art – time. ■ *Kinetic Construction* consists of a metal rod connected to a motorised device, which causes the rod to vibrate in a wave-like fashion. The speed and the frequency of the oscillations are such that the eye registers only a volumetric shape balancing on the verge of materiality. The viewer is presented with a projection of movement, an inexistent volume, a visual echo. The eye is incapable of grasping the movement itself, perceiving instead the outline of a three-dimensional image. ■ '[*Kinetic Construction*] was done in a primitive way, but the only way I could have done it at that time, when conditions were such that looking for elaborate mechanism was to search for a golden plate from the Moon. This is how I did it. The standing waves had attracted my attention since my student days, in particular the fact that when you look at a standing wave, the image becomes three-dimensional. In order to show what I meant by calling for the introduc-

40 El Lissitzky, 'Art and Pangeometry', in Sophie Lissitzky-Küppers, *El Lissitzky. Life, Letters, Texts*, Thames and Hudson, London 1968, p.356.

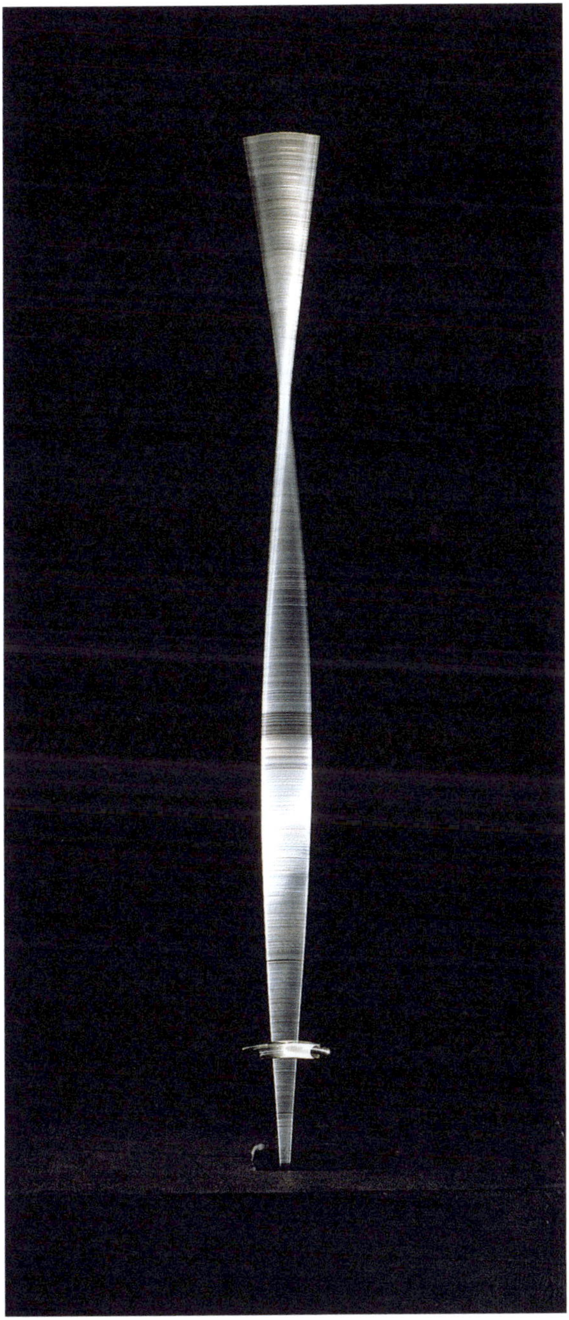

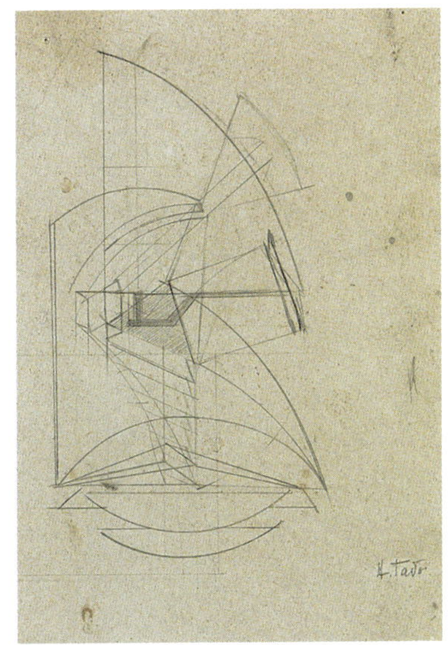

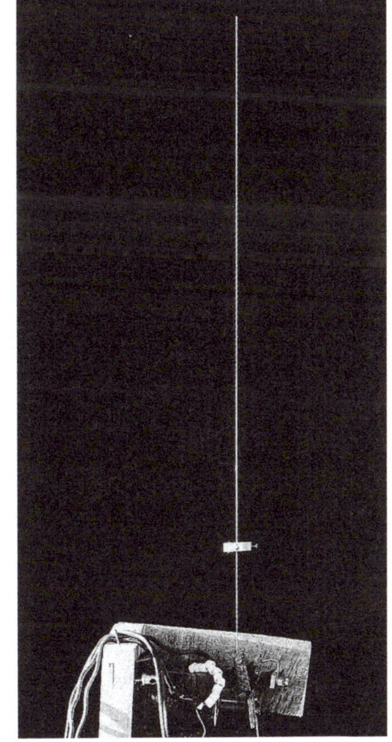

Sketch for a Kinetic Construction 1922
Pen and ink on graph paper, 43.2 x 31.4

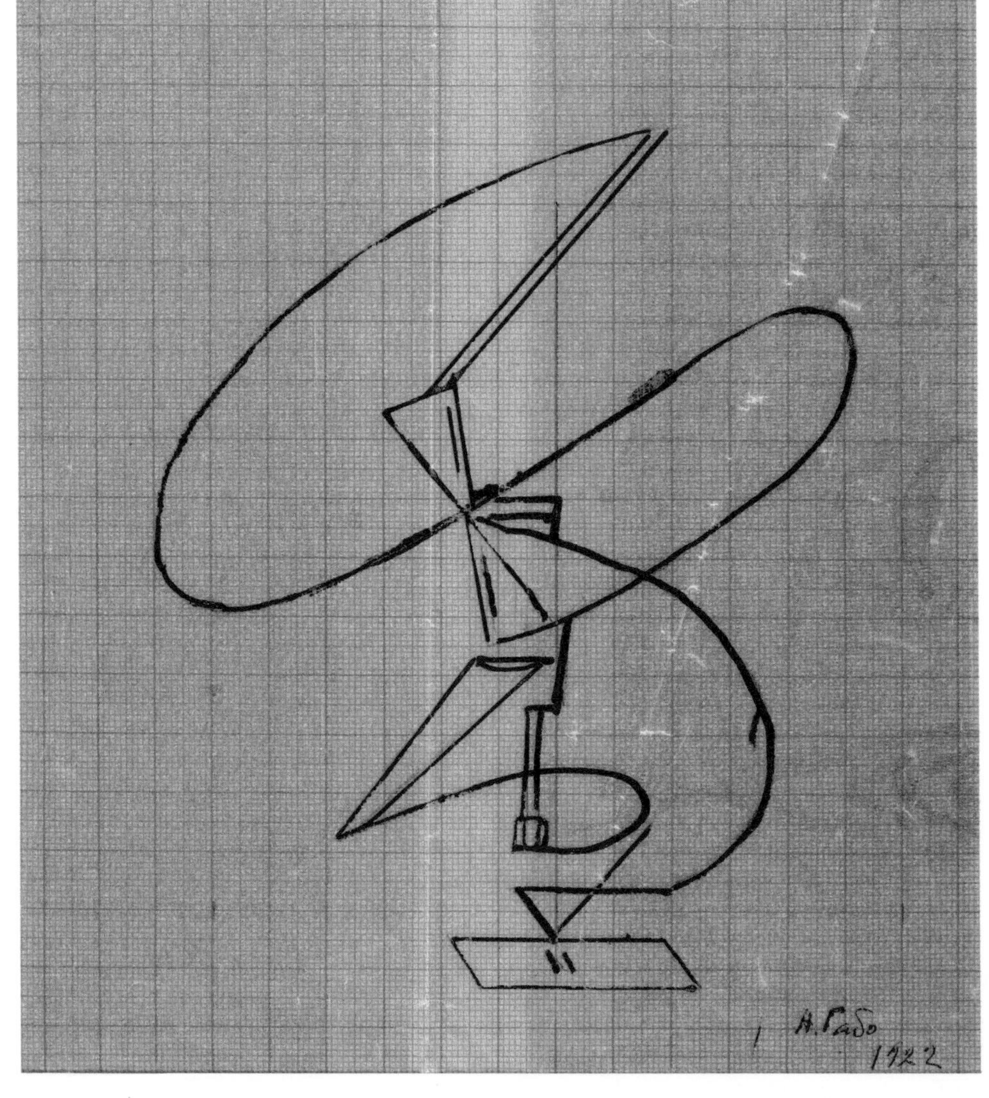

tion of kinetic rhythms into a constructed sculpture, I chose [sic] that standing wave was a good illustration of the idea – so I decided to construct a standing wave which would be vibrating on one fixed point and rigid enough to be indeed a "standing wave" … When I showed it to the students I made it emphatically clear that this was done by me in order to show them what I mean by "kinetic rhythms". This piece is only a basic example of one single movement – nothing more.'[41]

■ Gabo created a number of works in which the mobile element played an important role – suspended constructions, rotating sculptures and paintings, as well as a few uncompleted sculptural projects – the majority being created between 1950 and 1976. Several of the works were set in motion by an electrical device; only in *Kinetic Construction* did Gabo produce a singular object whose form was shaped entirely by the motion itself. In employing the term 'kinetic', Gabo once more referred to the world of natural science: in physics, the term describes a branch of mechanics that deals with motion and its causes (forces). Gabo became acquainted with the principle of the 'standing wave' during his studies in Munich with Professor Leo Grätz. This phenomenon characterised by a wave that remains in a constant position was an unsolved enigma for physicists until 1981. During the 1910s, when Gabo was a student, it was widely believed that studying the nature of electromagnetic waves was the key to solving a number of problems in physics. It is not surprising that Gabo chose this particular phenomenon to illustrate his principle of kinetic rhythm in art. ■ *Kinetic Construction* epitomised Gabo's notions of the time-space continuum in art, which he outlined in *The*

41 Naum Gabo, 'The Kinetic Construction of 1920', *Studio International* (London), vol.178, no.914, 1969, p.89.

Realistic Manifesto: 'space and time are the only forms on which life is built and on which therefore art must be built'.[42] The creation of such a unique object in which volume was formed not by matter or space but by motion itself was the direct fruit of Gabo's technical skills and his knowledge of the latest discoveries in physics. What for Gabo was a mere exercise was in fact a breakthrough in sculptural technique that was ahead of its time and has since then been reinterpreted, transforming what was conceived as a demonstration tool into a prodigious work of art.

COLUMN: A SYMBIOSIS OF SCULPTURE AND ARCHITECTURE In 1919, Gabo took to experimenting with non-objective forms. Beginning with relief structures, he moved swiftly towards working with architectural forms. Gabo's rapid shift from figurative to non-objective art between 1920 and 1922 was a natural consequence of his encounter with the Russian avant-garde artist community, at the time one of the most vibrant, audacious and creative artistic circles in the world. Such artists as Tatlin, Malevich and Rodchenko introduced Gabo to the world of non-figurative art. He first experimented with relief compositions assembled according to his stereometric method, such as *Construction in Space C* c.1920–1 and *Square Relief* c.1921. Although the originals are considered lost, they have been preserved in photographs and later reconstructions by the author. The early studies for the constructions, such as *Sketch* c.1917 in the Tate Collection, reveal the still hesitant hand of an untrained draughtsman in his quest for a clear understanding of the spatial development of voluminous form. The early 1918–19 studies for

42 Naum Gabo, Noton Pevzner, 'The Realistic Manifesto (1920)', translated from Russian by Christina Lodder, in *Gabo on Gabo* 2000, p.32.

his abstract relief constructions, such as *Design for a Construction in a Niche* c.1918 and *Sketch for a Relief Construction* 1917–19, reveal the influence of cubism and Russian cubo-futurism on Gabo's works. Of particular interest is the surviving photograph of his *Construction en Creux* c.1921, where the introduction of transparent materials is clearly visible. ■ In the early 1920s, Gabo executed a series of constructions known as *Columns* or *Towers* – the first works that demonstrate his search for unity between sculpture and architecture. This leaning towards the most 'technical' form of art – architecture – marks the end of the figurative period in Gabo's transition from the world of science towards that of art. By the early 1920s, Gabo considered himself first and foremost an artist, applying his knowledge of engineering to his artistic creations. In his 1957 monograph, Gabo noted: 'From the very beginning of the Constructive Movement it was clear to me that a constructed sculpture, by its very method and technique, brings sculpture very near to architecture … My works of this time, up to 1924, are all in search for an image which would fuse the sculptural element with the architectural element into one unit.' ■ *Column* 1920–1 is the key work of Gabo's Moscow period (1917–22). He returned to the construction throughout his life, as he did with *Constructed Head No.2*, reinterpreting it by experimenting with different media and dimensions. By 1975, the work had grown to a monumental transparent glass construction 193cm high and 156cm in diameter. The earliest known example of the work is the *Model for Column*, now in the Tate Collection. It was created between 1920 and 1921 from celluloid planes (now yellow with age), which rise vertically from its circular base. The geometric precisions of the construction build from subtly coloured plastic planes, and its upwards-projected form is fused with such characteristics as transparency, so utterly dissociated from tectonic volume. Every detail in particular and the entire structure of the construction in general are visible; from any given angle, one may simultaneously perceive both the details and the work as a whole. In his use of transparent, synthetic materials, hitherto practically unused in art, Gabo achieved the total penetration of sculptural and external space. The formal language of his *Model for Column* resembles one applied to his earlier stereometric works in that it is built up of intersecting flat planes structured outwards from its central core. ■ Gabo adapted the stereometric method of his figurative sculptures to create non-objective architectonic constructions with the new feature of total transparency, soon to become the sculptor's signature technique: 'Transparent materials give me the chance to dematerialize as much as possible the content of my work of art. By dematerialization I mean to make it as near as possible to a spiritual object'.[43] ■ Even the smallest model of *Column* is endowed with the essential quality of monumentality. Gabo saw most of his constructions as models for public monuments destined to transform the streets and squares of contemporary cities. It was his conviction that they were to play an important role in society's expression of the new social order envisaged in Vladimir Lenin's Plan for Monumental Propaganda of 1918. He pictured *Column* as towering over a town square, lit from below at night to reveal the text of the first Soviet constitution inscribed on the glass panels that were to make up the construction.

[43] Teresa Newman, *Naum Gabo. The constructive process*, Tate Gallery, London 1976, p.17.

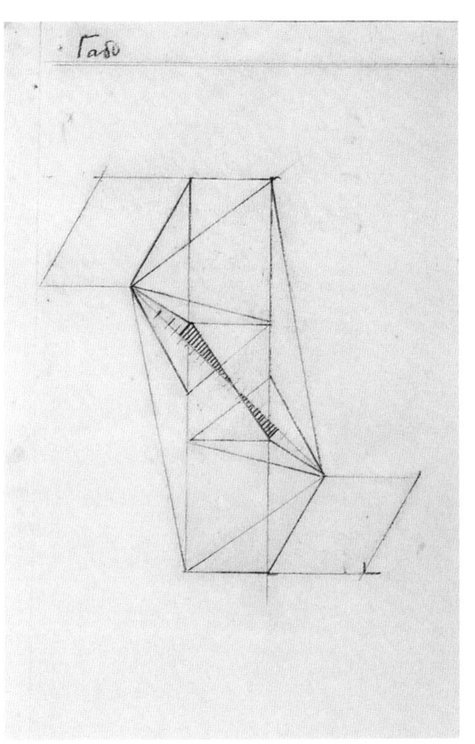
Габо

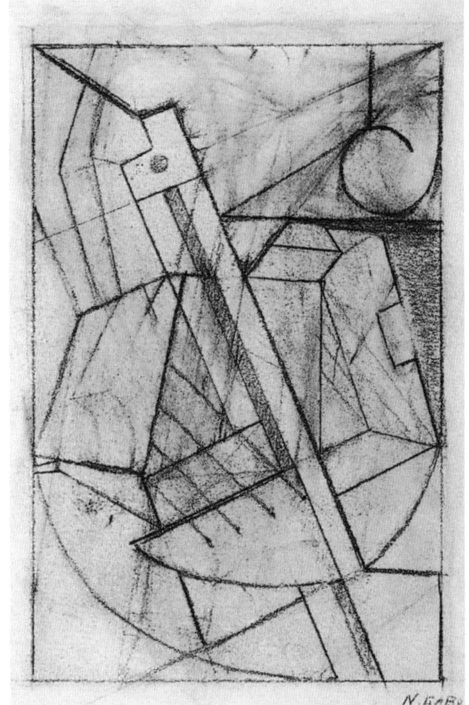
N. GABO

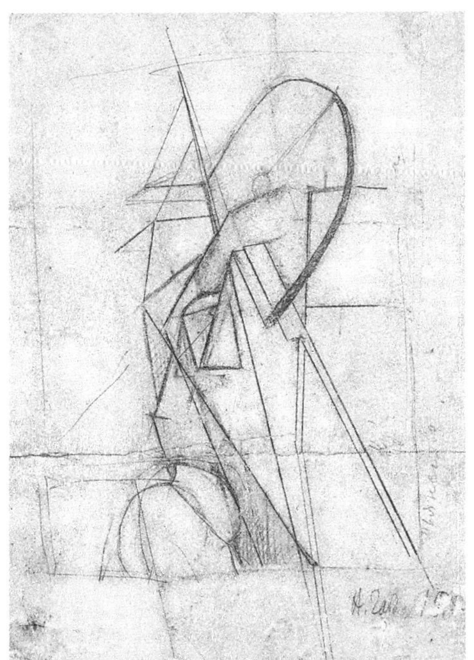

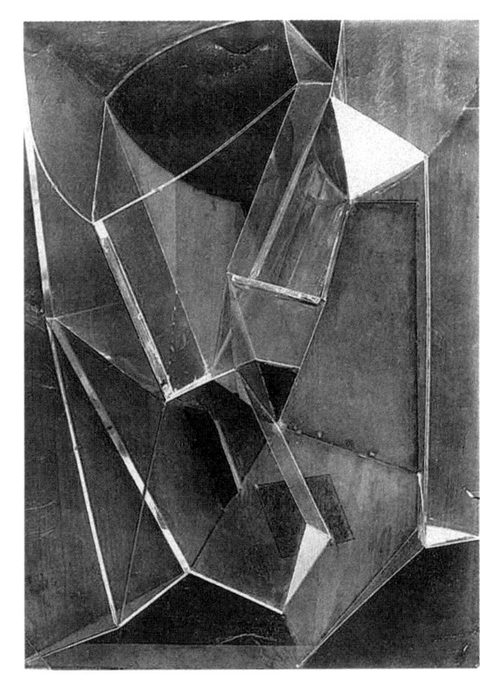

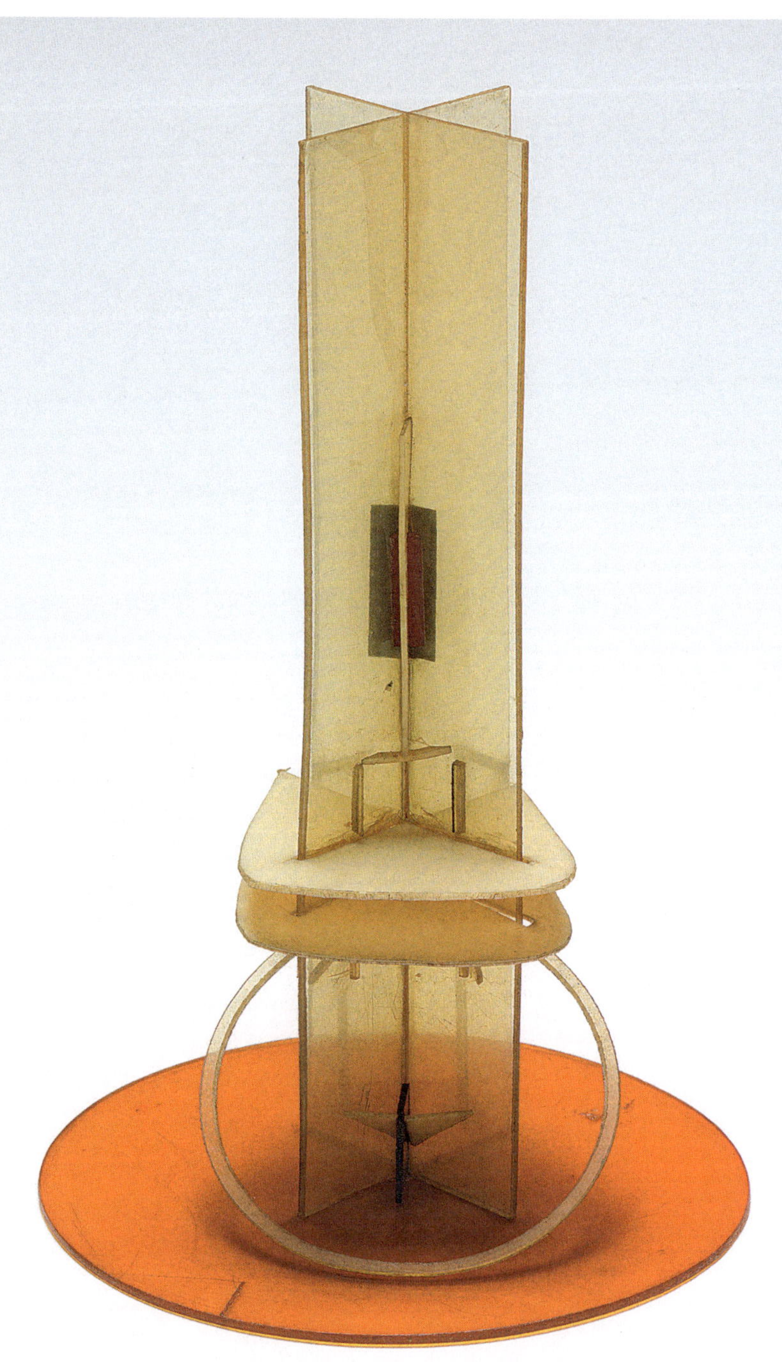

←

Model for Column 1920–1
Cellulose nitrate, 14.3 x 9.5 x 9.5

The concentric circles at the base of the monument were to serve as a podium for speeches.[44] In a letter to his brother, Alexei, Gabo described the construction process: ■ 'They are building my old Column from glass. It will be two metres high – one for the Louisiana Museum and the second for me … The official date of its creation is 1923, although the idea came to me much earlier. It is essentially just a prism, that is to say a stereometric cube like those I introduced to sculpture in my 1915–1916 busts. Frankly speaking, I don't consider this form to be out of date … I didn't envisage my first Column as a skyscraper but rather as a community building to fulfil the same role as temples or churches in the past'.[45] ■ During the late Moscow period (1920–2) and the years he spent in Berlin (1922–32), Gabo applied the skills that he had acquired during his engineering studies in Munich to create a series of constructions exemplifying the symbiosis of sculpture and architecture. Many of these works are known only through surviving photographs and drawings, such as *Model of a Monument for an Observatory* c.1922 or the bronze and glass *Illuminated Tower* 1921–5. The ideas propagated by the newly emerged Russian constructivist movement – synthesis of the arts, the monumental qualities of non-objective forms and the utopian notion of the impact of art and design on the development of the new social order – all influenced Gabo in shaping his own artistic principles. He was well aware of Tatlin's tower project, *Model for a Monument to the Third International* 1919–20, and actively participated in debates between supporters and opponents of imple-

44 Helen Adkins, 'From a Talk with the Artist Charles Wilson, Assistant to Naum Gabo', in *Competition for the Palace of Soviets* 1993, p.39.

45 Naum Gabo, Draft letter to Alexei Pevsner, 12 June 1970, TGA.

Column 1947
Perspex on aluminium base
28.2 x 19.2 x 19.2

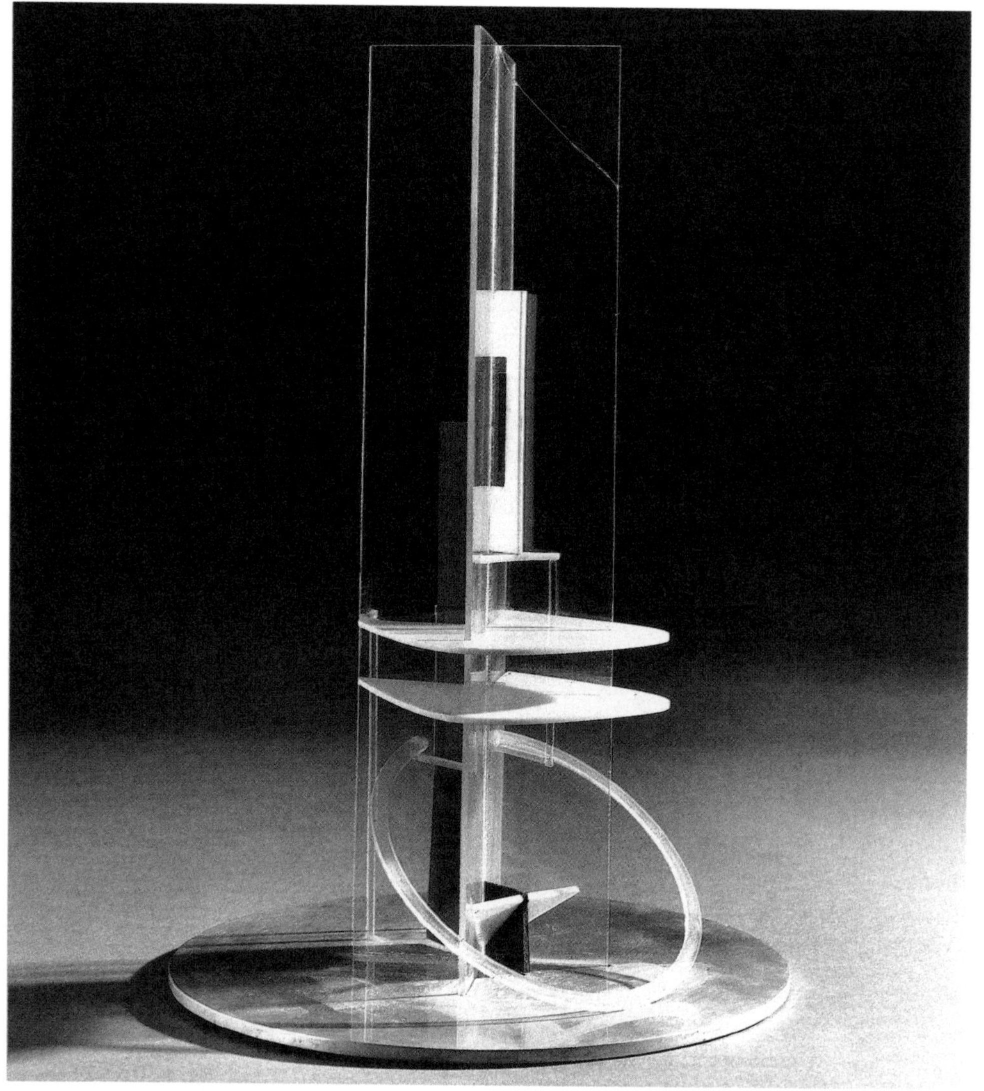

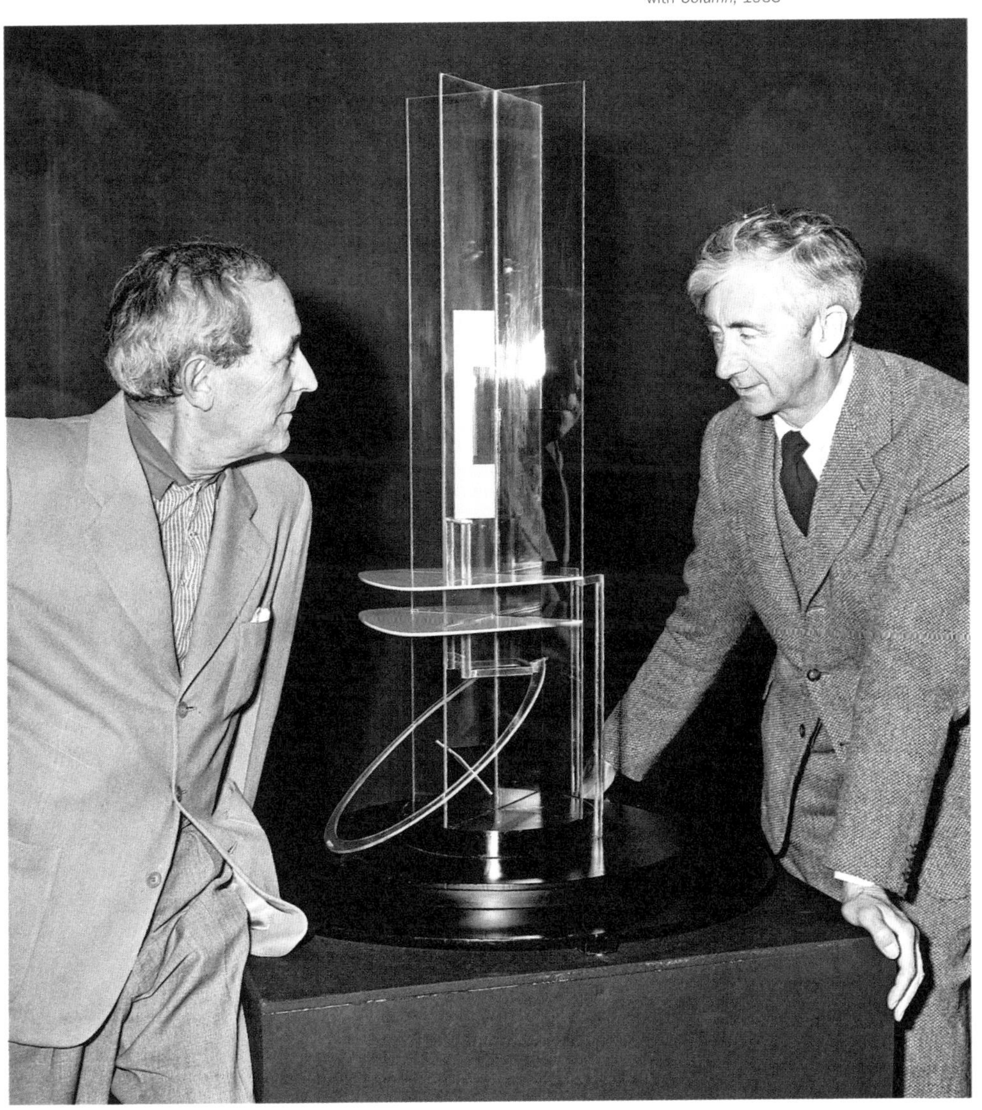

Photograph of Gabo and Herbert Read
with *Column*, 1953

→
Photograph of *Illuminated Tower*, 1921–5

menting the project. To Gabo, its spiral structure was reminiscent of the Tower of Babel.[46] ■ From 1920–22, Gabo was preoccupied with combining his technical skills and scientific knowledge to create a new self-identity as an artist. He was inspired by the same ideas as the Russian constructivists of the time. His experiments with the fusion of sculpture and architecture in one spatial construction are of the same order as those of Rodchenko and members of the Obmokhu group – Karl Ioganson, Konstantin Medunetsky, Georgii and Vladimir Stenberg – who exhibited their works in the *Second Spring Exhibition* of 1921. Soviet Russia provided the perfect environment for experimental spatial constructions to be transformed into designs for real objects, such as various agitation or propaganda constructions (Gustav Klutsis), kiosks (Aleksei Gan) and furniture (Rodchenko). Gabo at this time continued developing non-objective sculptural forms.[47] ■ Gabo's memoirs provide the richest source of information on his life and work during the Moscow period. Russian sources of information are rather limited – only occasionally is his name mentioned in the diaries of his fellow-artists,[48] by critics in periodicals,[49] or in documents of official organisations. Judging by the artist's own records, he was actively engaged in creative and social activities, participating in public debates on the role of art in the new social order, and collaborating with the Fine Art Department (IZO) of Narkompros in the organisation of the Acquisitions Committee and Pricing Board.[50] In

[46] Naum Gabo, *Iz moei rechi o Bashne Tatlina. Otvet Mayakovskomu*, p.8, TGA.

[47] Christina Lodder, *Russian Constructivism*, Yale University Press, New Haven and London 1983, p.230.

[48] Varvara Stepanova, *Chelovek ne mozhet zhit' bez chuda*, Sfera, Moscow 1994, pp.74–5.

[49] A.A. Sidorov, 'O novom realizme', *Tvorchestvo*, nos.5–6, Moscow 1920, pp.32–3.

[50] Letter from Naum Gabo to Herbert Read, 24 June 1958, Yale.

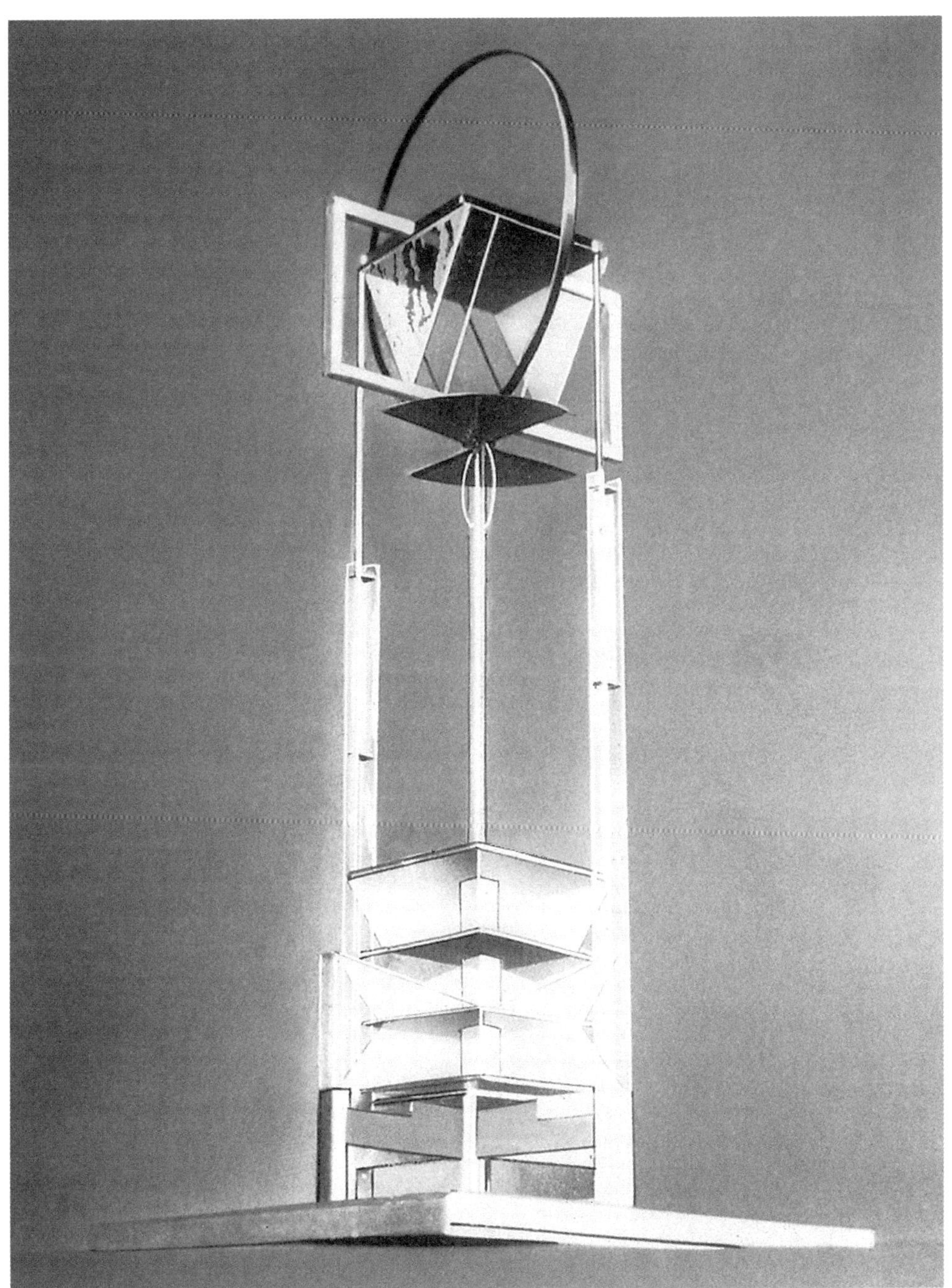

Sketch 1920–1
Pencil on paper, 30.5 x 22.2

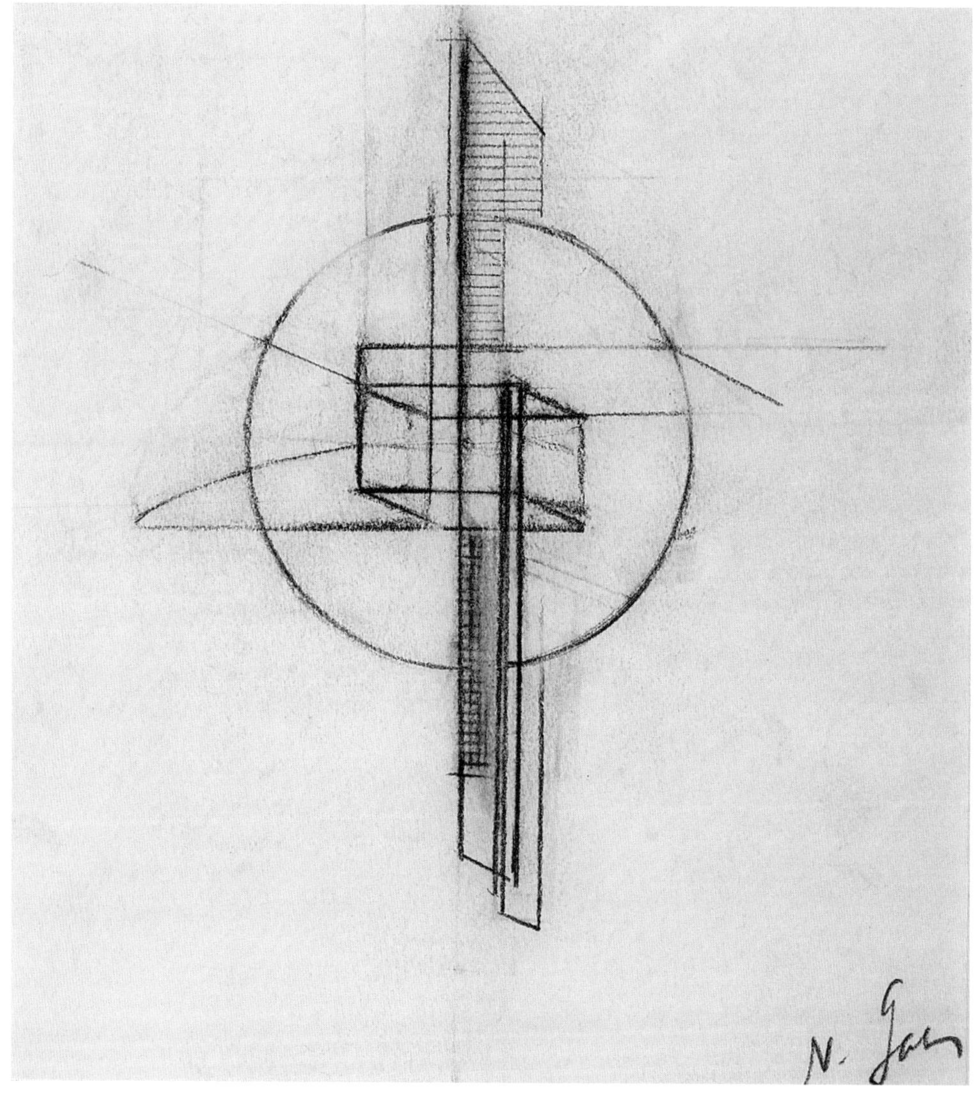

*Sketch for a Monument for an Institute
of Physics and Mathematics* c.1921
Pencil on paper, 33 x 22.9

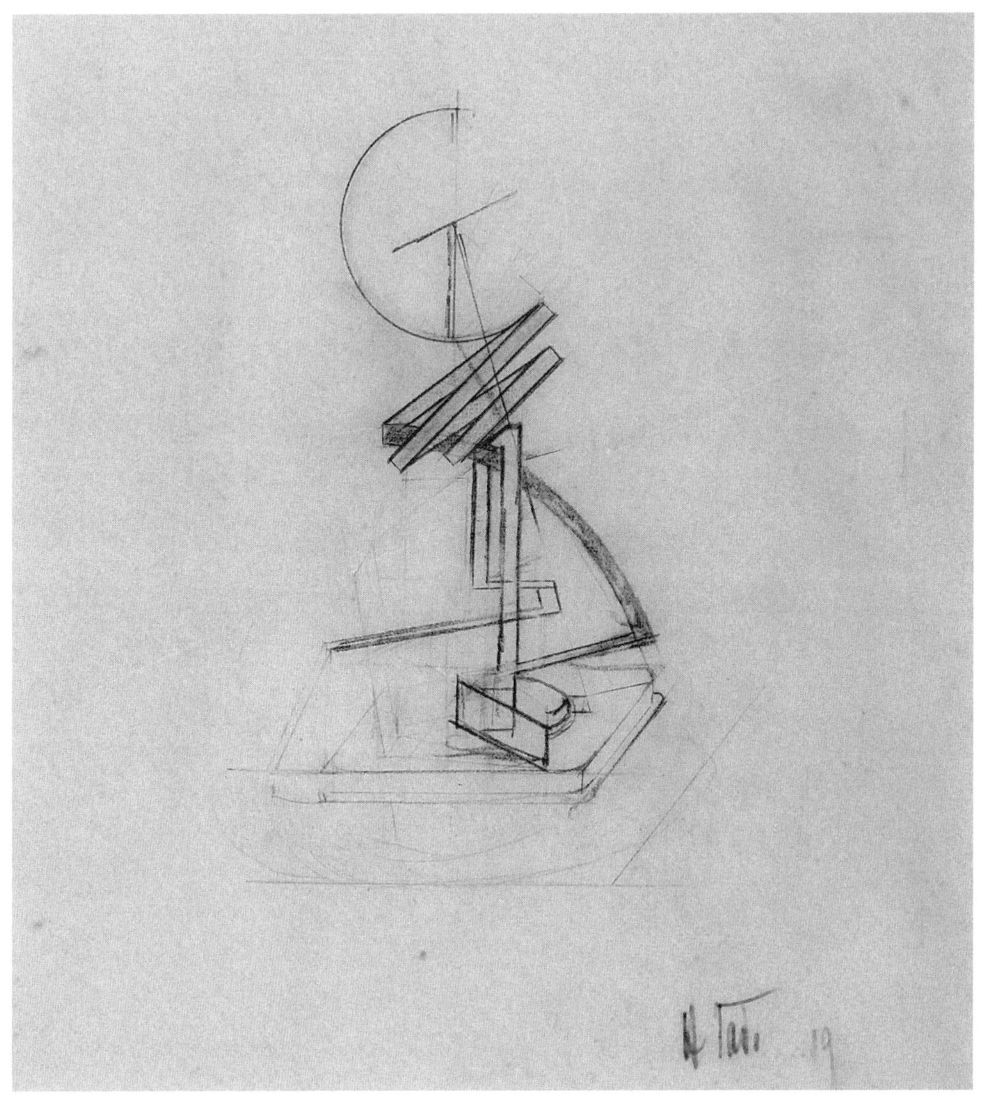

addition, he worked with the students of Antoine's Vkhutemas studio.[51] All of these activities were, nevertheless, unofficial and Gabo did not hold an accredited government position. Gabo's recollections are confirmed to a limited extent by his contemporaries. Stepanova, Rodchenko's wife and herself an artist, mentioned Gabo as a member of the 'group of nine' who devised and published the IZO department magazine *Iskusstvo*. The Acquisitions Committee selected Gabo's works to be purchased by the state and sent to regional museums, and later asked him to participate in the organisation of the large-scale *First Russian Art Exhibition* to be shown abroad. For the first time, the Soviet government was to reveal the entire range of traditional and cutting-edge Russian art to the West. This wealth of activity is witness to the fact that Gabo, while holding no official position, played an important role in the post-revolutionary Russian art scene. ■ Gabo's constructions from 1917–22 display striking similarities to the artistic experiments of the early or 'laboratory' stage of the Russian constructivist school; these experiments immediately preceded its more practical or 'productivist' trend of architecture and object design. Both Gabo and the artists of the 'laboratory' period were absorbed with the utopian idea that the transformation of the visual environment would bring about social change. While the constructivists attempted to achieve such a change through new concepts in architecture and object design, Gabo maintained a purely artistic line, developing a fusion between sculpture and architecture that would transform the notion of monumental sculpture and its role in society altogether. When the Working Group of Constructivists was founded in March

51 Naum Gabo, Draft letter to Antoine Pevsner, August 1947, pp.3–4, TGA.

1921, bringing together advocates of employing scientific ideas and engineering tools in art, Gabo felt all the more reassured in his own artistic experiments. ■ The propaganda of quintessentially new ideas and principles in art through exhibitions, museum displays, street art, manifestos, public debates and lectures was prevalent in all trends of the Russian avant-garde, including constructivism. Gabo demonstrated his allegiance to such an approach in *The Realistic Manifesto*, which was released on the streets of Moscow in the form of a wall poster. This self-promotion proved to work as the poster, hung on the walls of the capital, attracted crowds of people expecting to find a new government proclamation or order. The *Manifesto* was written on the occasion of the opening of the *Exhibition of Paintings by Natan Pevsner, Sculpture by N. Gabo and the school of Pevsner, Gustav Klutsis* on 5 August 1920. It took place on the open stage of Tverskoy Boulevard in Moscow and lasted a month. The *Manifesto* reflected on the stereometric method that Gabo had already put into practice: ■ 'We reject in sculpture mass as a sculptural element. Every engineer has known for a long time that the static force of bodies, their material resistance, does not depend on the amount of their mass. Examples: a rail, a flying buttress, a girder etc … But you sculptors of all shades and tendencies, you still cling to the age-old prejudice that volume cannot be freed from mass. Here we take four planes and build from them the same volume as a mass of four hundred-weights'. ■ When questioned about the meaning of the word 'realistic' in the title of the text, Gabo replied that his works were as real as if Nature herself had created them through the hands of an inspired artist. The notion of 'reality' was

Photograph of Vladimir Tatlin by the *Model
for a Monument to the Third International*
1919–20, Petrograd, 1920

Georgii Stenberg 1900–33
Construction for a Spatial Structure c.1921

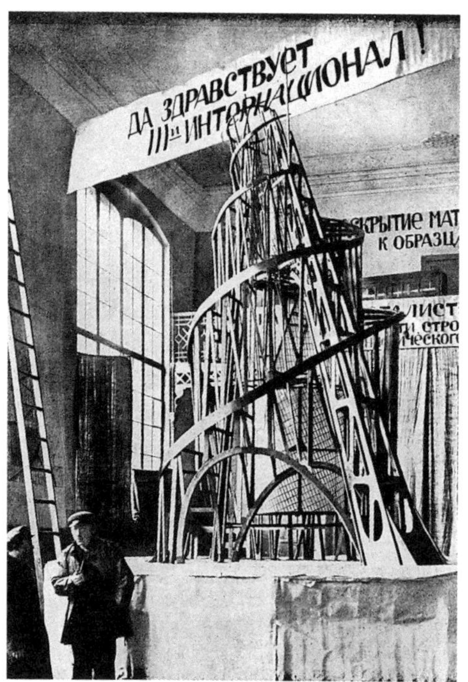

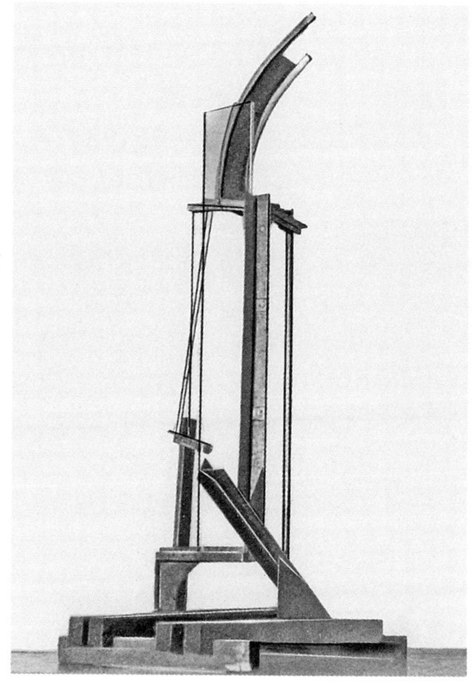

Aleksandr Rodchenko 1891–1956
Spatial Construction 1921

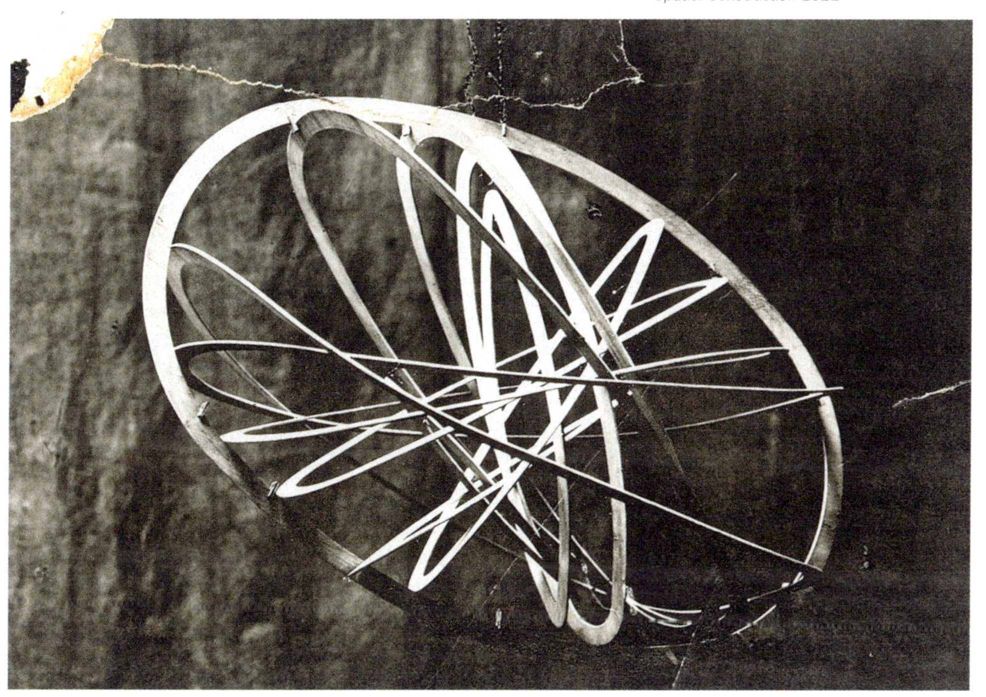

widely employed at the time by followers of various artistic trends, including the suprematists who considered themselves to be the creators of a new reality. Gabo recalled with amusement obtaining permission for the publication of the poster right after the end of the Civil War, when paper and printing materials were decidedly scarce. A party official glanced at the title and, believing it to be a proclamation of realist artists, issued Gabo with an authorisation to print.[52]

■ Alexei Pevsner, who witnessed at first hand his brother's artistic activity of the time, recalled Gabo putting together the text of the *Manifesto* in the few remaining hours before the opening of the Tverskoy Boulevard exhibition. Gabo's ideas were no revelation to Alexei as the sculptor had already shared them with his brother during their stay in Norway. Gabo's fervour to articulate, publish and promote his ideas was not only a claim for his artistic independence but also a reaction to the forthcoming opening of Tatlin's Model for the *Monument to the Third International* – the most anticipated artistic event of the time. It was paramount to Gabo that he should not be counted among Tatlin's followers, and *The Realistic Manifesto* was a means of expressing his independence. Contemporary critics were impressed by the concept of self-promotion by means of the poster revealed on the opening day of the exhibition, but they failed to recognise the singularity that it expressed. 'The author has had difficulty in expressing his opinion of the exhibition of comrades Pevsner, Gabo and Klutsis', wrote Aleksei Sidorov in his review *August exhibitions in Moscow*, published in the journal *Tvorchestvo*. He continued: 'The author is prepared either to accept the main ideas of

52 'Russia and Constructivism. An interview with Naum Gabo by Abram Lassaw and Ilya Bolotowsky', in *The World of Abstract Art*, G. Wittenborn, New York 1957, p.93.

Naum Gabo and Noton Pevsner
The Realistic Manifesto 1920

РЕАЛИСТИЧЕСКИЙ МАНИФЕСТ.

the Manifesto and rejoice in its criticism of Futurism ... or to celebrate the Tverskoy Boulevard artists as mere followers of Picasso. But it would appear that his conscience refuses to make a connection between words and deeds'.[53] ■ *The Realistic Manifesto* was written by a young sculptor, familiar with the achievements of European avant-garde artists, who was himself a prominent player in the revolutionary changes in Russian art of the 1910s–20s. Although the *Manifesto* reflects many influences, trends and ideas, its foremost principle was that of space and time: 'We say: Space and Time were born for us today. Space and Time are the only forms on which life is built and on which therefore art must be built'. The idea would remain central to Gabo's aesthetic thinking and, as the artist himself stated, the sole concept of the whole *Manifesto* to remain constant throughout his life. ■ Gabo was challenged by the concept of expressing the dynamic development of volumetric form throughout his artistic career. The Tverskoy Boulevard exhibition confirmed that his complex aesthetic ideas could be expressed only through the non-objective form of sculpture. The transitional period of compromising with figurative forms was reaching its end, as was the sculptor's time in Russia. In 1922 Gabo left for Berlin, expecting the sojourn to be a temporary one. He would be allowed to return to his homeland only in 1962, during Nikita Khrushchev's 'thaw', as one of a number of American tourists permitted to visit the Soviet capital following decades of isolation.

[53] A.A. Sidorov, 'Po vystavkam. O novom realizme', *Tvorchestvo*, nos.5–6, Moscow 1920, p.33.

A RUSSIAN CONSTRUCTIVIST IN EUROPE (1922–36)

THE INTRODUCTION OF A NEW MEDIUM In the spring of 1922, Gabo took his constructions to Germany to participate in the *First Russian Art Exhibition.* This unprecedented showcase of the widest range of contemporary Russian art in Western Europe took place in the Galerie Van Diemen in Berlin.[54] The exhibition created a long-lasting impression in Europe, although it went virtually unnoticed in Russia.[55] Contemporary reviews stated only that: ■ 'The Revolution has awoken in us dream-like, life-changing urges which are forestalled by our lack of technical means, preventing their materialisation and forcing us to sketch them on canvases for the time being … Give us the advanced technical means to build life, construct houses and machinery! Then, one can only hope, instead of the "art of falsification" we will once again feel the urge to produce paintings, an urge which has lain dormant since the Revolution.'[56] ■ The official commissars of the state exhibition were the Head of IZO, David Shterenberg and Natan Altman. Gabo was among those who assisted with the organisation and installation. The event was a turning point in

54 For further information on the exhibition see: *The First Russian Show. A Commemoration of the Van Diemen Exhibition, Berlin 1922*, Annely Juda Fine Art, London 1983.

55 Anatolii Strigalev, 'Iskusstvo konstruktivistov ot vystavki k vystavke (1914–32)', *Sovetskoe iskusstvoznanie*, issue 27, Moscow 1991, p.149.

56 Ya. Tugenkhold, 'Russkaya khudozhestvennaya vystavka v Berline', *Russkoe iskusstvo*, no.1, 1923, pp.100–2.

Gabo's career – not only did participating in the organisation of the exhibition enhance his reputation in Berlin's artistic milieu, but also his constructions were a success with critics and art collectors. He took the opportunity to exhibit the entire range of his works, eight sculptures and one drawing altogether, from the figurative *Heads* to the transparent *Reliefs* and the mobile *Kinetic Construction.* By comparison, Tatlin was represented by a single *Counter-Relief* in the sculpture section and Rodchenko by one *Spatial Construction.* Judging by the display photographs, the exhibition catalogue did not include all the works shown but, nevertheless, the number of Gabo's sculptures displayed was impressive. He also acquired a first buyer for his works in the connoisseur Katherine Dreier, the founder of America's most prominent contemporary art foundation, the *Société Anonyme.* Dreier's acquisition of *Construction in Space C* c.1920–1 laid the ground for a long-lasting friendship between the artist and the collector. ■ Despite his eight-year absence from Germany, Gabo rapidly became an integral member of Berlin's creative milieu. Prominent members of Russian artistic and literary circles such as Archipenko, Ilya Ehrenburg, Vladimir Mayakovsky and Jean Pougny were sojourning in Germany's capital at the time. In addition, he formed close friendships with German avant-garde artists Hans Richter and Kurt Schwitters. When the *First Russian Art Exhibition* moved on to Amsterdam's Stedelijk in 1923, Gabo was unable to follow it because of illness; he remained in Berlin to be nursed by Hans Richter's ex-wife, Elisabeth (née Steinert). Trained as a nurse during the war, she was 'one of the richest girls in Berlin'.[57] Their romantic involve-

57 Cleve Gray (ed.), *Hans Richter by Hans Richter*, Thames and Hudson, London 1971, p.28.

ment was to last until Elisabeth's tragic death in November 1929.
■ The period spent in Berlin (1922–32) was one of the most intense in the sculptor's artistic career. During this time, he produced a series of ground-breaking constructions, participated in a competition for a large-scale architectural project, created design projects, lectured at the Bauhaus, and produced an impressive theatre stage set and costume designs. He achieved recognition as a sculptor and gained a reputation as one of Europe's leading masters of non-objective art. ■ In 1923, Gabo was involved in the publication of the first issue of the magazine *G: Materials for Elemental Form-Creation*, with a key editorial that documented the latest innovative tendencies in art, architecture, design and film in the Weimar Republic. This issue included an extract from Gabo's own translation of the *Manifesto* and Lissitzky's explanation of his *Proun Room* at the *Grosse Berliner Kunstausstellung*.[58] From 1922–30, Gabo exhibited extensively in Germany, France and the USA. In 1923, he encouraged his brother, Antoine, to adopt the stereometric method and associated construction technique. Subsequently, Antoine abandoned painting to become one of the most prominent sculptors in France. The brothers demonstrated their most recent works at a joint exhibition, *Constructivistes Russes: Gabo et Pevsner – Peintures, Constructions*, at the Galerie Percier in Paris.[59] They would henceforth refer to themselves as Russian constructivists, while they began to consider the members of the Working Group of Constructivists in Soviet Russia as 'productivists'. In Gabo's opinion 'the Constructivists proper, under the leadership of

[58] Detlef Mertins and Michael W. Jennings (eds.), *G: An Avant-Garde Journal of Art, Architecture, Design, and Film. 1923–26*, Tate Publishing, London 2010, pp.7, 100.

[59] *Constructivistes Russes: Gabo et Pevsner*, exh.cat., Galerie Percier, Paris 1924.

Tatlin, were a group denying any value to art and were entirely denying its usefulness and proclaiming that art has lost its purpose as a social factor … They demanded from art that it should turn from creating social values to making utensils and home appliances.'[60] In reality, Gabo and Pevsner had left Moscow during the early years of the Russian constructivist movement and their respective careers came to represent an alternative route integrating international non-objective trends and steering away from the development of Russian constructivism. ■ The years 1923–7 marked a creative boom for Gabo and are traditionally associated with his interest in machine aesthetics in art. *Construction in Space: Diagonal* c.1925 was conceived in Russia but executed from coloured plastics in Berlin; the *Monument for an Institute of Physics and Mathematics* c.1924 celebrated achievements in science and technology; the *Rotating Fountain* c.1925 reflected Gabo's first attempt to employ the kinetic energy of water. ■ In the 1920s, Gabo made press cuttings of various apparatus and tools,[61] revealing his exploration of machine aesthetics, or rather its formal side concerning a machine as an image or an object. His works of this period are constructed from transparent materials such as glass and plastic mounted on metal frames, and are characterised by stark, geometrically simple shapes. Gabo envisaged them as models for monuments to science and technology. Their shapes, proportions and symmetrical composition are reminiscent of the apparatus of a scientific laboratory: the *Model of a Monument for an Observatory* c.1922 seems to be based on the form of a microscope; *Construction in Space: Diagonal*

[60] Naum Gabo, Lecture notes 9313/2/2/37, p.28, TGA.

[61] *Constructing Modernity* 2000, p.182.

Photograph of the organisers of the
First Russian Art Exhibition at Galerie
Van Diemen, Berlin, 1922

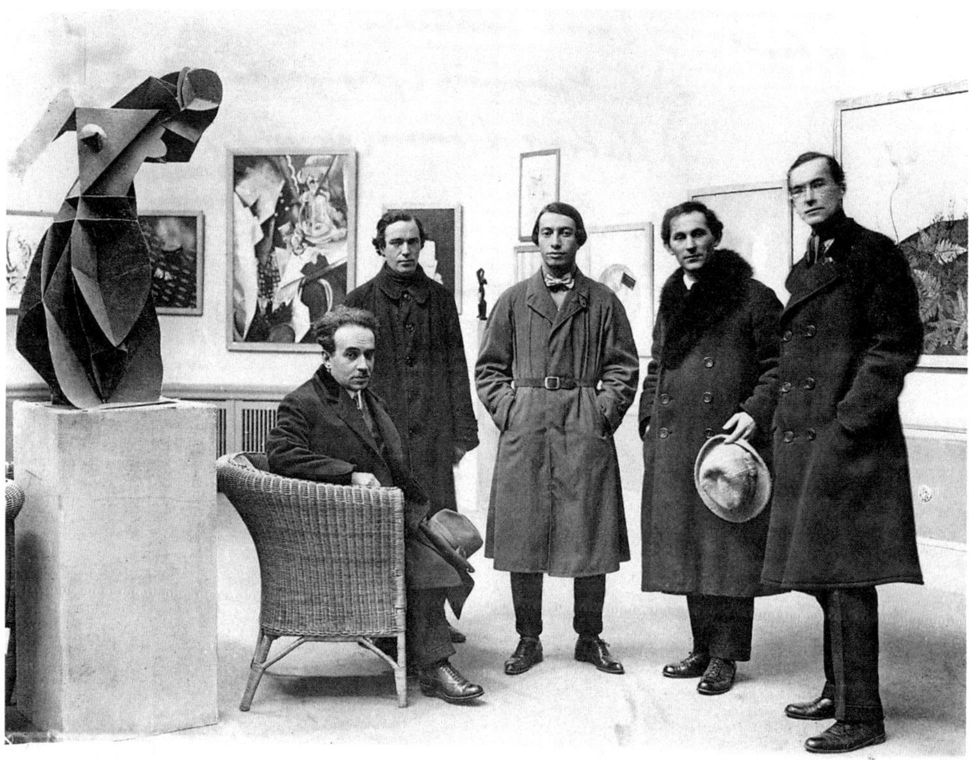

1.
RUSSISCHE
KUNST
AUSSTELLUNG
AMSTERDAM
1922
STEDELIJK MUSEUM

←

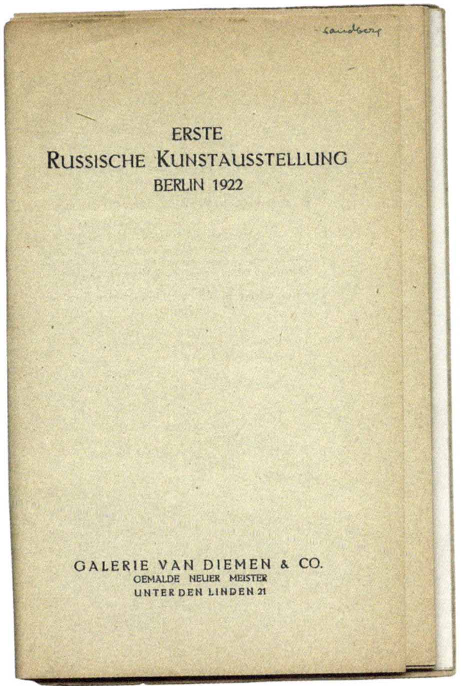

Cover of the *First Russian Art Exhibition* catalogue, Berlin, 1922

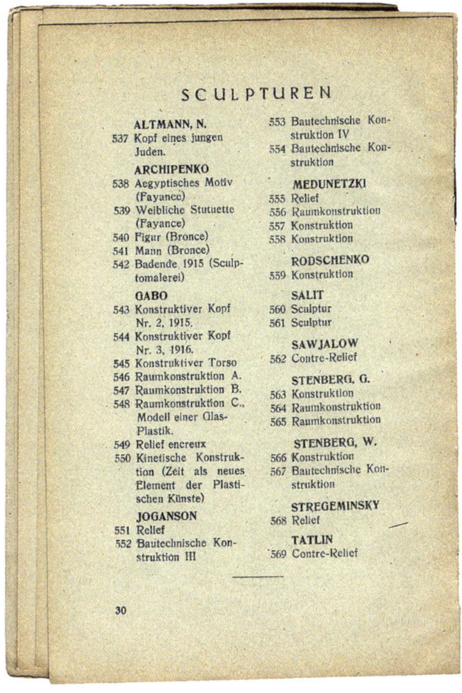

SCULPTUREN

ALTMANN, N.
537 Kopf eines jungen Juden.
ARCHIPENKO
538 Aegyptisches Motiv (Fayance)
539 Weibliche Stutuette (Fayance)
540 Figur (Bronce)
541 Mann (Bronce)
542 Badende 1915 (Sculptomalerei)
GABO
543 Konstruktiver Kopf Nr. 2, 1915.
544 Konstruktiver Kopf Nr. 3, 1916.
545 Konstruktiver Torso
546 Raumkonstruktion A.
547 Raumkonstruktion B.
548 Raumkonstruktion C., Modell einer Glas-Plastik.
549 Relief encreux
550 Kinetische Konstruktion (Zeit als neues Element der Plastischen Künste)
JOGANSON
551 Relief
552 Bautechnische Konstruktion III
553 Bautechnische Konstruktion IV
554 Bautechnische Konstruktion

MEDUNETZKI
555 Relief
556 Raumkonstruktion
557 Konstruktion
558 Konstruktion
RODSCHENKO
559 Konstruktion
SALIT
560 Sculptur
561 Sculptur
SAWJALOW
562 Contre-Relief
STENBERG, G.
563 Konstruktion
564 Raumkonstruktion
565 Raumkonstruktion
STENBERG, W.
566 Konstruktion
567 Bautechnische Konstruktion
STREGEMINSKY
568 Relief
TATLIN
569 Contre-Relief

30

Title page and list of Gabo's sculptures in the *First Russian Art Exhibition* catalogue, Berlin, 1922

recalls the instruments of a physicist. By the mid-1920s, Gabo had clearly moved away from the pure abstraction of his reliefs during the Moscow period. The aim of his constructions now was to reflect the new constitution of a world undergoing remarkable changes through advances in science and technology. ■ Gabo's use of first-generation synthetic materials gained him a reputation as a sculptor directly inspired by science. Some would attribute his European success, as opposed to his relative anonymity during the Russian period, to his access to superior quality materials unavailable to his

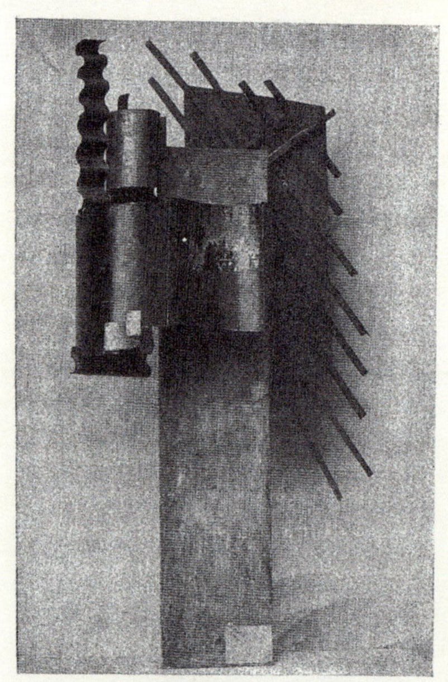

TATLIN: Contre-Relief

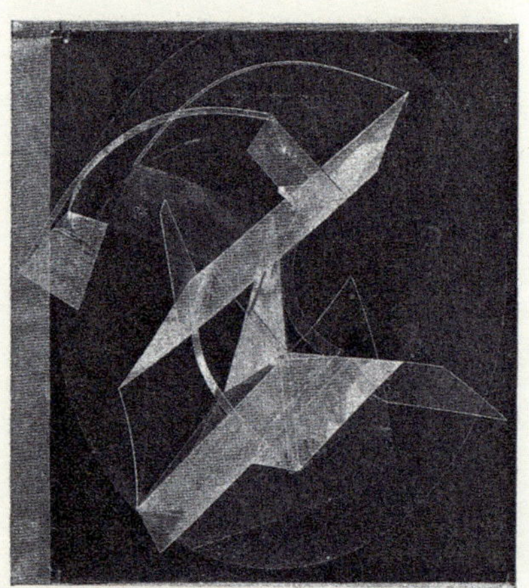

GABO: Raumkonstruktion C (Modell zu einer Glasplastik)

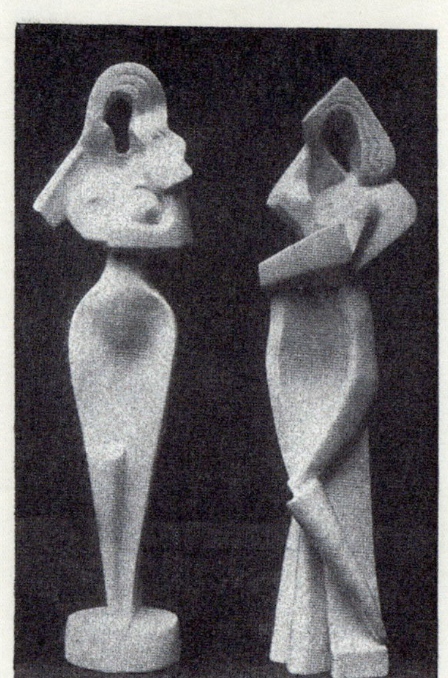

ARCHIPENKO: Aegyptisches Motiv (Fayance), Figur (Bronce)

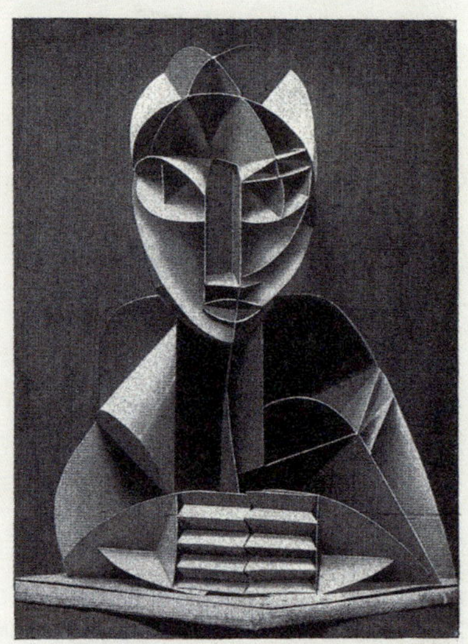

GABO: Konstruktive Kopf Nr. 2 1916 (Eisen)

Illustrations from the *First Russian Art Exhibition* catalogue, including Gabo's *Constructed Head No.2* c.1916 and *Construction in Space C* c.1920–1

fellow artists in Soviet Russia.[62] It was also assumed that the invention of a new generation of plastics inspired Gabo to search for novel spatial forms in his sculpture.[63] In reality, a number of constructions of the Berlin period had been conceived by Gabo in Moscow and were subsequently executed in Germany where synthetic materials were widely available. Throughout his artistic career, Gabo's creative imagination anticipated the invention of new materials. Miriam Gabo, the artist's widow, mentioned in a letter to art collector Jim Ede: 'He [Gabo] has always been an artist with a long backlog of works unexecuted – he shows me sketches sometimes … Sometimes it takes ten years or even more before materials catch up with his ideas or before he can find the technical means.'[64] ■ In working with such a fragile, short-lived medium as plastic, Gabo did not expect his constructions to be as durable as those made from traditional materials. For Gabo, an idea or an image itself was far more important than the chemical characteristics or the durability of the medium employed to translate his mental pictures into spatial objects. Some of the early plastics used by Gabo between 1920 and 1940, such as celluloid, are easily degradable, leading to the loss of a number of works even during Gabo's lifetime. Gabo was a pioneer in introducing synthetic materials as one of the main mediums of sculpture and it was his works that first raised concerns about the 'inherent vice' of artworks executed from plastics – a problem that remains unsolved to this day. ■ Most of the above-mentioned works were unknown to the gen-

62 Selim Khan-Magomedov, *Pionery sovetskogo dizaina*, Moscow 1995, p.93.

63 Christopher K. Green, *Naum Gabo in England*, MA thesis, Courtauld Institute of Art, University of London 1967, pp.7–8.

64 Letter from Miriam Gabo to Jim Ede, 7 February 1968, Kettle's Yard Archive, Cambridge.

eral public from the 1940s to the 1970s. Disassembled and tightly packed in boxes as Gabo fled Nazi Germany in 1933, the works travelled with the artist from Berlin to Paris, then to London and finally the USA. Unexhibited and untouched for decades, they were discovered in the attic of Gabo's Connecticut house by his assistant Charles Wilson in the late 1960s. The gradual process of unwrapping, restoring and reassembling the works began in Gabo's lifetime and was continued by Wilson throughout the 1980s, when the works were exhibited for the first time in almost fifty years. The story with the *Heads* had repeated itself, only this time the group Gabo chose to censor was that which he considered to be the most influenced by machine aesthetics.

CURVED SPACE AND THE TRANSITION TOWARDS ORGANIC FORMS The achievements of the first fifteen years of Gabo's creative life were shown in November 1930 at his first one-man exhibition *Gabo: Konstructive Plastik* at Kestner-Gesellshaft, Hanover.[65] On this occasion, Gabo gave a lecture on *'The rational and irrational in modern art'*, expressing his belief that constructive art is a reflection of the irrational side of a human being, whereas science is concerned with the rational side of life scrutinised through logic. For Gabo, constructive art was based on scientific principles, as it was 'for in these laws, however real and rational they might appear, we felt that the highest spiritual potential of the irrational was revealed'.[66] ■ Gabo became increasingly concerned with articulating and explaining the ideas and values behind his art. In order to demonstrate the basic principles of his stereometric method

[65] *Gabo: Konstruktive Plastik*, exh. cat., Kestner-Gesellschaft, Hanover, 6–23 November 1930.

[66] Translation by Christina Lodder, in *Gabo on Gabo* 2000, p.70.

Cover of the *First Russian Art Exhibition*
catalogue, Amsterdam, 1923

Cover and list of Gabo's sculptures in the
*Constructivistes russes: Gabo et Pevsner –
Peintures, Constructions* catalogue,
Galerie Percier, Paris, 1924

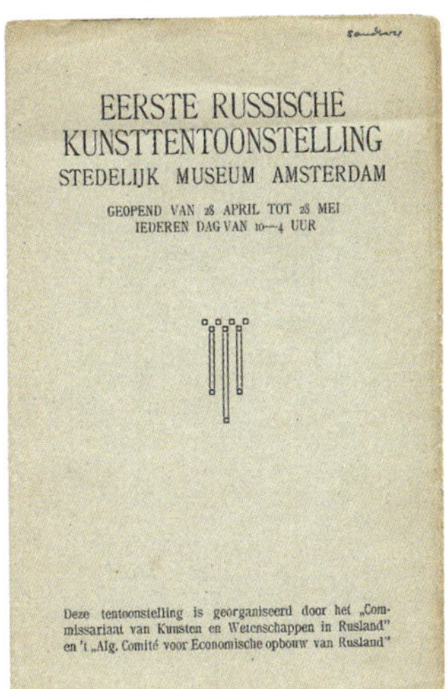

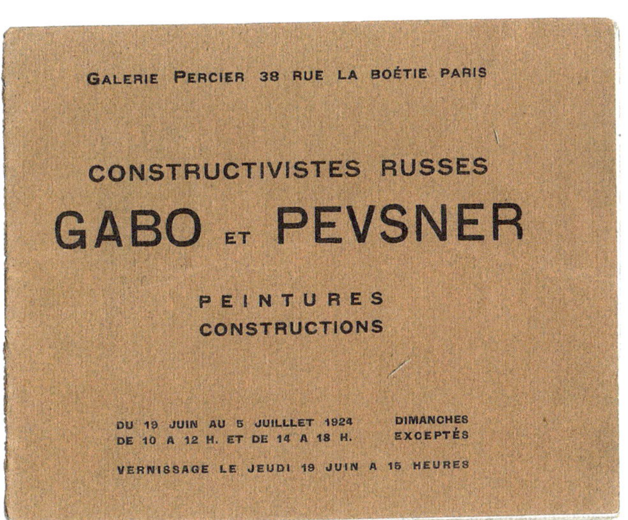

Ils libellent leurs principes en des termes exacts, c'est-à-dire en
des formes parfaitement adéquates à leur pensée intime. Arti-
sans experts, ils apportent un soin particulier à l'exécution
manuelle de leurs œuvres. Ils ont le goût du travail accompli et
de la mise au point qui confèrent aux objets qu'ils fabriquent la
haute tenue technique des instruments de précision, parfaits
dans leur absolu dénuement et dans leur stricte adaptation aux
besoins en vue desquels ils ont été créés.

Waldemar GEORGE.

CATALOGUE

GABO

1	Construction tête (1915).	*wood*
2	— torse (1915).	*Jane Heap's*
3	— en creux.	
4	— d'un monument pour une place d'observatoire.	*Dreier*
5	Construction (1923).	
6	— (1924).	
7	— (1924).	
8	— d'une maison.	

at the Hanover exhibition, Gabo displayed *Two Cubes* 1930, one conventional, representing solid volume, and the other stereometric, constructed out of intersecting planes. They were shown alongside *Constructed Head No.1*, annotated *The first application of stereometric system in sculpture.*[67] While the stereometric method mirrored the traditional space of Euclidian geometry, the new series of constructions reflected the contemporary understanding of the curved, spatio-temporal continuum or Einsteinian four-dimensional space. Developed from the mid-1920s through to the end of the 1930s, the series consists of a number of works defined by curvilinear forms or helical shapes, such as *Red Cavern* c.1926, *Construction in Space: Two Cones* 1928 and *Torsion* c.1929. ■ The 1930 Hanover exhibition also featured *Circular Relief* c.1926, one of the first works of the series. Mounted on a wall, the shape of the relief develops from a circular black wooden base coated with shiny black paint. A transparent spiral structure springs in an outward motion from its centre. The round base and the curvilinear aspect of the central element liberate the construction from such characteristics as upper and lower, left and right, front and back, while the transparent element ensures the interplay of the inner and outer volume of the sculpture. ■ Jörn Merkert's description of Gabo's creative output during the Berlin period expresses a widely accepted opinion: 'Gabo's sculptures in those years became fully free non-objective geometric spatial constructions, made up of many parts. Clear form, modern materials, the regularity of strict geometry and the precise calculation of an engineer's imagination inspired by nature were the artistic recourses with which new aesthetics were

67 Catalogue Raisonné 1985, p.200.

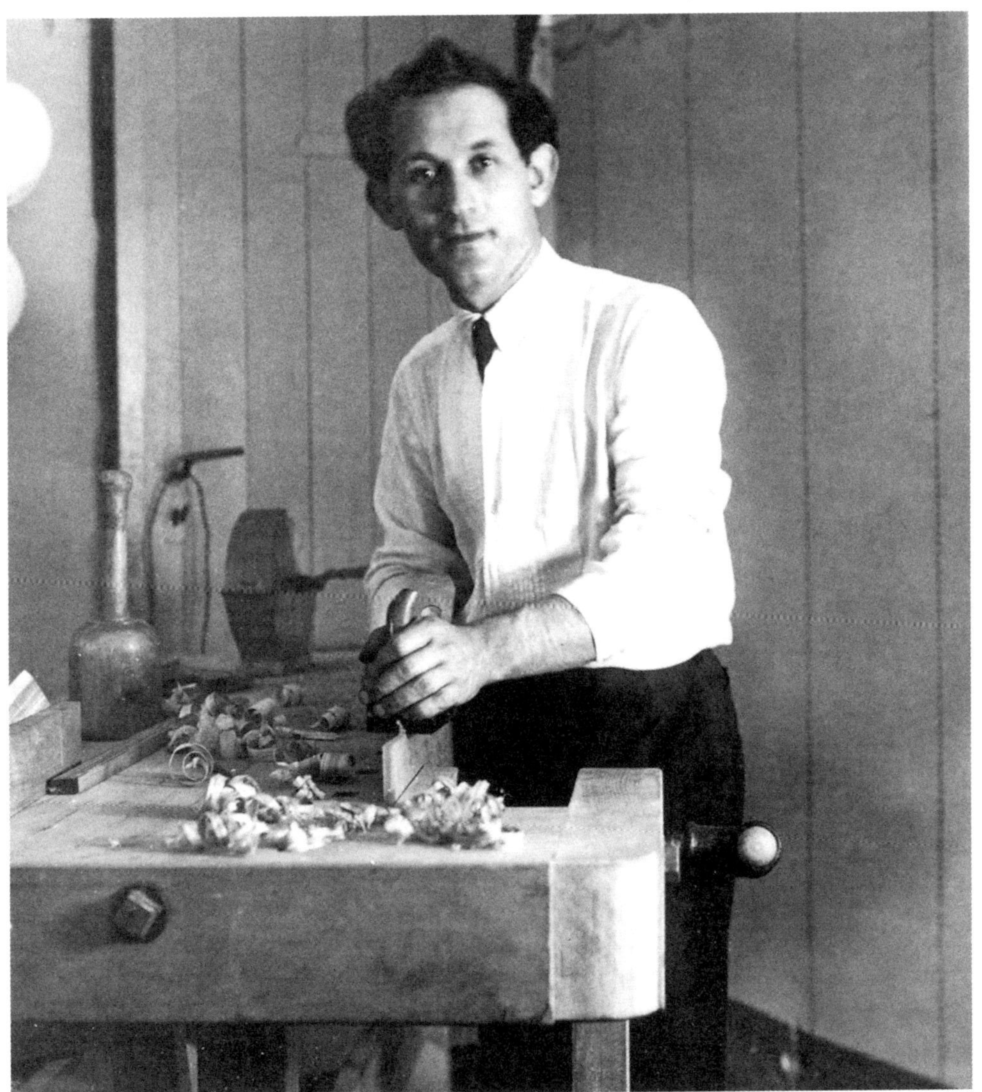

Photograph of Gabo in his studio,
Berlin, 1920–30

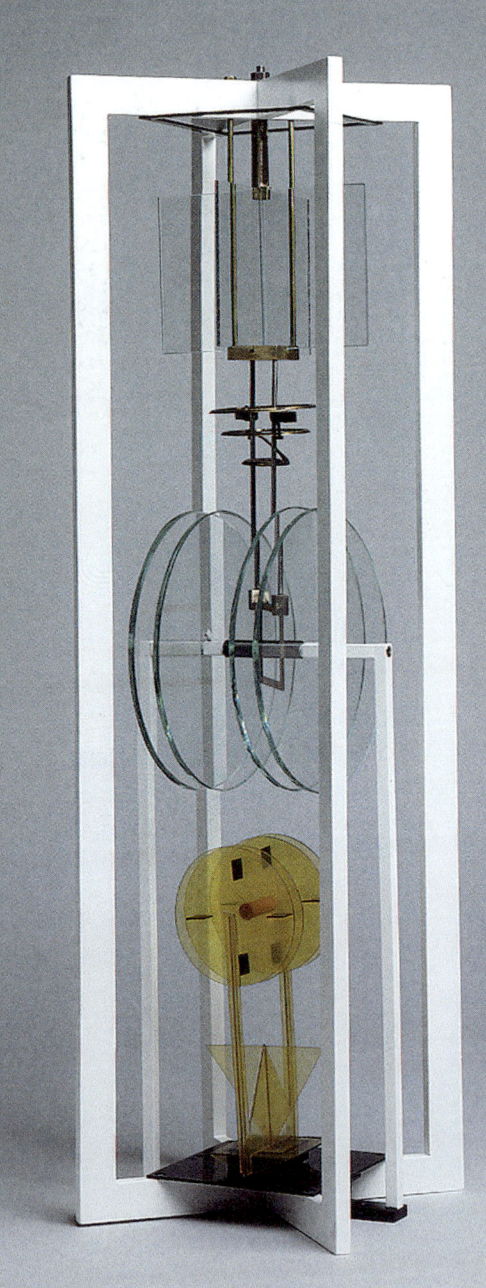

Construction in Space: Diagonal c.1925,
reassembled 1986
Glass, metal and celluloid, 61 x 16.3 x 16

Monument for an Airdrome (Variant of 1924)
c.1933, this version 1948
Perspex and brass, 41.6 x 108 x 57.7

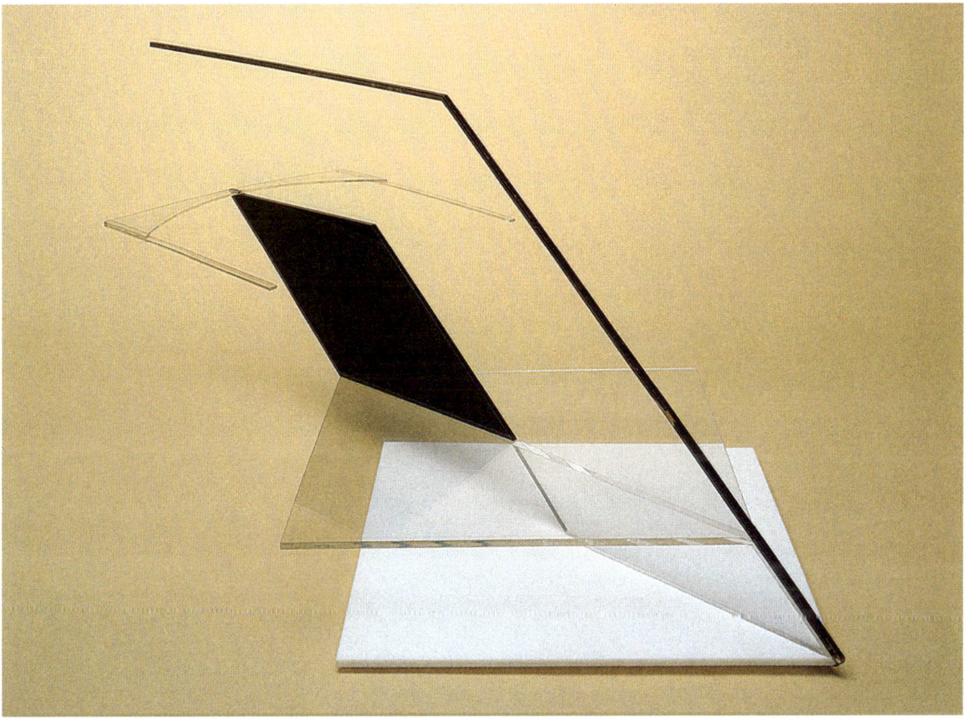

*Monument for an Institute of Physics and
Mathematics* c.1924, reassembled 1990
Brass, plastic and crystal, 44 high

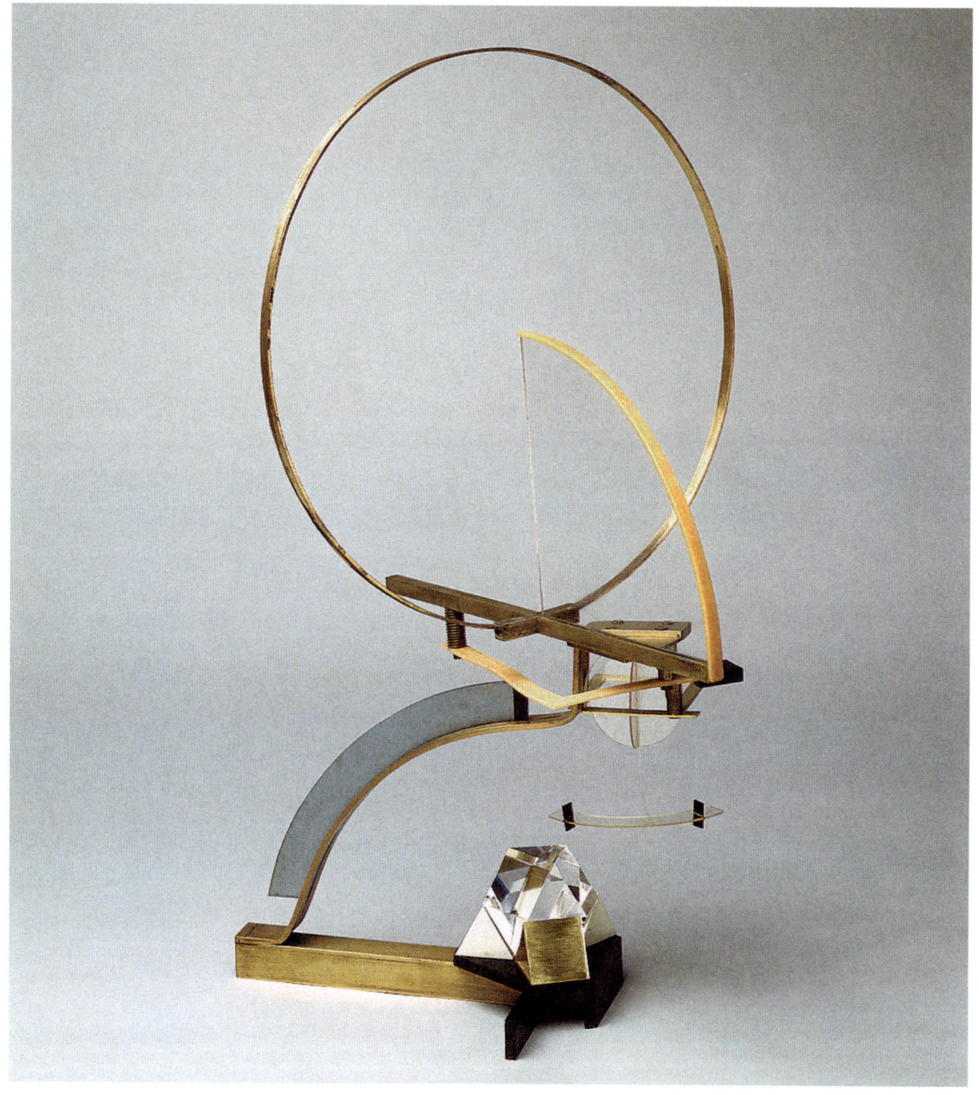

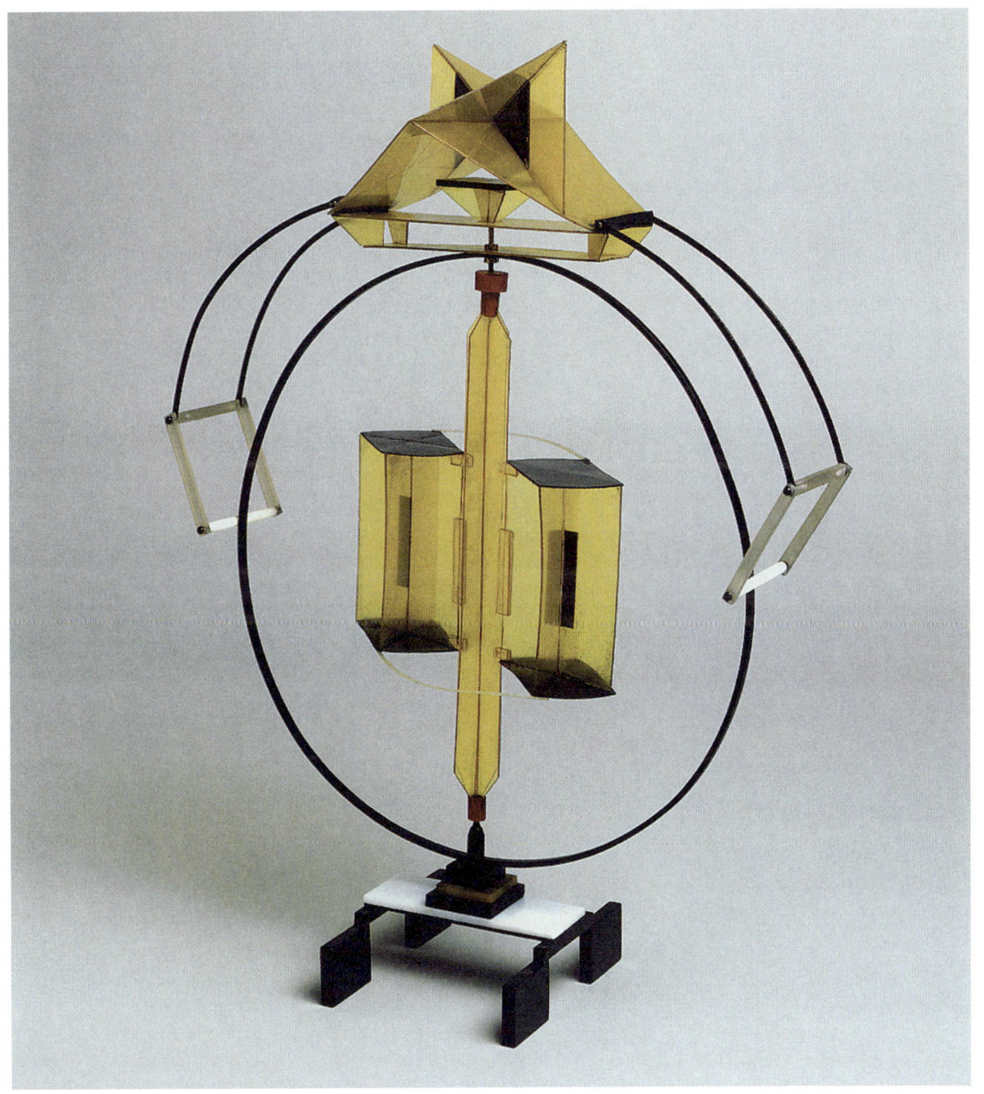

Rotating Fountain c.1925,
reassembled 1986
Metal and plastic, 44 x 40 x 40

being voiced.'[68] Gabo's works from 1925–32 do indeed give the impression of being calculated, precisely balanced constructions in which every element fits perfectly into place. From his very first constructions, Gabo employed a hands-on approach, working with card templates each cut and repeatedly reshaped, and each element of the construction attached and detached, adjusted and readjusted, until all parts were in precisely the right place. He worked in this meticulous manner throughout his artistic career. Gabo was also perceived as a 'scientist-sculptor', calculating his models as an engineer does a bridge. Many of his sketches and drawings were executed on graph paper and some contained calculations and formulas in his own handwriting pencilled into the margins. Closer analysis confirms that they are very basic computations giving the rough proportions of sections of the constructions and the angles of their intersections. The rest was done by painstaking, manual artisan-like work. ■ In 1993, the Tate Gallery acquired Gabo's family archive, and the unique documents that it contained, including correspondence, sketches, templates and unrealised projects, became publicly available. Detailed examination of the visual material sheds valuable light on the artist's creative method. For example, if one were to make a case study of *Torsion*, another work of the curvilinear series, the entire genesis of the sculpture could be reconstructed from the first preliminary study to the final large-scale construction. ■ The late 1920s to the early 1930s saw a new trend in Gabo's works as he developed an interest in more organic shapes. One of the first works to reflect the gradual departure from purely geometric forms was

68 Jörn Merkert, 'Naum Gabo: Constructivist and Constructor', in *Competition for the Palace of Soviets* 1993, p.14.

Torsion, conceived in about 1929. Its simple outline, lack of small detailing and use of just one basic element in the construction of its elaborate shape differentiates *Torsion* from works of the previous period. Its shape is determined by six identical triangles with a semi-aspheric incision at their base, joined at their apex in a slightly twisted motion. The genesis of the work could be traced to *Stereometric Tetrahedral Study* c.1929, a card pyramid that Gabo constructed in order to work out the basic shape of the triangular element, then transferred to a large sheet of thick paper as a pencil drawing. In turn, the symmetrical drawing was divided vertically, with its right side cut out to be used as template. It corresponds to the exact shape and size of the template used to create each of the identical triangular elements of the construction. It was executed using the same, or enlarged, template, first from transparent plastic in *Torsion* 1929/37 and later from bronze in *Torsion: Project for a Fountain* 1960–4 and stainless steel in the monumental *Revolving Torsion: Fountain* erected in 1976 by the Thames in the garden of St Thomas's Hospital, London. The fountain's water jets and slow rotating motion create a particularly expressive public monument. Gabo had a very precise idea of the fountain's appearance and functionality: ◼ '… the jets will give a certain kind of form by themselves. So the direction of the water is dictated by the form of the wings of the structure, and it goes round and then it becomes like a ball of water, and then it goes down, you know … In ten minutes one movement, so you stay there and look at the whole thing and then you suddenly see a totally different thing in the middle … I made it in stainless steel, so it has the same tone as water to a certain extent,

Circular Relief c.1926
Plastic on wood, 49.8 x 49.8 x 22.9

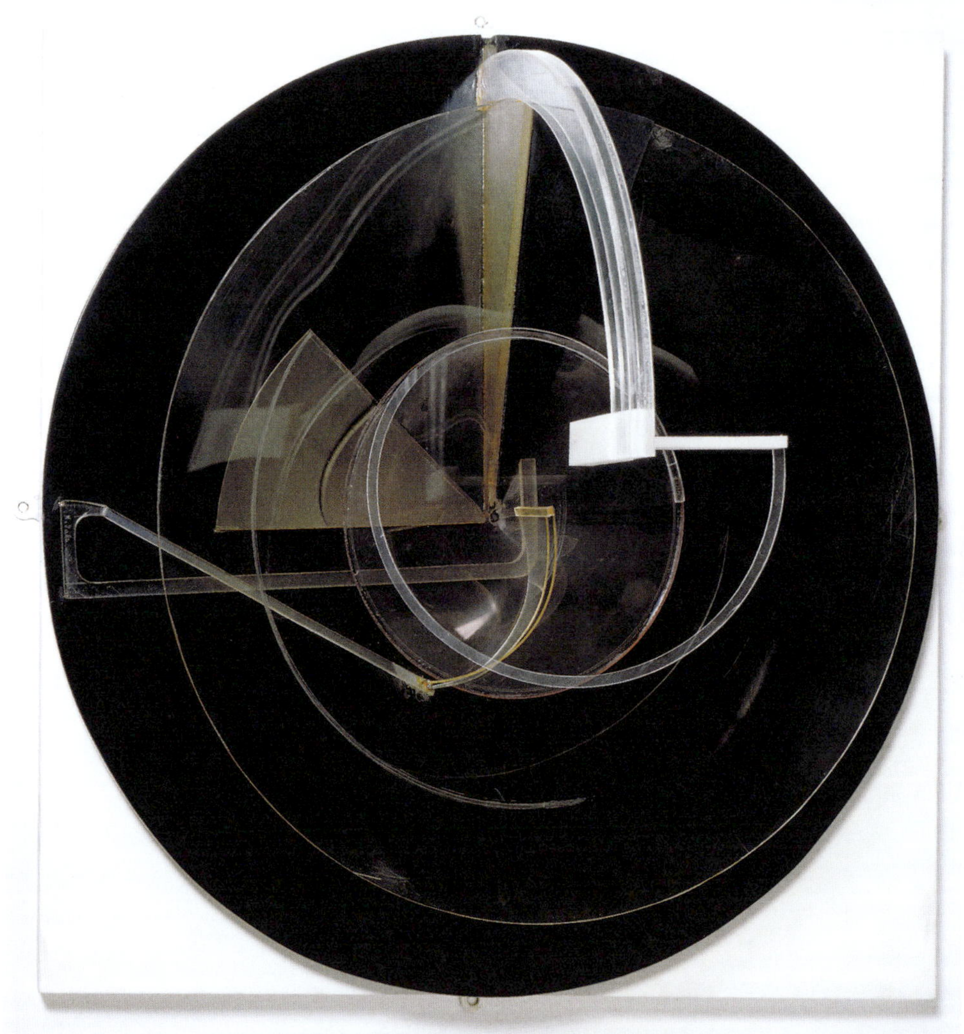

Torsion c.1929, this version 1937
Perspex, 35.2 x 41 x 40

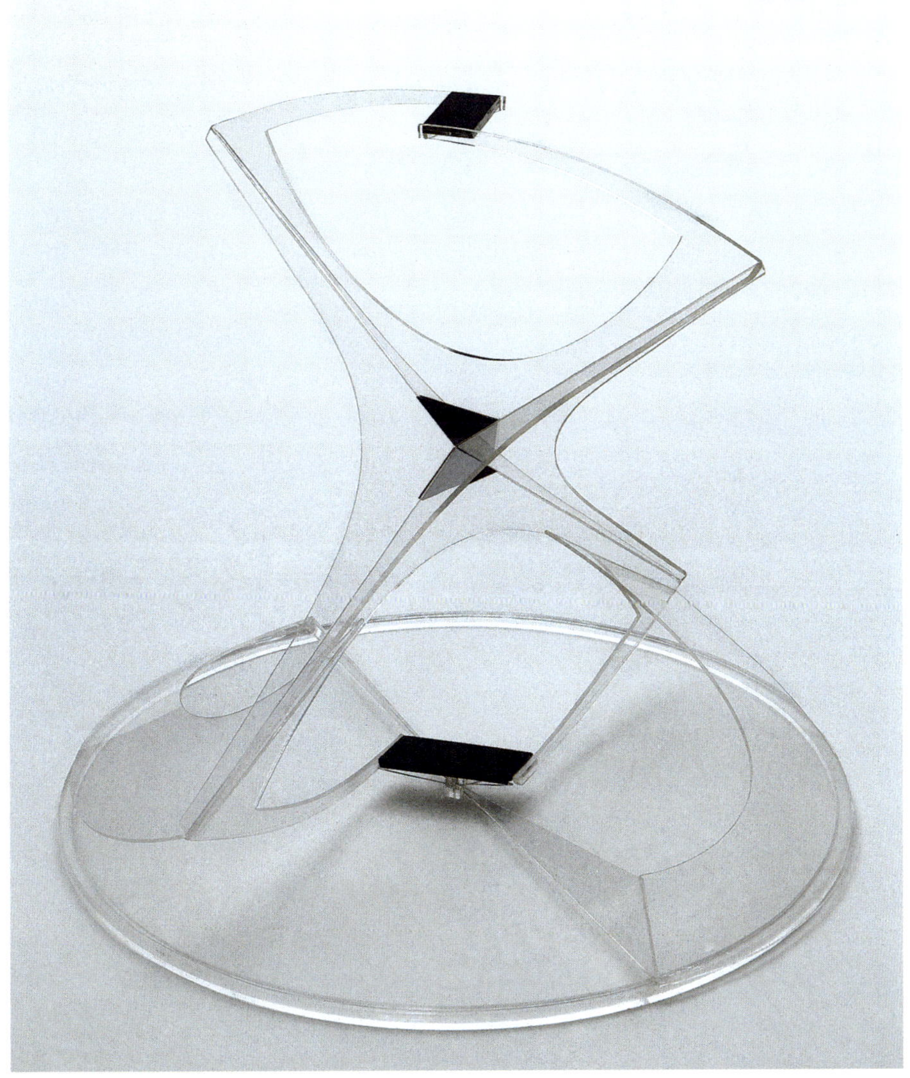

but its shadows you can see, and you ought to see, in the water.'[69]
■ The Berlin period saw the genesis of many ideas that Gabo was able to bring to life only at a much later stage of his career. While the execution of *Revolving Torsion: Fountain* dates from the 1970s, Gabo had first had the inspiration to use water as a new kinetic element bringing motion to his artworks in the mid-1920s. At the same time, he embarked on the completely new and exciting experiment of introducing his kinetic rhythms to a field previously unexplored by him – the theatre.

GABO AND DIAGHILEV Gabo's ideas of organically fusing formal and dynamic elements into an integral whole were fulfilled in his work on the stage set for Sergei Diaghilev's ballet production, *La Chatte*, premiered in Monte Carlo on 30 April 1927. This experience was the culmination of Gabo's search for non-mechanical motion in sculpture. From the mid-1920s, he displayed a particular interest in abstract film and music, as suggested in his diary entry of 4 January 1929: ■ 'Take the gems of sounds in handfuls and string them up. Polish them as a jeweller would do, the treasure of sound is waiting to be unveiled in our humdrum everyday life. How many of them are hidden in a waterfall, how many are lying about the streets, buildings and factories, produced by cars and people, in the air and on the ground, an entire spectrum of it in every thing! I am seriously considering all these possibilities with regards to my film on kinetic constructions. Without music it would be a legless invalid. The rhythm must be musically sound in order to keep the viewer in tempo.'[70] ■ His opportunity to fuse music with motion and

[69] 'Naum Gabo talks to David Thompson', *Art Monthly*, London, no.4, February 1977, p.10.

[70] Naum Gabo, Diary, 4 January 1929, BG.

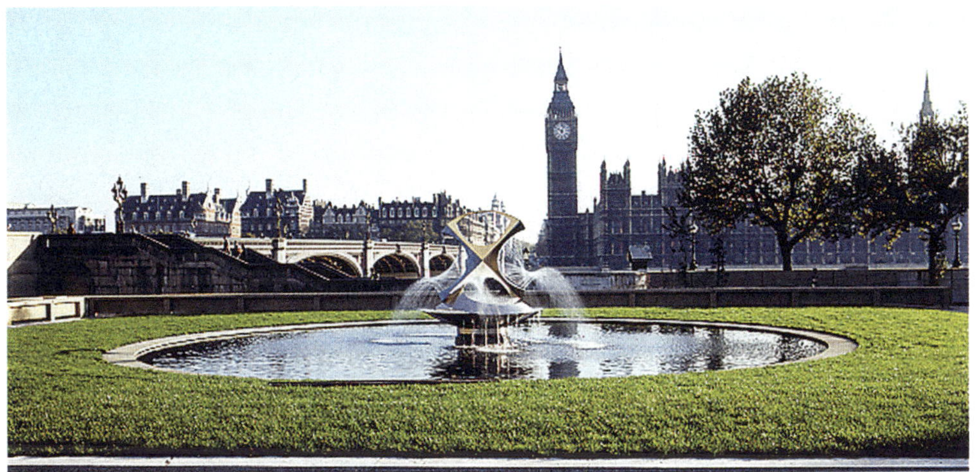

Photograph of *Revolving Torsion: Fountain* 1972–3 outside St Thomas's Hospital, London

form came in the long-awaited invitation from Europe's most successful entrepreneur, Diaghilev, to collaborate on a ballet production. ■ It appears Gabo himself approached Diaghilev in 1926 with a proposition for a kinetic set design. Diaghilev, who was in search of cutting-edge décor for *La Chatte*, recalled Gabo's project while compiling the programme for the 1927 season. Extensive correspondence between Gabo and Antoine, who was also involved in the project, sheds light on how it was possible to complete the design for the first constructivist ballet in history in just a couple of months. ■ Antoine to Gabo, 11 February 1927 ■ '... Upon returning home I found a telegram from Diaghilev addressed to you which read "Dear Gabo, come at once to me at the Grand Hotel I must see you immediately." I telephoned Diaghilev ... he wants to talk not about that kinetic set you had shown him in Paris, but a completely new one ...

→ (p.100)
Antoine Pevsner 1884–1962
*Model for the Statue of Aphrodite
in the Ballet* La Chatte 1927
Plastic, 14.9 x 4.4 x 5.1

→
Production photograph of *La Chatte* 1927

Photograph of stage set for *La Chatte* 1927

→ (p.101)
Photograph of Alice Nikitina in her *La Chatte*
costume, dedicated to Gabo, 1928

The kinetic set with which he is familiar doesn't suit him at all at this moment because of the following: the 20th anniversary of the Diaghilev Ballet will be celebrated in Paris in two-and-a-half months. On the occasion he indeed wants to make an ultimate splash. He wants something new and cutting-edge and this is why he has called upon you and me … It has been decided to produce one of Aesop's fables. ■ Naturally, the self-promotion and publicity for us will be huge. It would be unthinkable to create such a commotion with an exhibition. The fact that it is Diaghilev's jubilee makes it particularly attractive as he will commission only the best artists. As you know, Picasso is painting the stage curtain for the jubilee etc … Think about it urgently and [reply] straight away.'[71] ■ Gabo went immediately to Paris, where he promptly produced a design model to present to Diaghilev. Surviving sketches, models and archival documents indicate that Gabo worked on the stage set and costumes while Pevsner created the large *Statue of Aphrodite*, which towered over the stage set. The one-act play was a collaboration between the innovative choreographer George Balanchine and the young composer Henri Sauget, on a scenario by Boris Kochno based on the surprisingly classical theme of Aesop's fable. The story tells of a cat transformed into a girl by Aphrodite, the goddess of love, at the insistence of a young admirer. The goddess then sends a mouse to test the girl's true nature. Unable to resist her instinct, the girl chases the mouse away and is transmuted back to her animal state. Her lover dies of sorrow. Gabo chose an entirely new approach to his set design. He covered the walls and floor of the stage with black shiny oilcloths as a background

71 Letter from Antoine Pevsner to Naum Gabo,
11 February 1927, TGA.

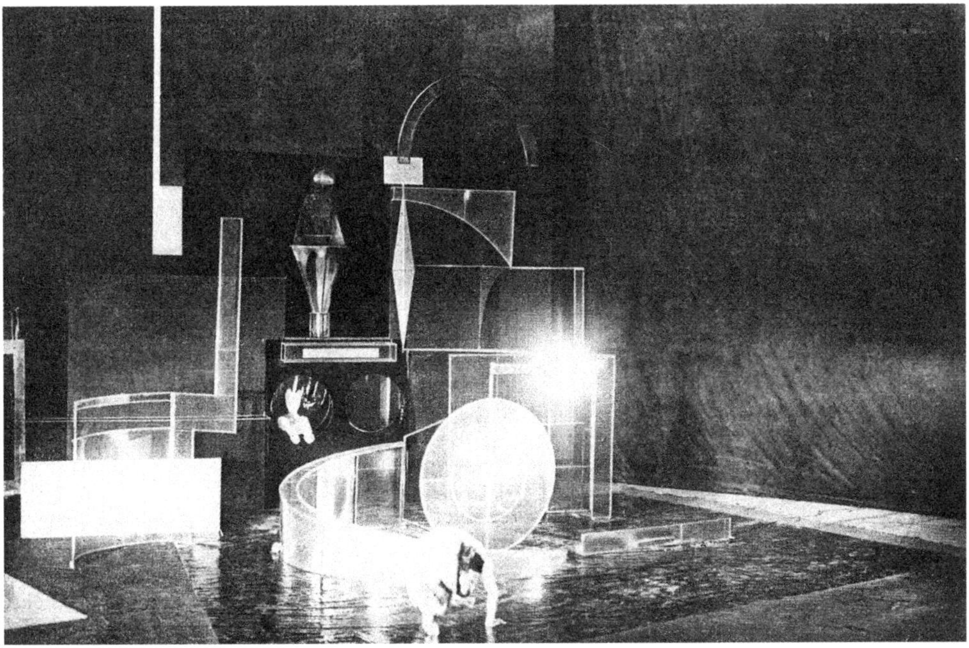

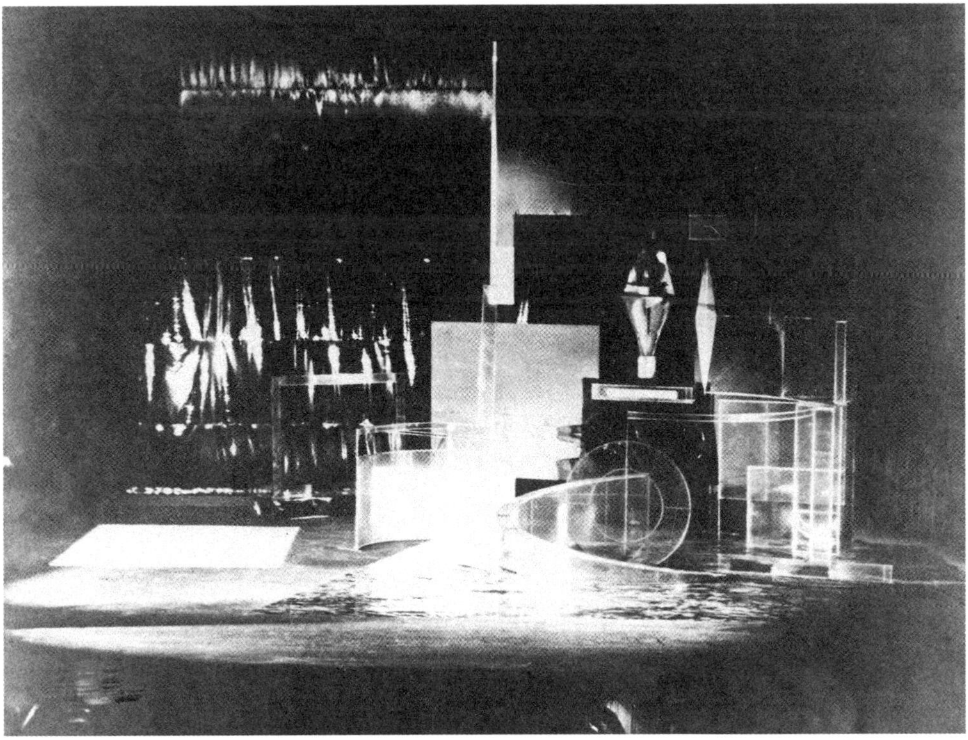

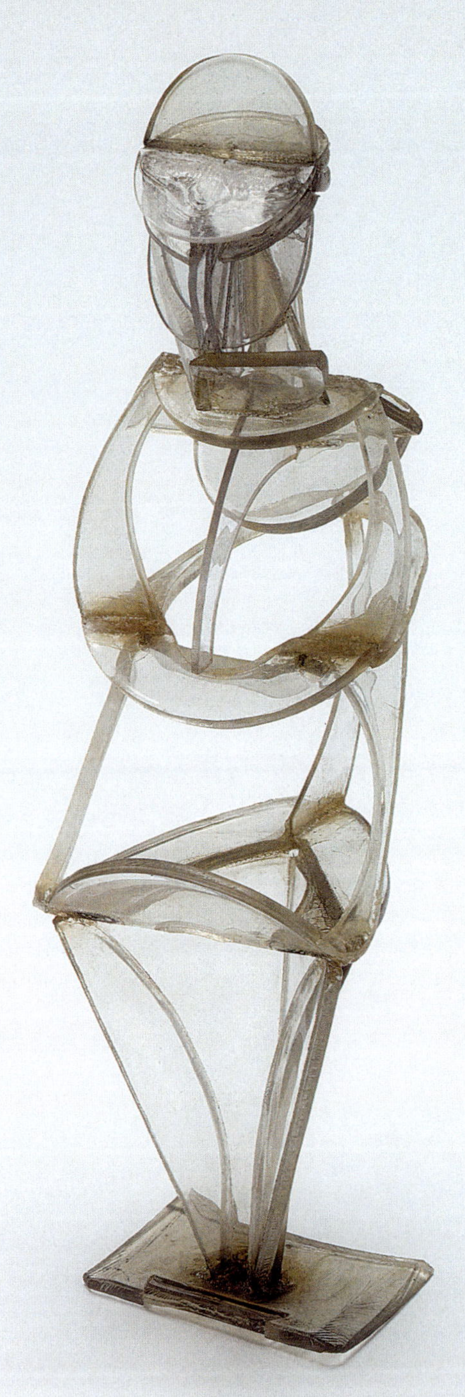

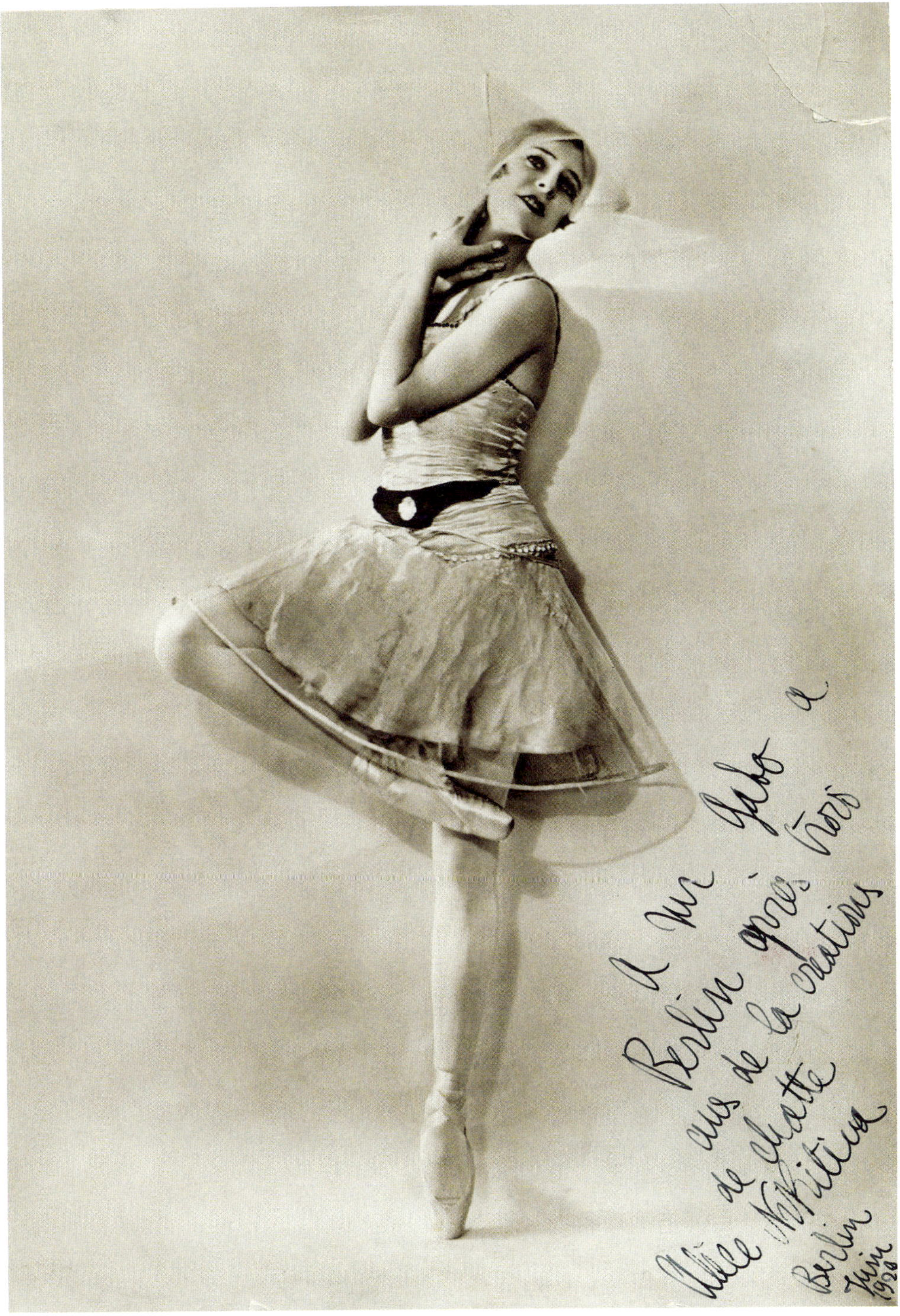
A Mr Gabo à
Berlin après bons
aus de la création
de chatte
Alice Nikitina
Berlin
Juin 1928

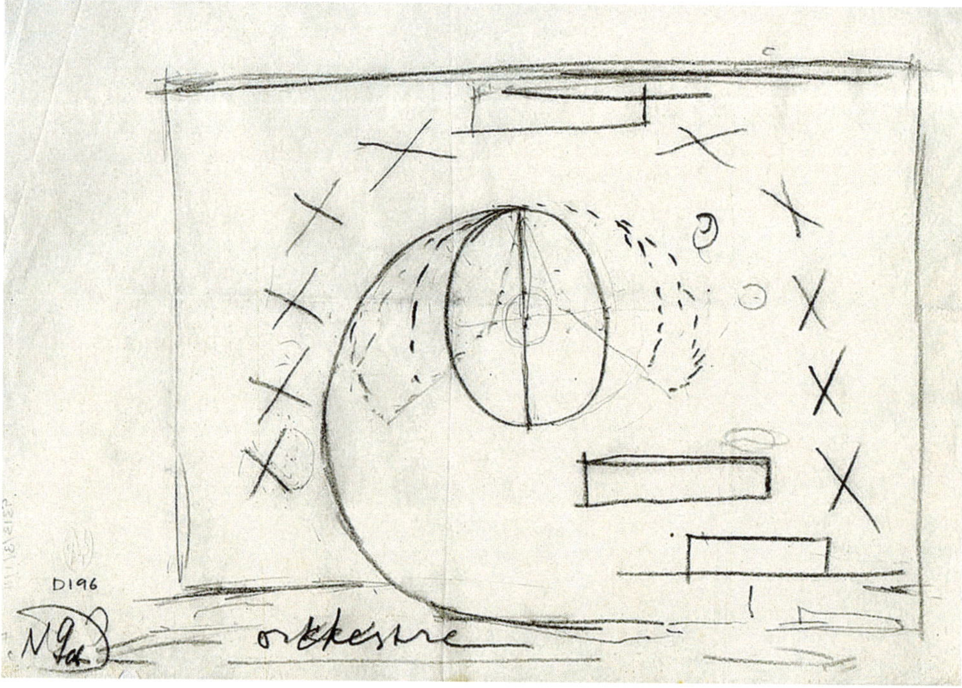

D196

orkestre

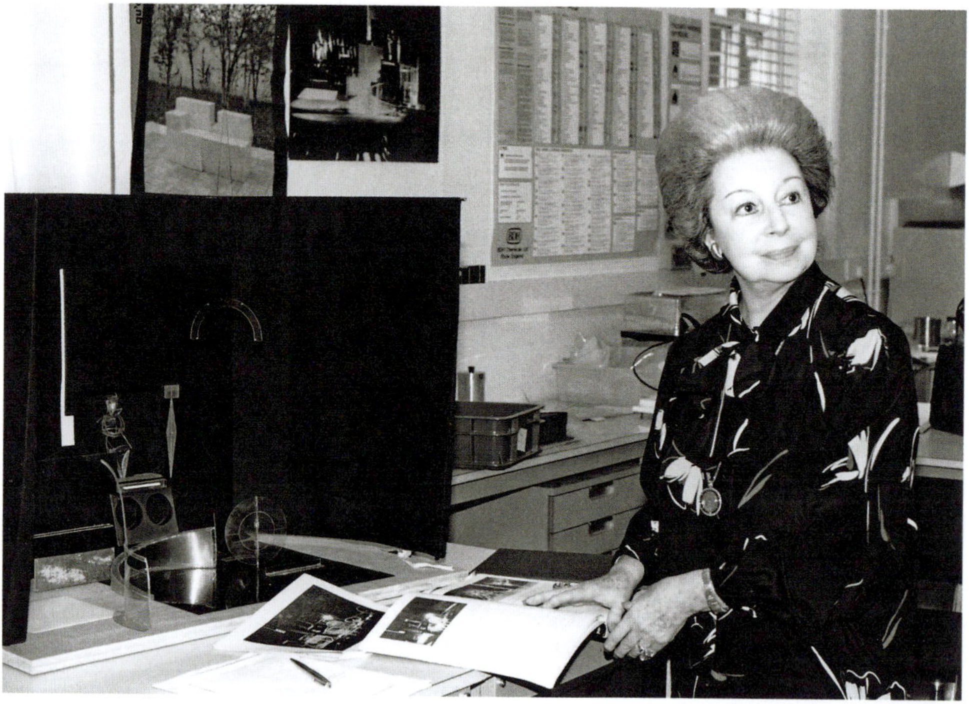

←

Drawing of the Stage Design for La Chatte
1927

Photograph of Alicia Markova with the *Model
for the Set of* La Chatte 1927, at the Tate
Sculpture Conservation Department, 1988

for his transparent set, which was based on a combination of simple geometric shapes. The dancers' costumes were enhanced by transparent plastic elements such as headdresses, breastplates and embellished skirts and sleeves. The main emphasis was on the illumination of the stage.  The ballet, although devised for the star duo of Serge Lifar and Diaghilev's prima ballerina Olga Spessivtseva, was later played by the young dancers Alice Nikitina and Alicia Markova, each partnering Lifar, who have left vivid recollections of the production. Nikitina describes the stage as lit from below as well as from the sides, making the oilcloth shine. Such illumination created the blurry, mirage-like illusion noted by critics and the public. In order to achieve the desired visual effect, Gabo suggested introducing new dynamic elements to the final scene. The young man's friends were to rotate geometrical frames in their hands – squares and circles painted black on one side and white on the other. During the final *marche funèbre*, the body of the young man was to be encased in these same frames.[72] Many years later, Markova recalled how unnerving it was for the dancers to perform on the shiny oilcloths covering the stage, which seemed so glossy and slippery. The use of synthetic materials was something of a novelty in set design. Pevsner reported to Gabo how fragile the set proved to be during the numerous transportations and installations: ■ Antoine Pevsner to Gabo, 9 February 1928 ■ ' … Our décor travelled with Sergei Pavlovich [Diaghilev] across most of Europe … Can you imagine what became of it? They themselves were constantly repairing it, altering it – they broke the celluloid and replaced it … But you can't even imagine what became of the God-

72 Richard Buckle, *Diaghilev*, Weidenfeld and Nicolson, London 1979, p.484.

Photograph of Gabo, Antoine and Virginie
Pevsner in Berlin, 1920–30

Costume Sketch for La Chatte 1927
Graph paper, pencil and pastel, 25.5 x 19

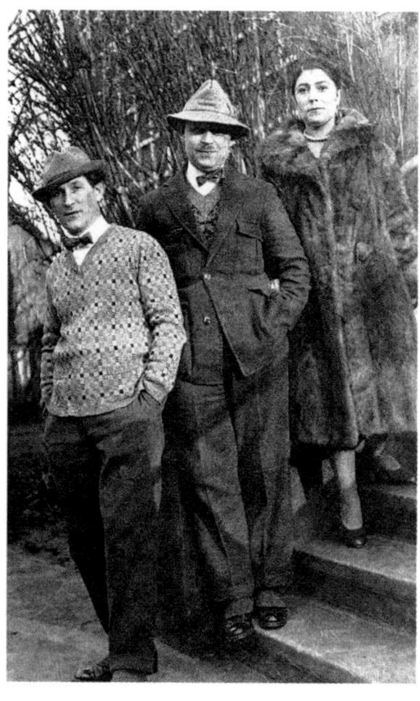

$\rightarrow$

Costume Sketch for La Chatte 1927
Paper, pencil and pastel, 26.7 x 21

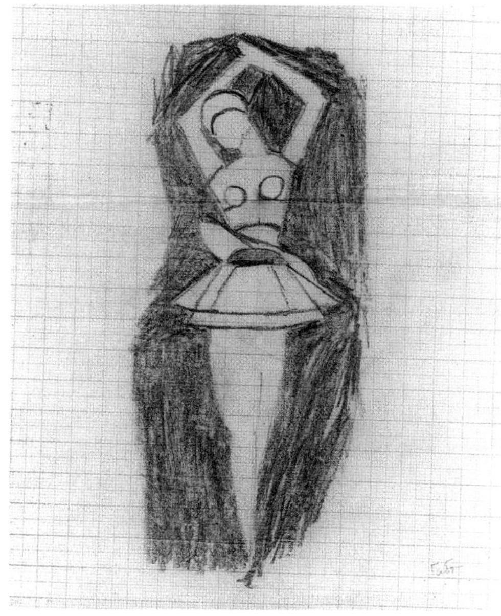

dess! … Everything was torn apart and my soldering didn't hold as the material was raw and, consequently, the road and time destroyed it completely! So, as far as my strength permitted, I put everything right and managed to make it presentable. Yesterday, on the 8th, *La Chatte* was staged once again at the Sarah Bernhardt Theatre – it was packed like herrings and was a tremendous success, despite the extremely tatty state of the set. What do you say? But Sergei Pavlovich remains silent; he will not admit that his only *pièce de résistance* is our decor. I learned quite some time ago that he is planning on travelling to America with our set …'[73] ■ It is clear from

[73] Letter from Antoine Pevsner to Naum Gabo, [9 February] 1928, TGA.

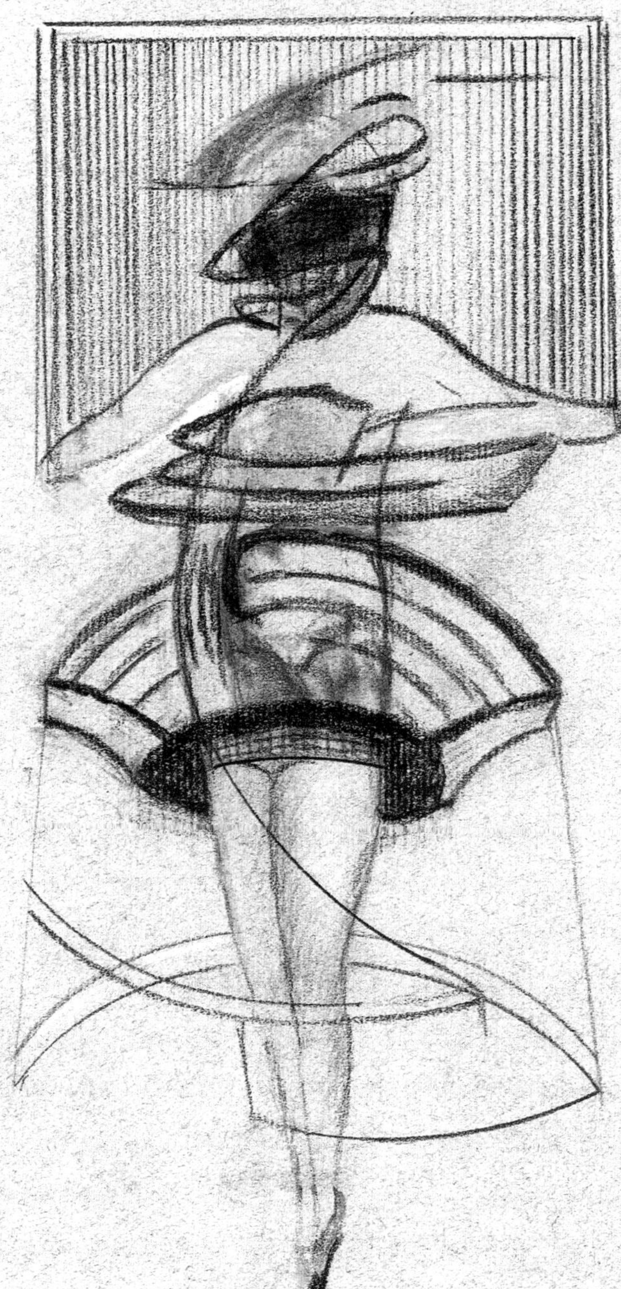

the decor for *La Chatte* that Gabo had observed closely the work of Russian constructivists in the field of Soviet theatre and film design and, in particular, Alexandra Exter's costume and stage design for Yakov Protazanov's silent film *Aelita* (1924). He introduced new elements, such as the light reflection and absorption of the surface of synthetic materials and the pure forms of the transparent geometric constructions, which embodied the concept of kinetic rhythm outlined in his *Realistic Manifesto* of 1920. Gabo followed the success of his first theatrical oeuvre and was immensely proud of his work: 'Yesterday. Another premiere of Diaghilev's *La Chatte* – it is still very popular. Among all the decadence and trash of contemporary ballet, our production stands out as being the most sane and avant-garde.'[74] Later he added: 'I have to give Diaghilev credit for keeping his ballet afloat during the entire fifteen-year period. Now he, too, has been claimed by death and the ballet cause will be lost. The *La Chatte* production was the final spark of a dying flame.'[75]

■ The year 1929 marked the beginning of a deep personal and creative crisis for Gabo. Not only was the last hope of creating a democratic society in Germany lost in the rise of the Nazi movement but also, on a personal level, Gabo lost his partner, Elisabeth, who passed away in November. Gabo's desperation was reflected in a verse that he composed following his tragic loss: ■ 'Too many windows! Too many windows! ■ The buildings are shouting at me, ■ Thundering nets of cables, ■ And roaring cars, ■ Dragging themselves along the wires, ■ Should I retire?, ■ I have no desire to live… ■ The streetcar rolls and buzzes, ■ Like a monster set on fire.'[76]

[74] Naum Gabo, Diary, 19 June 1929, BG.

[75] Ibid., 20 August 1929, BG.

[76] Naum Gabo, Diary, 17 March 1930, BG.

■ It was the end of the period of unreserved experiments and uto-pian belief in a new society that was to be built on scientific and technological progress. Gabo's last endeavour of the Berlin period was his participation in the most daring and grandiose project of the time – the 1931 architectural competition for the Palace of Soviets.

THE END OF UTOPIA: THE COMPETITION FOR THE PALACE OF SOVIETS, 1931
In the first decades of the twentieth century, Germany emerged as a cradle of the period's most avant-garde architecture. Pioneering masters of modernist architecture such as Walter Gropius, Erich Mendelsohn, Ludwig Mies van der Rohe and Bruno Taut were work-ing in Berlin at the time of Gabo's arrival. During his involvement with *G* magazine, Gabo found himself among the leading architects of Europe, all of whom contributed to the short-lived periodical, edited by his close friend Hans Richter. The sculptor was also close to members of the *Novembergruppe*, which brought together 'revolu-tionary spirits' of young, up-and-coming international artists and architects. Gabo taught at the Bauhaus, Europe's most innovative school of architecture and design. Thus his decision to enter the competition for the largest and most ambitious architectural project of the interwar period came as no surprise. ■ The Moscow Palace of Soviets, that Tower of Babel of the twentieth century, was part of the state's 1931–5 General Plan for Reconstruction of Moscow, aiming to modernise the city's medieval concentric circular plan. The Palace was to be the dominant edifice in the city, its new core. Blending the capital's political and social life, it was to 'accommodate congresses and large public assemblies', including theatrical and musical productions. Most importantly, it was to become the emblem

of the young Soviet state, symbolising new communist power. The international competition was announced on 13 July 1931, proposing the territory of the Christ the Saviour's cathedral as the future construction site. The cathedral would be demolished only a few days after the closing date for project submissions in December 1931. Gabo, who had lived for some time in 1918–19 in the attic studio of the Pertsov House directly opposite the church, was the only foreign competitor who knew the site intimately, and not solely from the plans. He firmly believed that only architects were capable of creating a new means by which future generations would grow: ■ 'Nowadays architects work on style, combining the forms of buildings, sketching city plans and forgetting that their entire work will rise and fall together with the social way of life in which and for which they are working. A capitalist city must be destroyed from the inside – only then can a truly new architectural form grow out of the void … Contemporary cities have outlived themselves. Not only have they grown out of their old superficial clothing, but their inner core has been emaciated by the worm of capitalist chaotic lifestyle, ugly commercialism and disgraceful, beastly an-archy …'[77] ■ The competition for the Palace of Soviets was one of the most important architectural projects of the first half of the twentieth century. For an entire generation of architects it was a dream to be able to construct on such a scale within one of Europe's largest historical cities. The Soviet government understood very well the resonance that their plans for the Palace of Soviets would create in the West. Leading Soviet and European architects such as Gropius, Nikolai Ladovsky, Le Corbusier and Mendelsohn were commissioned by the

[77] Naum Gabo, Diary, 17 April 1929, BG.

Soviet state to present designs. ■ Working on the project enabled Gabo to realise long-dormant architectural ideas and to combine his engineering prowess with practical experience in construction. For the first time in months, he wrote the following happy entry in his diary: ■ 'I haven't picked up my diary for five months. What has been achieved in this time? A great deal: the project for the Moscow Palace of Soviets. It's been a long time since I've been as satisfied with a work as I am with this one. In eight designs I found a quite satisfactory solution to a grandiose and very difficult problem. This is a lot. I say "quite satisfactory" as it is through no fault of my own that my solution is not flawless. It's the lack of time: an incredibly short deadline was set by Moscow. The façades and the basic structure were done in a hurry and the result is sloppy. My calculations could have been more precise but the basis of the project, the essence of the solution and the method are correct. ■ I do not believe in the impartiality of the Moscow commission of experts – other than the scientific experts … I don't expect to win, but it is with great joy that I recall the past two months of feverish activity. I literally worked as though I had a fever, I slept no more than two to three hours a day during this period, many nights I didn't go to bed at all and the following day worked without stopping as though it were perfectly normal … This project has convinced me all the more how deeply the roots of my constructivist sculptures stretch into the future of architecture.'[78] ■ Gabo proposed a complex redevelopment of the site and adjacent territories with a compact Palace at its core, exactly on the site of the destroyed cathedral. The basic architectural concept presented a tower

78 Naum Gabo, Diary, 10 December 1931, BG.

Design for Palace of Soviets: Plan of First
Level and Foundations 1931
Pencil and india ink on paper, 99 x 86

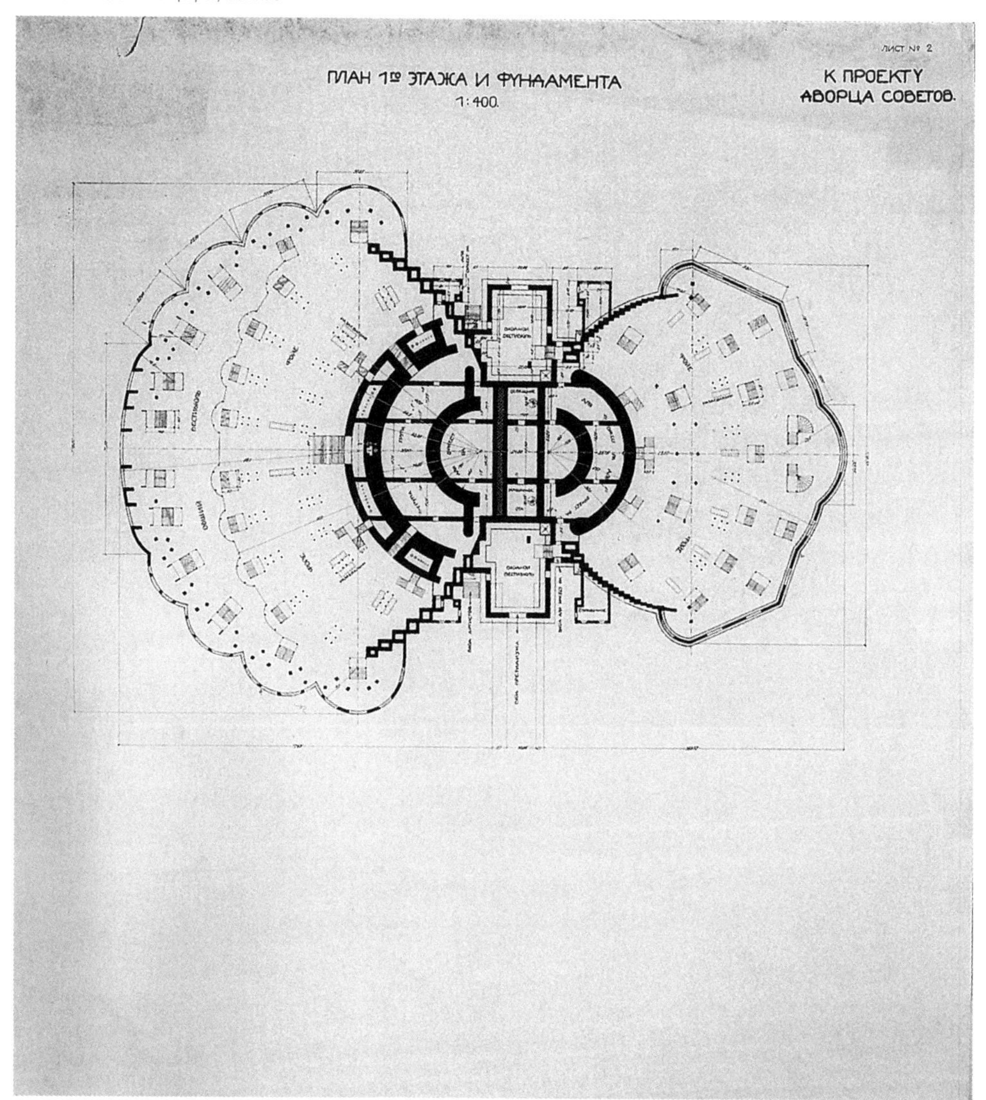

Design for Palace of Soviets: Plan of Main Hall and Section 1931
Pencil and india ink on paper, 98.3 x 85.5

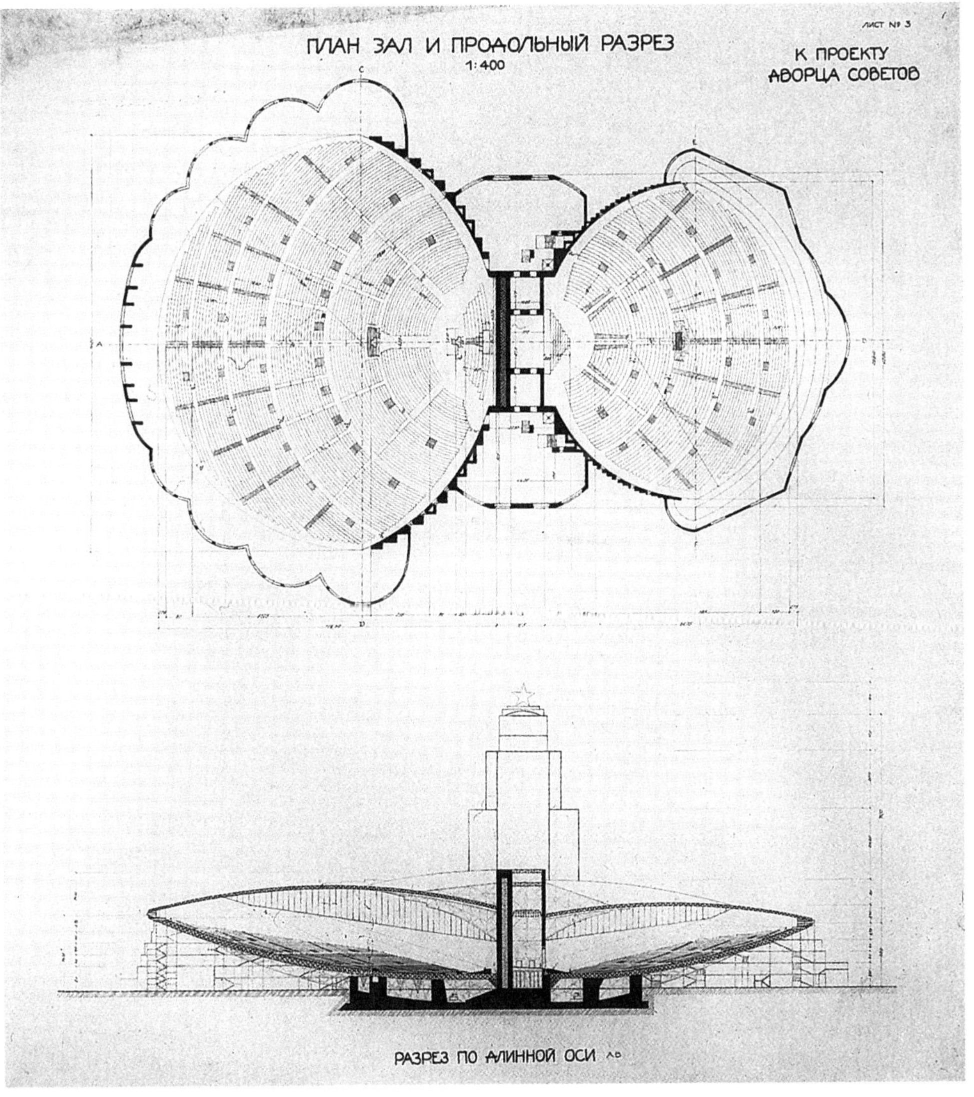

→

*Design for Palace of Soviets: Two Elevations
and Section* 1931
Pencil and india ink on paper, 98 x 145.3

*Design for Palace of Soviets, Façade of
the Small Hall* 1931
Pencil on graph paper, 23.2 x 26

of administrative offices at its axis with two main auditoriums canti-levered out from the central support. Each hall, elliptical in shape, was designed to hold 15,000 and 6,000 people respectively, accessible directly from beneath through a system of escalators. Gabo's main challenge was the continuous skin of the main hall's shell, for which he invented an original supporting structure. ■ Gabo was right: the project was not entirely thought through. His design developed just half of the building site proposed, reducing the grandiose scale expected from the competing projects. He had not had time to solve the complex issues of exterior decoration or even to create a layout of the Palace's central section above the auditorium level. However, his idea of large and open elliptically shaped auditoriums was very innovative. Gabo was extremely proud of the roofing supporting structure that he developed, and later patented it first in Germany (1932) and subsequently in France, the UK and the USA.[79] Before sending his designs to Moscow, he took several photographs of the blueprints. For many years, they were the only proof of the existence of the project, which was considered lost. ■ One of today's leading architects, Norman Foster, chose Gabo's Palace of Soviets project for his Master's degree thesis at Yale University. His research was based mainly on interviews, information and photographs provided by Gabo. Carefully sifting and interpreting the information that he provided to Foster, Gabo seemed to have managed to turn the failings of his project into its virtues: ■ 'It is restricting not to be able to see the full set of drawings because one suspects that many details which would be vital to the formal success of the scheme were never really

[79] Martin Hammer and Christina Lodder, 'Gabo's Design for the Palace of Soviets', in *Competition for the Palace of Soviets* 1993, p.267.

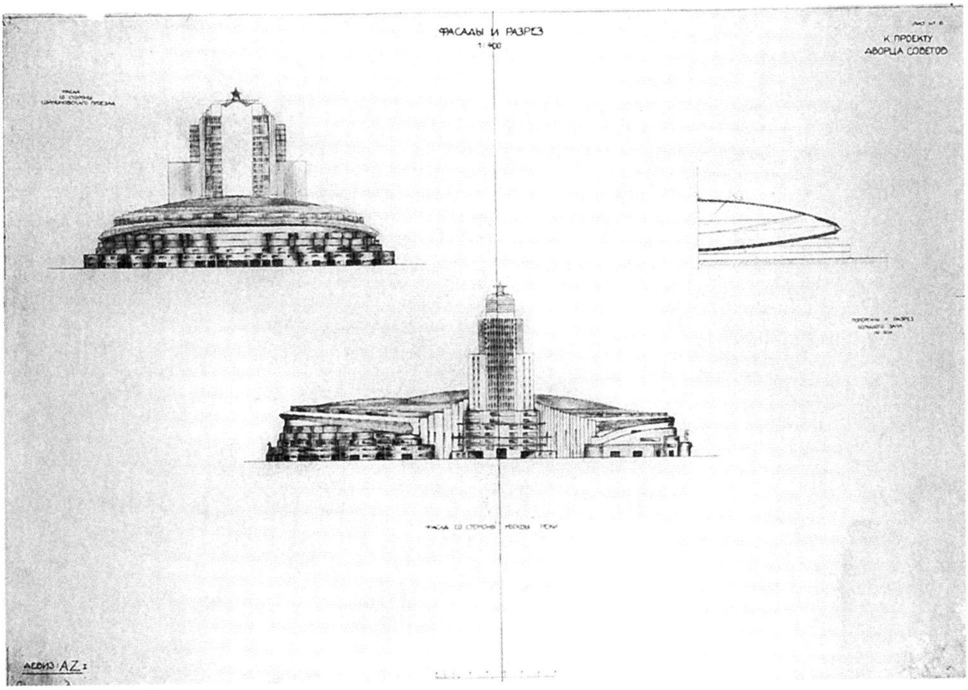

ФАСАДЫ И РАЗРЕЗ
1:400
К ПРОЕКТУ
ДВОРЦА СОВЕТОВ

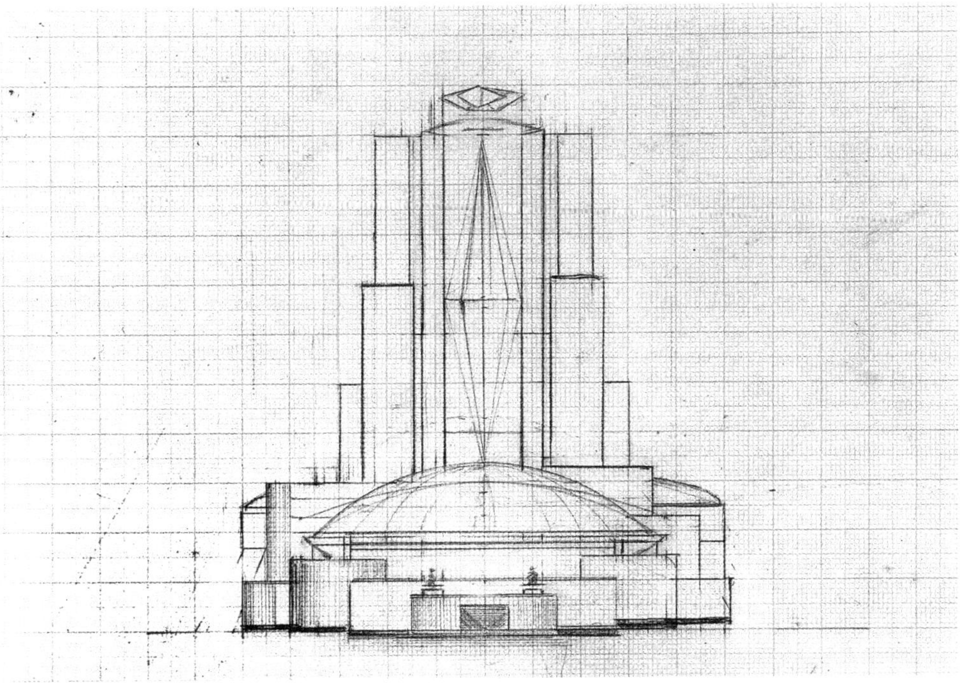

worked out. This is partly understandable in a scheme of this size, because it doesn't matter, for example, that the towers were never planned internally and are different on each drawing … The importance of Gabo to architecture is his capacity to suggest the way in which surfaces can enclose volumes with all the intuitive awareness of the forces at work and their relationship to form … On an architectural scale this is the quality we expect to find today in a small élite of architect-engineers …'[80] ■ For someone with no architectural background, the idea of completing plans for a complex building on a professional level in under five months would seem practically impossible. The endeavour to undertake such a task was stimulated by Gabo's close encounter with leading European architects, his knowledge of basic engineering and his dedication to the idea of the higher social significance of new age architecture. This is yet another testimony to the sculptor's unique spatial imagination, enabling him first to establish a general outlook of the building as single compact hub and only then to proceed to precise calculations and the resolution of technical problems. Gabo's assistant, Charles Wilson, remarked in a 1992 interview: 'Technically, he was no engineer but he came to those things in an intuitive fashion … He could think better than he could draw … He fully conceptualized the image, without having to do so through this process of drawing.'[81] ■ In 1992, the exhibition *Naum Gabo and the Competition for the Palace of Soviets, Moscow 1931–1933* opened at the Berlinische Galerie in Berlin, travelling the following year to A.V. Shchusev State Research Museum of Architecture in Moscow.

[80] Norman Foster, *Palace of the Soviets. Competition Entry by Naum Gabo.* Course 53B, Yale University [1962], TGA.

[81] Helen Adkins, 'From a Talk with the Artist Charles Wilson, Assistant to Naum Gabo', in *Competition for the Palace of Soviets* 1993, pp.36, 41.

It was organised on the occasion of the discovery and attribution of Gabo's designs for the project among the extensive holdings of the Shchusev Museum collection. In the exhibition catalogue, it was noted: 'Naum Gabo's entry to this competition remained a legend for decades. The ground plan and cross-section have appeared from time to time in exhibition catalogues, but it wasn't known where the original project documents were to be found.'[82] For many years the project was considered lost, due to the common practice of marking the competition design sheets with mottoes rather than with the architect's name. This rule applied to all projects in order to ensure the impartiality of the jury, who could have been influenced by the names of renowned architects. Gabo's motto was 'AZ', located in the lower left corner of each sheet of the project, which had been long held anonymously in the museum of architecture. Or so it was assumed. ■ Actually, in 1967 Gabo became aware that his project was whole and untouched and was housed in the Shchusev Museum. Moscow-based Alexei Pevsner was the one to find the designs. In the 1960s, he actively sought to establish whether any works by his brothers, Naum Gabo and Antoine Pevsner, remained in the USSR. He discovered a number of Antoine's oil paintings at the State Russian Museum and the State Tretyakov Gallery, but was unable to locate any of Gabo's sculptures. After applying to the Director of the Shchusev Museum, Alexei received the unexpected news that the sheets of the Palace of Soviets project marked with the 'AZ' motto were recorded among the Museum holdings as an anonymous entry for the Competition and that the author of the project was unknown to the curators. Alexei

82 'Foreword by Professor Jörn Merkert and Vladimir A. Rezvin', in ibid.

visited the museum, spoke to the director, and asked him to organise the photography of the sheets and have them sent to Gabo. Alexei immediately reported to Gabo: ■ 'Dear Nekhemochka! I have found your Palace of Soviets project (!!!), it has been kept in the archives of the Shchusev Museum of Architecture in Moscow. I spoke with them and they have authorised me to make photographs of the project's six sheets and also of the Explanatory Note, if it has survived … they will not release the project, not to me, and not even to the author himself.'[83] ■ 'The director of the museum, having established that I am indeed the brother [of the author] and that the project under the motto "AZ" is your project, explained to me that it is out of [the] question to hand the project over … I'm glad, Nekhemochka, that my hard work and searching have not been in vain, that your project is undamaged and is housed safely in an established museum and that, besides, the project will now not only be kept under the motto "AZ" but catalogued under the world-famous name of the sculptor Gabo; the necessary changes have been made to the card-index of the holdings where it is being kept.'[84] ■ As such, the legendary status of the project, considered lost, was maintained to the end of Gabo's life and even for several years after his death. The blueprints became yet another link in the chain of enigmas and myths that Gabo left behind. The real reasons for his withholding the information are not entirely clear, but from Alexei's letter it appears that Gabo never lost hope of his designs being returned to him one day, and that stirring up excitement about discovering the project could have hindered his plan. It is also possible that, in his old age, Gabo preferred to stay

83 Letter from Alexei Pevsner to Naum Gabo, 28 August 1967, TGA.

84 Letter from Alexei Pevsner to Naum Gabo, 2 October 1967, TGA.

→ (p. 118)
Photograph of Gabo and Ben Nicholson
on the beach, Cornwall, c.1942

away from sensational 'discoveries', conscious, as was the case with Norman Foster's research, that if his original designs came under the magnifying glass of historians and experts, then they would undergo scrutiny, sceptical analysis and criticism and lose their legendary status. ■ As far as the story of the rediscovery of the project in the early 1990s is concerned, a recent investigation confirmed that the Shchusev Museum ledgers remained unaltered since the official acquisition of the designs in the early 1930s. Although the sheets were hand-marked as executed by Naum Gabo and curators were aware of the identity of the designer, the only paperwork confirming it is a card with a 1967 curator's note identifying Gabo as the author of the project under the motto 'AZ'. ■ Soon after completing the project, the sculptor, like many other avant-garde artists, decided to leave Germany and try his luck in Paris. Hitler's rise to power accelerated this process. The period 1933–6 was the most difficult of his life[85] – during the four years he spent in France, he produced a very small body of work and hardly exhibited at all, his financial situation becoming catastrophic as he was unable to find buyers for the few sculptures that he did produce. In desperation, he attempted to commit suicide. A short period of collaboration with the *Abstraction-Création* journal did not achieve its aim of bringing him closer to other artists working in Paris at the time and, moreover, he became estranged from his brother, Pevsner. Gabo's acquaintance with the young English abstract painter Ben Nicholson and a series of trips to England inspired him to leave France. From 1936 to the end of the Second World War Gabo lived and worked in Britain.

85 'Naum Gabo talking to Maurice de Sausmarez', in Maurice de Sausmarez (ed.), *Ben Nicholson: A Studio International Special*, London 1969, p.15

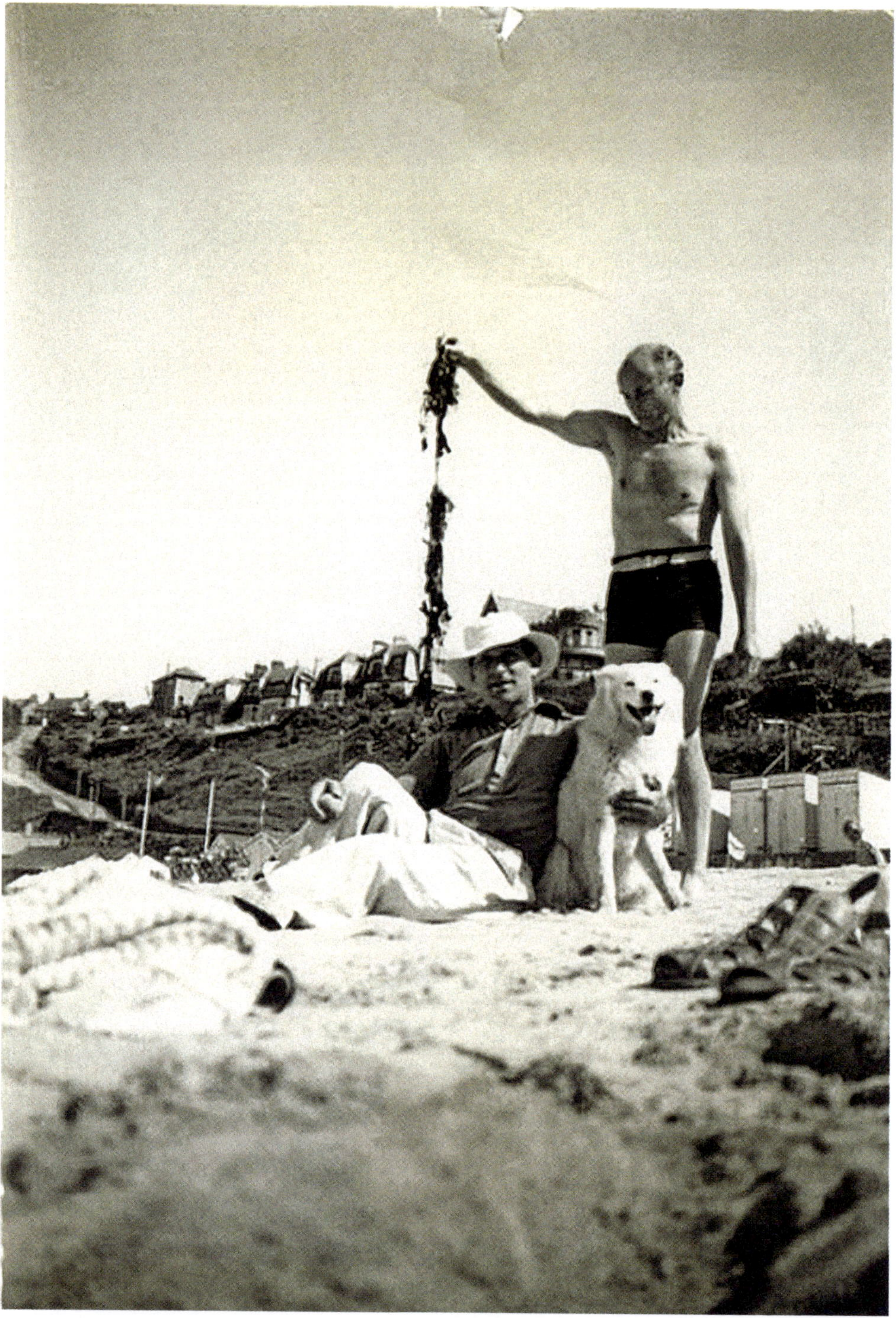

CREATIVITY AND THE WAR: THE BRITISH PERIOD (1936–46)

SURREALISM VERSUS GEOMETRICAL ABSTRACTION In his old age, Gabo's favourite chess partner was Marcel Duchamp. '[Dadaists] had a lot more fun than I did!',[86] remarked Gabo, sincerely regretting that he 'slightly missed the boat' with surrealists in the 1930s. However, at that time the antagonism of surrealism versus geometrical abstraction was as irreconcilable as the left and the right in politics. ■ The year 1936 was critical in the history of modernism. It was marked by the outbreak of Civil War in Spain, the growing personality cults in the USSR and Nazi Germany, and the general economic crisis in Europe. These events lead to depression and widespread emigration among the artistic intelligentsia. It was particularly apparent at the 1937 *Universal Exhibition* in Paris that realist art was fighting to re-establish its leading position in Europe. The proponents of the surrealist movement held a string of important exhibitions in continental Europe and Britain and were actively producing lectures, publications and artistic performances.[87] ■ For Gabo, the period after moving to Britain was an incredibly intensive one, both personally and professionally. In the decade from 1936 to 1946, Gabo firmly established his reputation as a

[86] Charles Wilson interviewed in Chicago by Derek Pullen and Jackie Heuman on 23 January 2008, Sculpture Conservation Department files, Tate, London.

[87] Norbert Lynton, *Ben Nicholson*, Phaidon Press, London 1993, p.121.

key figure on the contemporary art scene and one of the founders of the European constructive movement. If the Berlin period saw him become a leader of European constructive art, the years spent in Britain gave rise to an international master, a widely recognised pioneer of abstract sculpture. As a Russian artist, he was of great interest to British scholars as a first-hand source of information on avant-garde trends in Russian art. Gabo's outlook greatly influenced the leading art critic of the time, Herbert Read, in his position on Russian art.[88] ■ After a four-year lull in activity, Gabo once more felt capable of continuing his work – he had a massive influx of ideas. He took part in designer projects, gave lectures, wrote a great deal and published his texts about the theory of constructive art, took up oil painting and even mastered traditional techniques of stone carving. Generally speaking, a whole new creative period began for Gabo. In Britain, where abstract art was slowly and laboriously fighting to establish itself, Gabo received a creative stimulus that Paris, spoiled by the presence of so many renowned artists, was unable to give him. ■ Immediately upon arrival in Britain, Gabo felt the need to make himself an established independent artist, clearly outlining the ideas of which he was an exponent. It was of utmost importance to him to distinguish his 'constructive idea' (which is how he came to name the core principles on which his art was based) from all the other 'isms' of the time. Having only just arrived, he published a declarative article entitled 'Constructive Art',[89] although the core ideas of his new aesthetic platform were to be presented in the article 'The Constructive Idea

[88] James King, *The Last Modern. A Life of Herbert Read*, Weidenfeld and Nicholson, London 1990, pp.155–6, 210–16.

[89] Naum Gabo, 'Constructive Art', *The Listener*, London, vol.16, no.408, 4 November 1936, pp.846–8.

in Art', published in a book of articles, *Circle: International Survey of Constructive Art*, a year later.[90] *Circle* was originally intended to be a periodical and it was to be the voice of international geometric abstraction or so-called constructive arts, while its editors were recognised as the leading representatives of the movement in Britain: the painter Ben Nicholson, the architect Leslie Martin and the sculptor Gabo. The purpose of the publication was to consolidate a wide circle of artists, sculptors, designers and architects, reflecting the range of opinions surrounding the discussion of the issue of abstraction in contemporary art. The contributors, united under a general term of 'constructive artists', mainly represented the opponents of the surrealist trend led by internationally recognised figures such as Le Corbusier, Piet Mondrian and László Moholy-Nagy. ■ 'The Constructive idea … is not a technical scheme for an artistic manner, nor a rebellious demonstration of an artistic sect; it is a general concept of the world, or better, a spiritual state of a generation, an ideology caused by life, bound up with it and directed to influence its course… This idea can be discerned in all domains of the new culture now in construction … It is as young as our century and as old as the human desire to create. ■ … [The Constructive idea] has revealed a universal law that the elements of a visual art such as lines, colours, shapes, possess their own forces of expression independent of any association with the external aspects of the world; that their life and their action are self-conditioned psychological phenomena rooted in human nature; that those elements are not chosen by convention for any utilitarian or other reason

as words and figures are, they are not merely [90] *Circle* 1937, pp.1–10.

abstract signs, but they are immediately and organically bound up with human emotions.'[91] ■ In his creative work, Gabo continued to explore more organic forms, wholly repudiating the aesthetics of the machine age. The problem of synthesis of sculptural and architectural elements interested Gabo to a much lesser degree. He continued to experiment with the use of new transparent plastics, in particular Plexiglas. This material, invented in the early 1930s, was marketed in England under the brand name *Perspex* and became Gabo's favourite material. His daughter, Nina, remembers hearing the story of how, when he received his first sample of Perspex sheet, he heated it up in the oven and, impressed by the way it could then be bent into any shape, cried out: 'I've found my material!' ■ The sculptor's private life also underwent fundamental changes. Soon after moving to London, Gabo was introduced to an artist, Miriam Franklin (née Israels). Miriam was to be the love of his life, the inspiration behind his work, the mother of his only child and the secret of his success. They settled in London's Hampstead, where many modernist artists lived: Barbara Hepworth, Gropius, Moholy-Nagy, Mondrian, Henry Moore, and others. Most of these progressive artists were associated with Herbert Read, who became close to Gabo and played a major role in his life, both as a friend who shared his aesthetic values and views on art, and as the first art critic able to evaluate the sculptor's creative development in the context of the history of abstract sculpture at the outset of the early twentieth century.

DEMATERIALISATION OF THE FORM AND TRANSPARENCY IN SCULPTURE

Once in Britain, Gabo set to work in earnest. Even before the beginning of the Second

91 *Circle* 1937, pp.6–7.

Photograph of Gabo and Miriam in London,
c.1936

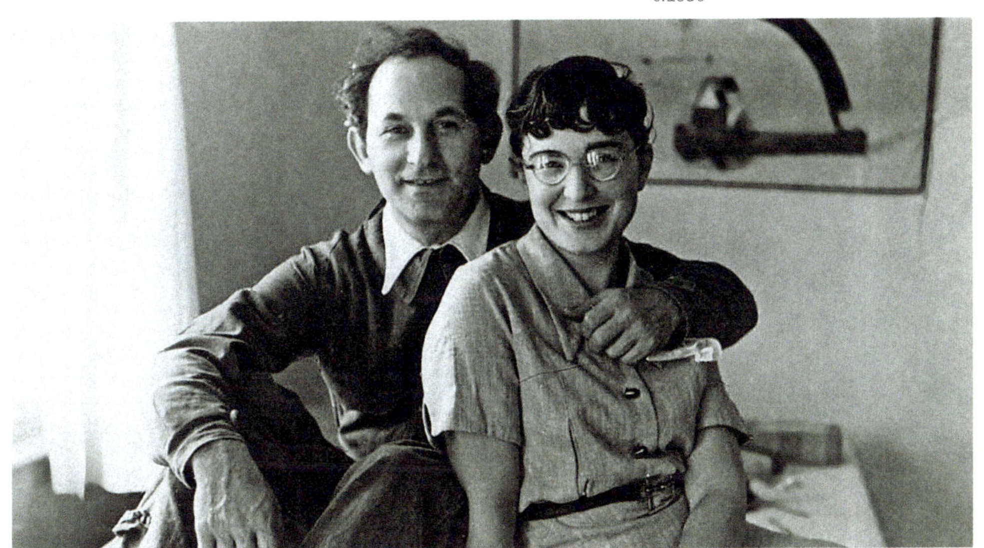

World War, he produced a whole series of works that can be considered among his best sculptures, including *Spheric Themc* c.1937,
Kinetic Stone Carving 1936–44 and the final version of *Construction
in Space: Stone with a Collar* 1933–7. Gabo started by developing
the ideas that he was unable to complete while still in Paris. His work
Construction in Space: Crystal 1936–7, the likeness of which to
a mathematical model may be considered provocative, served as a
link between the Paris and British periods. ■ At the *L'Exposition Sur-
réaliste d'Objets* at the Charles Ratton Gallery in Paris in May 1936,
among numerous objects such as African statues, books and Duchamp's 'readymades', various mathematical models made of plaster,
metal and card were exhibited. The models were borrowed from the
institute of research in mathematics, L'Institut Henri Poincaré. Of par-

ticular interest was the model of a 'tangent surface of cubic ellipse', a metallic cubic frame developed with strings stretched across it to fill the inner expanse of the framework. It is not known if Gabo saw this object before the exhibition at the Institut Poincaré, but his use of this mathematical model in particular as a prototype for his new work *Construction in Space: Crystal* the same year as it was shown at the surrealist exhibition can hardly be put down to chance.

■ *Construction in Space: Crystal* is Gabo's first fully transparent work. It is made of a plastic called Rhodoid and comprises the complex structure of a distorted polyhedron, defined by a centrifugal curve. The incised vectorial lines extend from the edges of the side planes to the centre, giving the effect of a string structure, twisting the whole construction, swirling the centre in and then uncoiling it outwards. This form seems to be dynamised by the effect of centrifugal movement. If we compare this work to the mathematical model, the likeness is striking, but *Crystal* remains a work of art, whereas the model is a graphic aid. Gabo explained that 'his idea was to take this complicated formula and change its realisation to prove that what is basically a fantasy (the intuition of the mathematician) could be seen through the intuition of an artist'.[92] He was also particularly attracted by the complete asymmetry of the model. Such an almost direct citation of science was something of a provocation, brought on by the general situation that Gabo experienced upon arriving in Britain, where he found himself in the centre of a heated discussion about the interrelation between science and art. At that time, the influence of surrealism in Britain was overwhelming. Among its proponents were

92 Anthony Hill, 'Constructivism – the European Phenomenon', *Studio International*, London 1966, vol.171, no.876, p.144.

Gabo's friends Read and Moore. It is possible that the use of a 'surrealist object' as the basis for a constructive work was for him an attempt at dialogue, a desire to initiate an exchange between the two principal tendencies in contemporary art: constructivism and surrealism.

■ *Construction in Space: Crystal* was the first in a series of entirely transparent works, not articulated by colour, which Gabo created between 1937 and 1941, approaching the fine line where the symbiosis of space and form pauses on the verge of total dematerialisation. The culmination of these experiments was the creation of a new method of modelling in sculpture, coined as Gabo's signature style – the stringing method.

IN SEARCH OF THE IDEAL FORM – THE SPHERIC THEME The most significant and consistent body of work, or 'themes', that Gabo worked on in the pre-war years was the *Spheric Theme*: 'In my entire life I have only created four such works (those in which I achieved perfection) ■ The Bust of 1916 (Head No.2) ■ The Column of 1923 ■ The Palace of Soviets, 1932 ■ The stereometric structure of a sphere (ball). I prefer the word "sphere" as the term "ball" implies a solid volume, whereas my structure is the space occupied by a ball. ■ I'm highlighting them in particular as each one represents an invention in an area to which it brought a vital improvement. The remainder of my works grew from these four.'[93] ■ The templates for this essentially astoundingly simple form are kept in the Gabo archive at Tate. The set consists of two basic flat circumferences with a removed core and a single slant along the radius. The edges along the slits of the two twisted circumferences are joined to each other in such a way

[93] Naum Gabo, 'Rassuzhdeniya o Mayakovskom, Rodine-Rossii i muzhike …', undated notebook [1960–70], pp.29–30, TGA.

$\rightarrow$

Spheric Theme: Transparent Variation
c.1937
Celluloid and Perspex, 21.5 diameter

Construction in Space: Stone with a Collar
c.1933, this version c.1936–7
Stone, cellulose acetate, slate and brass,
37 x 72 x 55

that they result in the surface of a double circumference that is no longer a plane figure but a volume, an endless spherical continuity. The construction has no surface, there is only scope created around the bent band, a vector that completes a full cycle, issued from and returning to itself. At first glance, it may seem that the series of works of the *Spheric Theme* develops the idea of the Möbius strip, but Gabo argued: 'To my mind the image of infinity could not be an image which turns back on itself. I feel this Spheric Theme to be continuity rather than infinity.'[94] ■ At various times, researchers into Gabo's works have suggested one or other area of mathematics from which Gabo may have drawn the idea of the *Spheric Theme*, although analogies can with equal justification be found in the natural sciences, such as biology (the artist received a strong grounding in the natural sciences during his studies in Munich). His archives contain photographs taken from the book *Art Forms in Nature* by Ernst Haeckel, the famous German naturalist working in the late nineteenth and early twentieth centuries.[95] The photographs in question are those of lithographic images of radiolarians, marine micro-organisms, intensely magnified so as to allow a study of their structure. They stand out for their polyhedral form and their complex symmetry, the basis of which is a filigree structure. Of particular interest are the consistent forms of nassellarian skeletons, similar in structure to Gabo's transparent constructions and to the tetrahedral motif of *Torsion* c.1929. The sculptor himself commented on the nature of his images as being completely unrelated to any scientific principles: 'I found no answer in graphic terms in science which would satisfy

94 Gabo 1957, note to illustrations 64–5.

95 Ernst Haeckel, *Kunstformen der Natur*, Verlag des Bibliographischen Instituts, Leipzig und Wien 1899–1904.

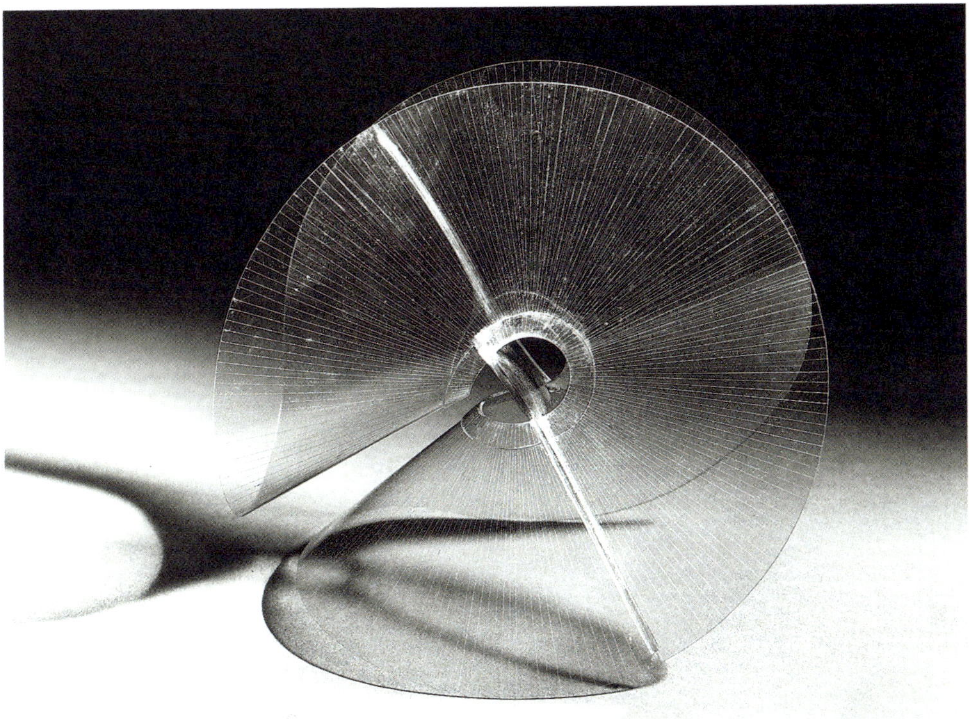

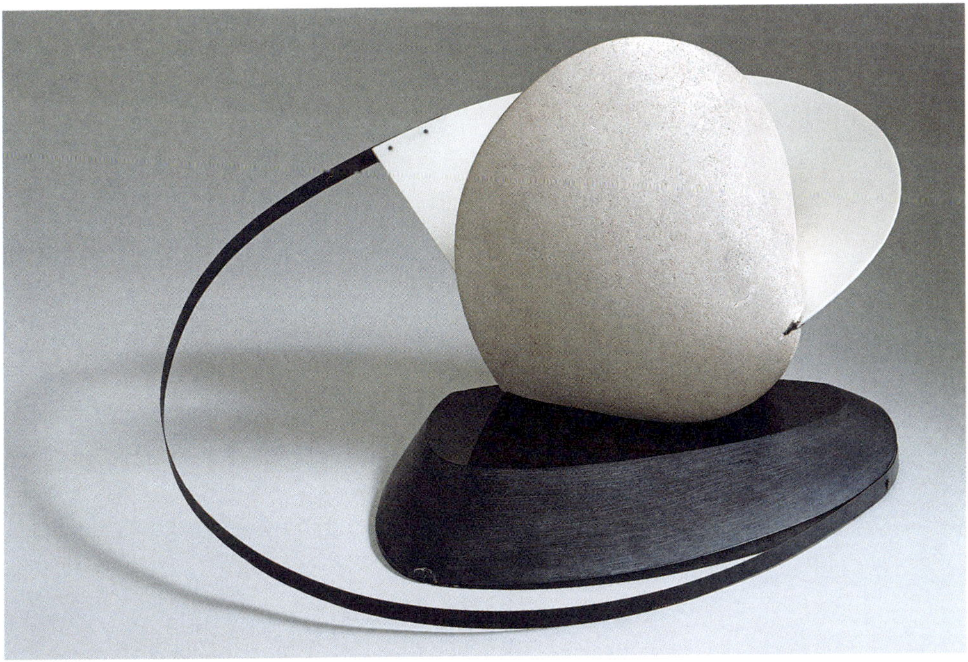

my vision of space. I considered that in this work of mine there is a satisfactory solution to that problem. Instead of indicating the space by an angular intersection of planes, I enclose the space in one curved continuous surface. I eliminate angularity in space construction and give the space the curved character which it has in my perception.'[96] ■ The structural system at the basis of the *Spheric Theme* was subsequently used in a whole series of original works. The idea of two planes with a disengaged core and a radial section that serves as a line of junction for the planes remained unaltered. It was only the template itself that became more developed as the discs were stretched, curved or angled. For example, in the *Model for a Monument to the Unknown Political Prisoner* 1952, the basic template is of elliptical elongated form and the minimalist, streamlined forms of the work resemble an arch. The *Monument* was never built, but its forms acted as a spur for the development of the design for the *Construction for the Bijenkorf Building* erected in Rotterdam in 1957. ■ In his *Construction in Space with Net* 1951, Gabo applied the same system – two discs with a disengaged core that evolve into a horseshoe-shape. The templates from which the metal mesh elements of the first version of the construction were cut out have survived in the Gabo archive. These card templates are covered with lines and markings in different coloured ink with which the sculptor outlined the edges, in search of the ideal form. He would settle for a particular shape and start cutting out around the final outline, then would change his mind and carefully stick the fragment back in place with adhesive tape. He had worked in the same way many years earlier with card

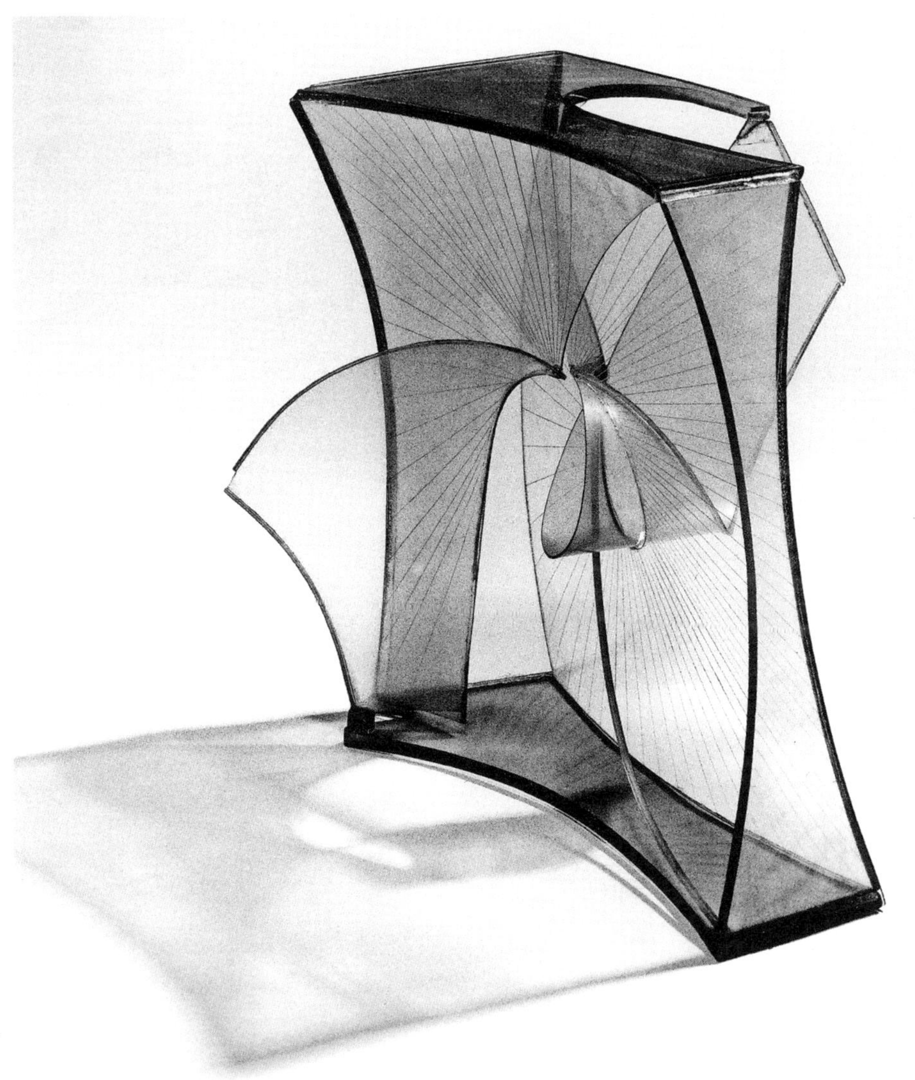

Photograph of *Construction in Space: Crystal* 1937

Study for Construction in Space:
Crystal c.1937
Pencil on paper, 24 x 20.5

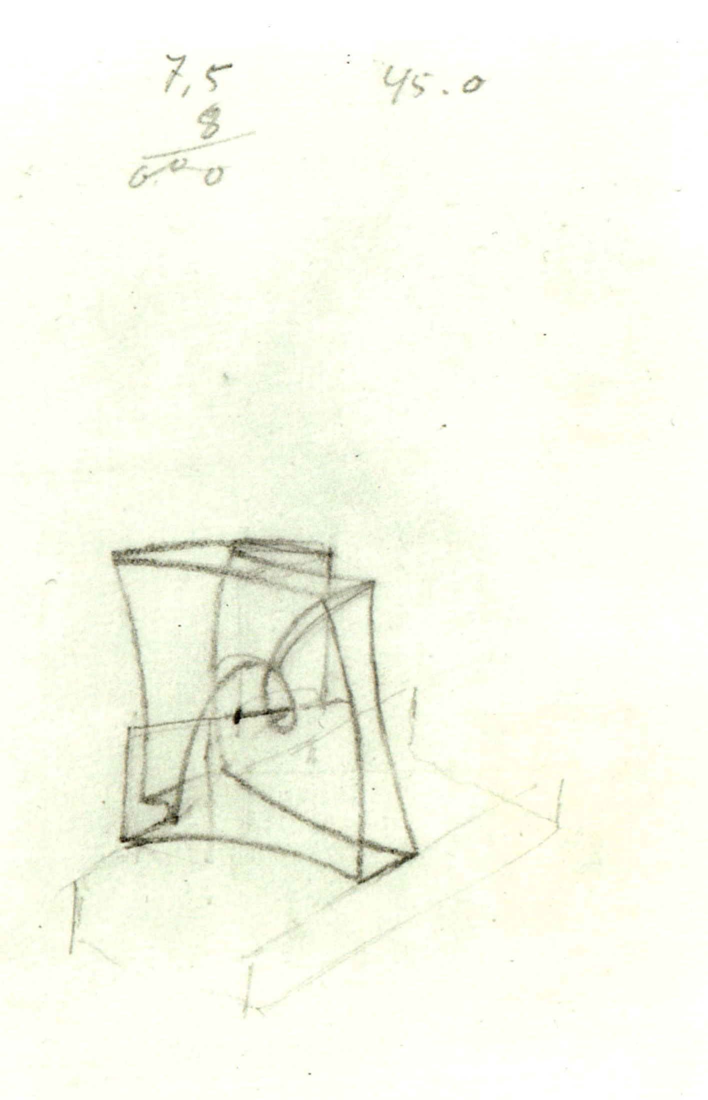

Photograph of *Construction in Space: Crystal* exhibited in Chicago in April 1953

Press cutting regarding Gabo's *Construction in Space: Crystal* 1938–9 at the *Decorative Arts exhibition*, San Francisco, 1939

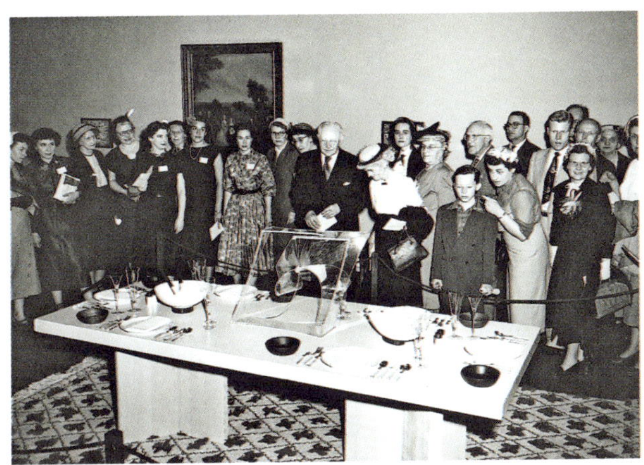

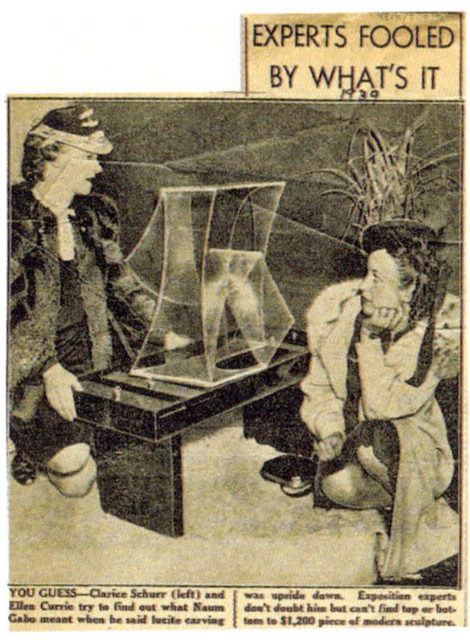

YOU GUESS—Clarice Schurr (left) and Ellen Currie try to find out what Naum Gabo meant when he said lucite carving was upside down. Exposition experts don't doubt him but can't find top or bottom to $1,200 piece of modern sculpture.

templates of his first *Heads*. Seen from a particular angle, the completed *Construction in Space with Net* appears as an impenetrable metallic structure; from another angle emerges a semi-transparent shroud, a golden filigree net, through which the surrounding space is visible. ■ *Construction in Space: Arch No.2* c.1958, with its shiny phosphor-bronze surface, reflects the light and movements of the viewer contemplating it like an ancient brass mirror. The centre of the curved arch-like sculpture, with its streamlined organic forms, is developed with stainless steel spring wire, drawing in the two wings of the construction as a corset tightens a woman's waist. Fragments of the unfinished *Arch No.2*, held in the archive, clearly show that the work was constructed on the same principle as the *Spheric Theme* – two flat bronze sheets, stretched into a curvilinear shape, preserve the same disengaged core and radial cut. ■ The *Spheric Theme* was the basis for some of Gabo's most expressive works.

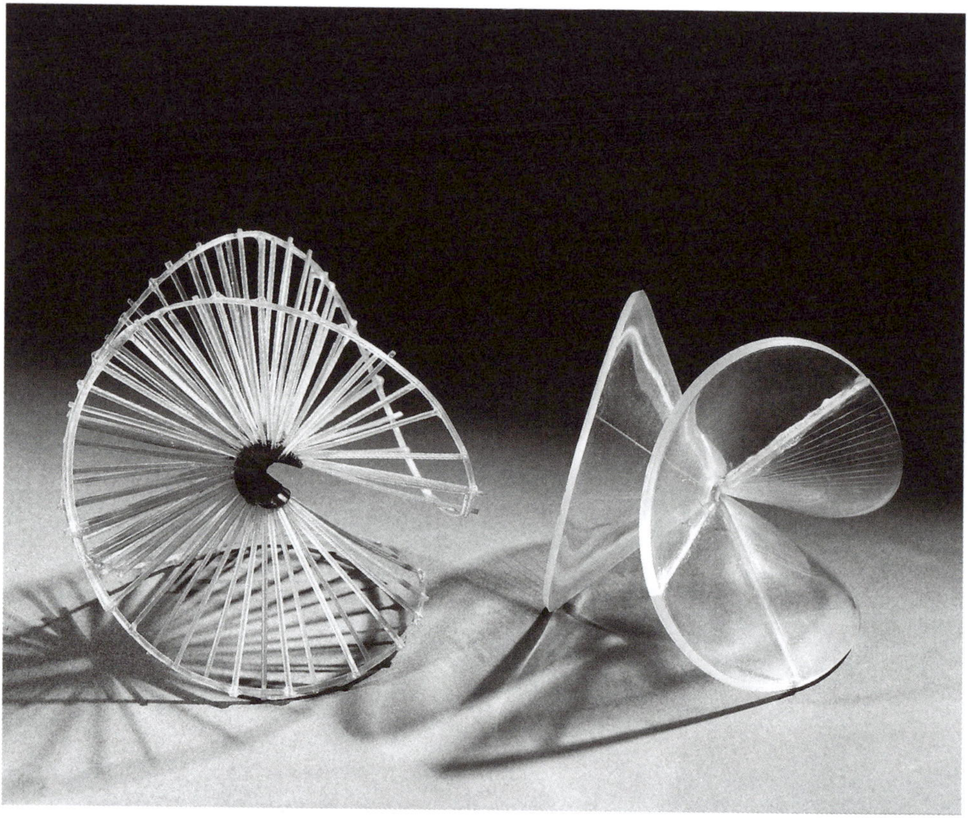

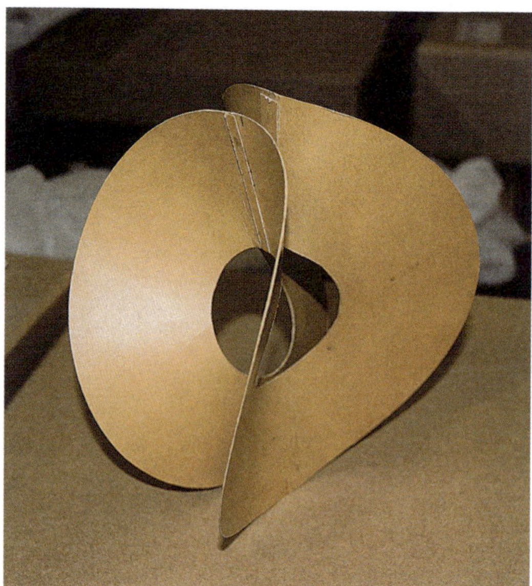

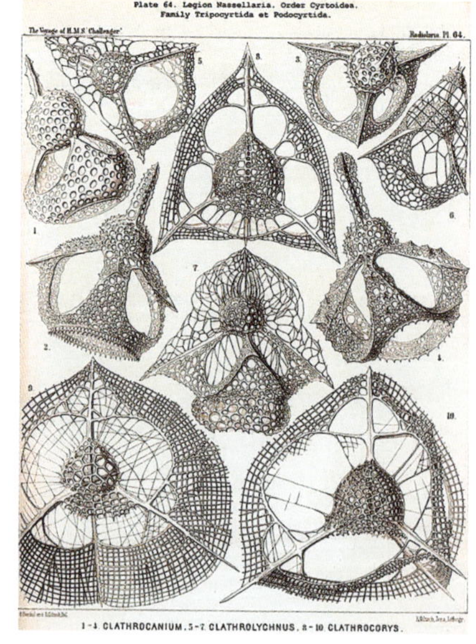
Plate 64. Legion Nassellaria. Order Cyrtoidea.
Family Tripocyrtida et Podocyrtida.
The Voyage of H.M.S. 'Challenger'
Radiolaria Pl. 64.
1-4 CLATHROCANIUM. 5-7 CLATHROLYCHNUS. 8-10 CLATHROCORYS.

← Photograph of *Model for Spheric
Construction: Fountain* 1938 and *Model
for Spheric Theme* 1937

Card Model for Spheric Theme [1936–51]

Ernst Haeckel 1834–1919
Legion Nassellaria, an illustration from
the *Report on the Scientific Results of the
Voyage of* HMS Challenger *during the Years
1873–1876*

→ (p.134)
*Model for a Monument to the Unknown
Political Prisoner* 1952
Plastic and wire mesh, 38.1 x 8.9 x 9.5

He produced transparent and opaque versions, steel monuments and bronze sculptures, models developed with strings or wire, and sculptures with a complex nucleus. Each version explores the theme of the interrelation between internal and external sculptural space, the symbiosis of which is possible due to the wave-like dynamic of the vane of the construction, which seems to inhale, allowing the surrounding space to pass through it.

'THE HIGHEST POINT OF AESTHETIC INTUITION OF A MAN' – THE SPIRAL THEME Created during the Second World War, the *Spiral Theme* stands out from the fully transparent works such as *Construction in Space: Crystal* and *Spheric Theme* that preceded it. Presented to the public in 1942 at the London Museum exhibition, *New Movements in Art. Contemporary Work in England: an Exhibition of Recent Paintings and Sculptures,*[97] *Spiral Theme* received great acclaim from visitors and critics alike, something that greatly surprised the artist, who was accustomed to a lack of understanding from the public. The following note in Gabo's diary describes the event: 'I have made one new construction, and have exhibited it together with some other earlier constructions to the London public at the London Museum; to my complete surprise this object has produced what I would describe as a wonderful effect on the mass of visitors … as well as upon the small number of critics from magazines and newspapers who have been impervious to my ideas until now … Speaking truthfully, the theme of this piece was worked out by me simultaneously with, if not earlier than, these two constructions (of 1937 and 1939).[98] Using the psychological calm which has resulted from an

[97] London Museum, 18 March – 9 May 1942.

[98] *Construction on a Line* 1937 and *Construction in Space: Crystal* 1936–9 accordingly.

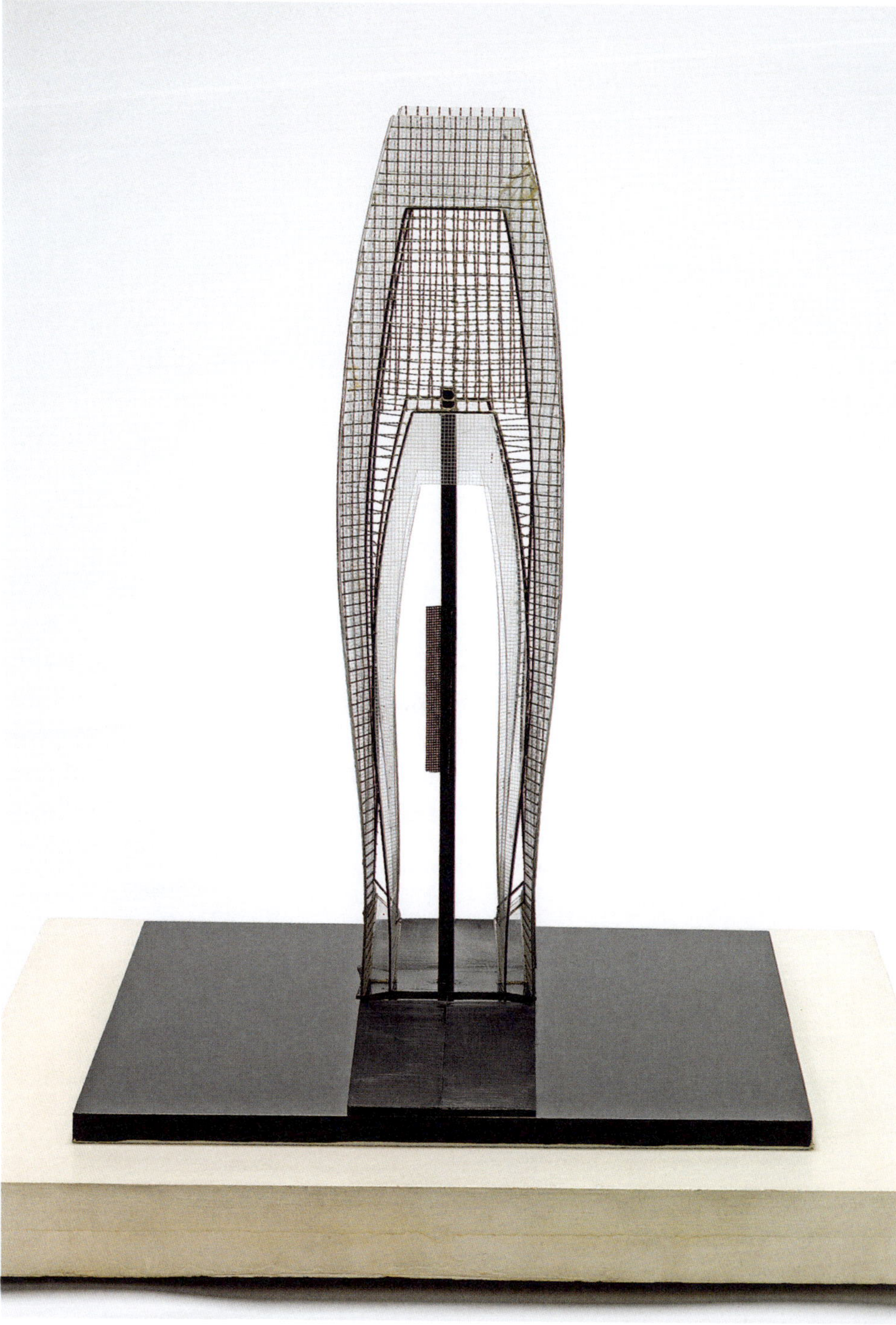

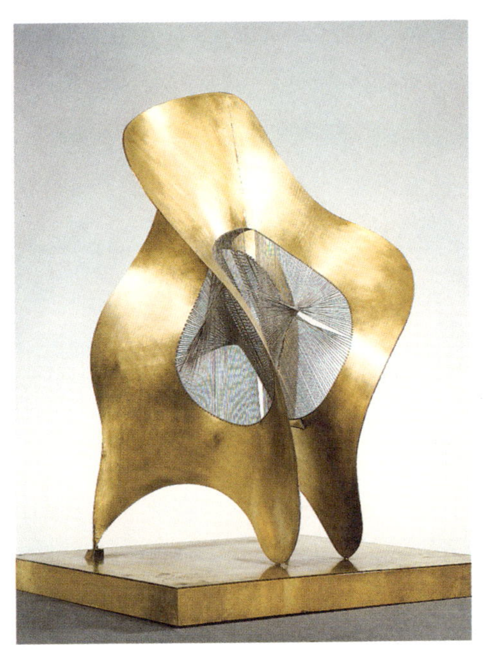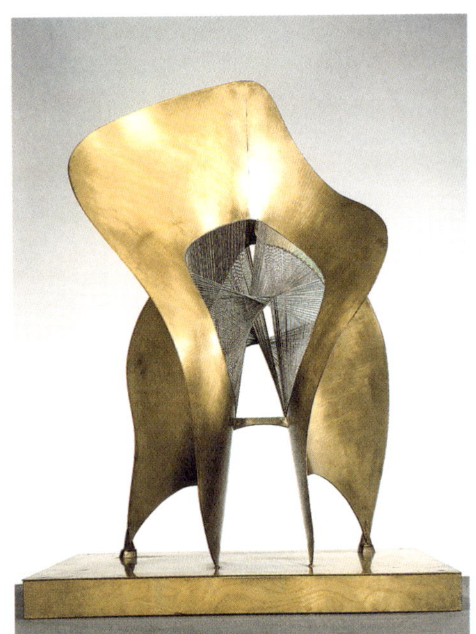

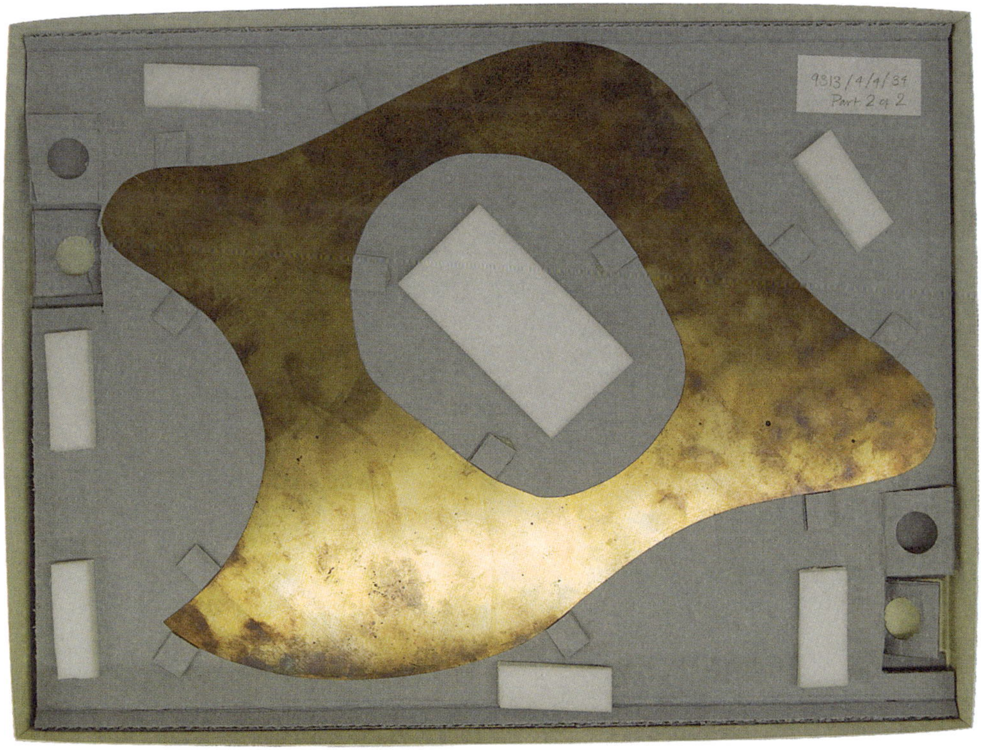

9313 / 4 / 4 / 34
Part 2 of 2

← (p. 135)
Construction in Space: Arch No.2 c.1958,
this version 1963
Phosphor-bronze, copper and stainless steel
spring wire, 82.6 high

Conservation photograph of a fragment for
Construction in Space: Arch No.2

Sketch for Spheric Theme 1937
Blue pencil on paper, 19.7 x 32.1

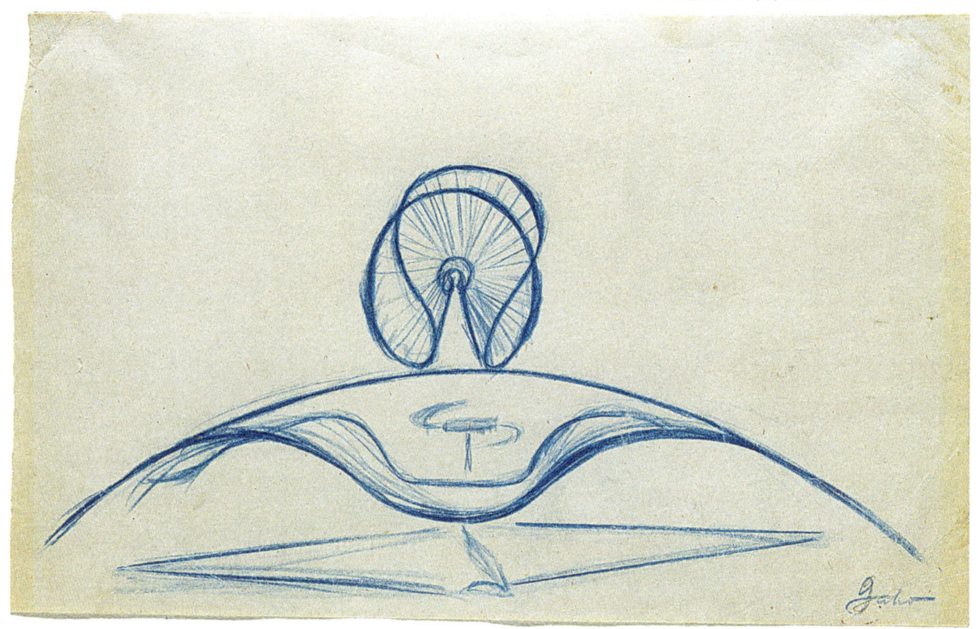

encouraging turning point in the course of the war I have devoted myself to the execution of this piece and have created it in every detail within these last three months. ■ Here is what Herbert Read, a poet and the best art critic in England, has written in the magazine *Horizon*:[99] ■ 'I must affirm in the first place that the art represented – to keep to a specific example – by Gabo's *Spiral Theme*, is the highest point ever reached by the aesthetic intuition of a man … Creation is a much abused word, applied loosely to imitations and logical constructions; it is justified only for that absolute lyricism we call "pure poetry", to music, to certain branches of mathematics and for constructivism in the plastic arts (which includes architecture). But even within this absolute world there is an hierarchy and at the summit I would place this spatial construction of Gabo's.'[100] ■ Such enthusiastic acclaim from the leading British critic was a significant event and a complete surprise to Gabo. They were close friends and Read, an advocate of the surrealist movement in art, had for many years preferred to abstain from openly expressing an opinion on the constructive work of his friend. ■ The structure of the *Spiral Theme* is composed of thin strips of transparent plastic presented on a base made out of a smooth, black, synthetic material, which, as a mirror, reflects the barely distinguishable forms. Each element of the construction is twisted, bent or otherwise dynamised. Although its form recalls the soft, organic contours of a shell, the inner energy concentrated in the work is evocative of the vortex-like contortions of celestial motion. The main element is established angularly, as if a rocket preparing to launch, whereas

[99] Herbert Read, 'Vulgarity and Impotence: Speculations on the Present State of the Arts', *Horizon*, vol.5, 28 April 1942, p.269.

[100] Naum Gabo, Diary, 23 May 1942, TGA.

the central vector, which evolves into a spiral, is directed inwards towards the centre of the construction. The torsion-like motion, the centrifugal kinetic and the overall outward dynamism of the structure all are united in one construction made of completely transparent elements. From above, the work exposes completely different forms to the viewer, reminiscent of an expanded, fan-like shell. ■ In one of his letters, Gabo noted that he had tried to create a construction that, depending on the angle from which it was viewed, would seem like an almost completely new work.[101] Here, for the first time, Gabo achieved what Read was to name one of the most important achievements in sculpture – an almost complete dematerialisation of form.[102] The outlines of the construction are so complex that they are particularly difficult to describe, as any references such as front/back or left/right are irrelevant. There is one endless movement in which each visible fluorescent surface appears only for an instant in the flashing twist of the perpetually moving, almost non-material substance. This work is the immediate predecessor of a new series of constructions created by applying the string method, and known as the *Linear Construction in Space* series.

THE WAR DIARIES With the onset of the Second World War in 1939, London, which was subject to regular bombing, became deserted by artists. Many of Gabo's fellow artists moved to the south-west of Britain, settling in Cornwall. A whole colony of artists, sculptors and potters was established around St Ives. Following in the footsteps of Nicholson and Hepworth, Gabo and his wife Miriam relocated to Carbis Bay near St Ives. Deeply shocked

[101] *Constructing Modernity* 2000, p.281.

[102] Herbert Read, *A Concise History of Modern Sculpture*, Thames and Hudson, London 1964, p.228.

by the act of war on the continent, Gabo began to keep a diary for the first time in years. Entries were always written in Russian, his native tongue, and referred to periods of extreme emotional tension. Four notebooks, the first beginning on 15 September 1939 and the last concluding on 13 May 1945, contain invaluable accounts of the sculptor's works, his artistic plans and his deeply personal experiences: 'Europe is once again engulfed in flames. The fire on her outskirts will be smouldering for long. The fire has started earlier than the wise predicted. Now everything is consumed. And it seems that it is my fate once again to be an observer. ■ I am living in a distant part of England (Cornwall). This is far away from any of the places threatened by air attack (although it isn't certain that the plunderers of the air will not fly over these fishing villages). But I am not intending to write about what is happening in the field. I shall write and indeed can only write about what I myself see, feel and think. I am one of millions living at this terrible time. ■ I am only a silhouette against the background of the volcanic conflagrations of history.'[103]

■ Gabo found it difficult to deal with his imposed inactivity backstage. As a Soviet citizen, up until the Soviet Union's entry into the war he found himself under the threat of detention, like many foreigners who were citizens of Germany or its allies. On 30 July 1940, almost a year before the Nazi invasion of the USSR, Gabo, concerned about the fate of his relatives and fellow countrymen who remained in the USSR, wrote in his diary: 'However strange and incompatible with the outward appearance of mutual cajoling between Stalin and Hitler, some intuitive voice whispers to my mind that Hitler is frantically preparing to strike not

[103] Naum Gabo, Diary, 15 September 1939, TGA.

$\rightarrow$

Spiral Theme 1941
Cellulose acetate and Perspex,
14 x 24.4 x 24.4

Spiral Theme 1941
Cellulose acetate and Perspex,
14 x 24.4 x 24.4

Sketch for Spiral Theme c.1941
Pencil on paper, 12.4 x 24.1

England, but the USSR. Hitler is desperately, they say, trying to keep the peace in the Balkans. … Hitler's understanding of peace has never changed and never will. For him, peace is where all resistance has been shattered and crushed under the boots of his horde.'[104]
■ A year later, on 22 June 1941, Gabo greeted the announcement of Hitler's declaration of war on the Soviet Union with what would seem strange enthusiasm: 'It has happened! The prediction I made ten months ago on 30 July 1940 has come true. Today Hitler declared war against Russia. My poor country! My long-suffering homeland …' For Gabo, the beginning of the Great Patriotic War meant the end of imposed inactivity. Now, as a citizen of an allied country, he was able to join the volunteer fire brigade (ARW). He yearned to know what was happening on the battlefield and his diary entries are full of newspaper cuttings and photographs. He followed events in the USSR very closely, dreading to see the names of familiar towns and places in the newspapers. ■ '27 September [1941]. For three months I haven't picked up my diary. I was paralysed by the events in the war in the Russian battlefields … When the German locusts were approaching Bryansk and one caught glimpses in the newspapers of the names of cities and villages so dear to me I felt only one thing – that my paternal home had been burgled, and my heart throbbed for the fate of those who were left inside.'[105]
■ Gabo and his friends, who read his diaries, perfectly understood the significance of the sculptor's notes as historical and cultural testimony. In the 1960s, Gabo's friend Thomas Whitney, a diplomat who spent a considerable amount of time in the USSR, helped prepare

104 Naum Gabo, Diary, 30 July 1940, TGA.

105 Naum Gabo, Diary,
27 September 1941, TGA.

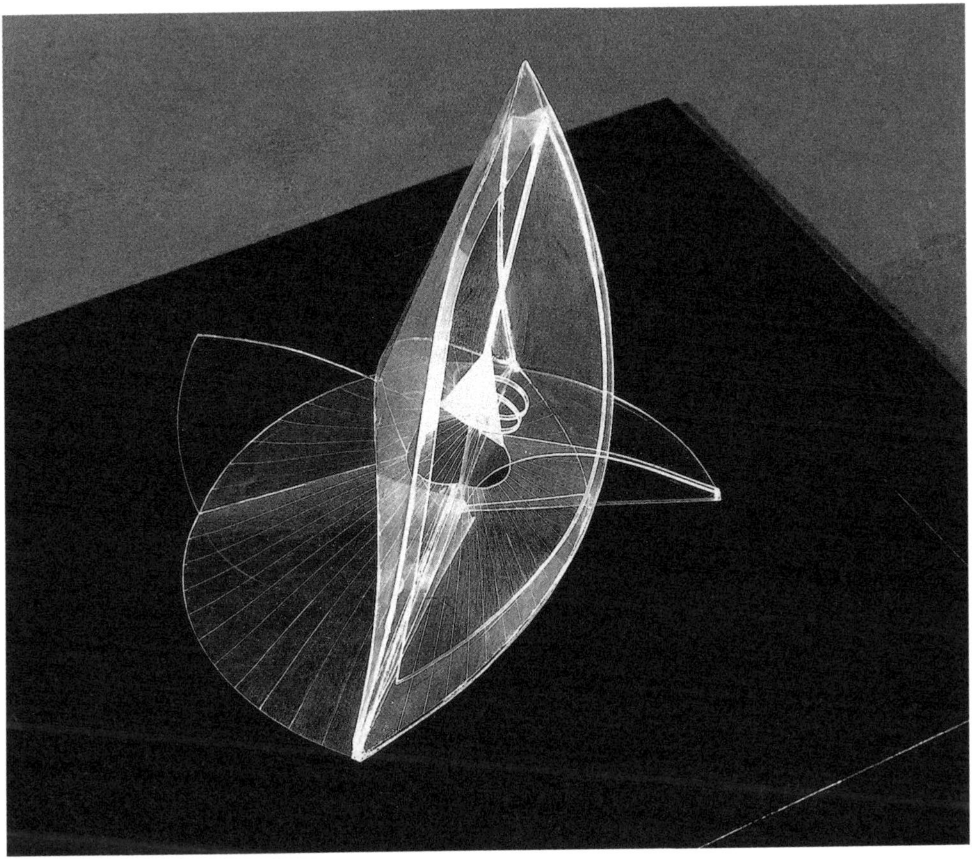

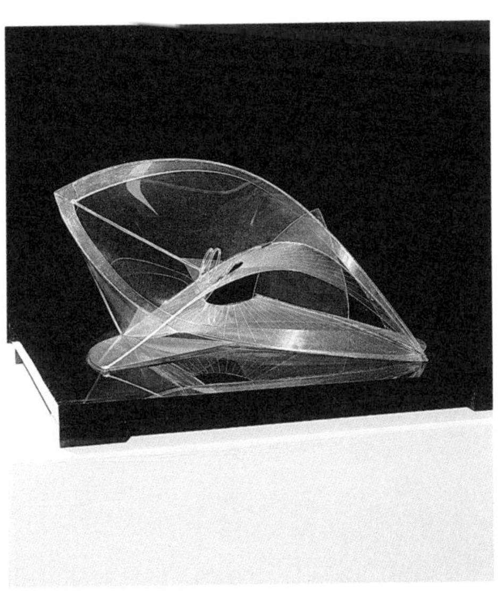

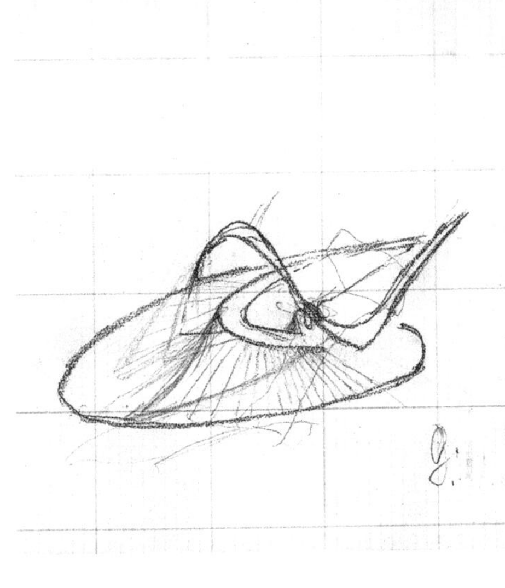

the Russian text of the diaries for publication. In his summary of the documents, Whitney stressed: 'Gabo's War Diary … is the artist's private and personal journal, giving his observations, including some major individual historical and philosophical essays, during the period of World War II … Gabo didn't shoulder a gun … and to his great anger he was turned down, because of being an alien, by the British Guard. Yet he was a very real participant in the war … So intensely did he feel a part of all that went on that it was only through this diary, in which he commented on the unfolding events … and in which he expressed his innermost thoughts about world affairs, that his creativity could find its full outlet in this particular period'.[106]

ST IVES Gabo spent the whole war in St Ives and those years were as fruitful as the pre-war period. Besides developing his ideas of various 'themes' and experimenting with a new stringing method, he worked on design projects, participated in radio broadcasts, wrote articles and published texts on his aesthetic thinking. He also began working with stone, possibly under the influence of his friend Hepworth. The fact that Gabo, a master who 'rejected mass', took to stone carving speaks of the long road that he had travelled from the 1920s, when *The Realistic Manifesto* was published, to the mid-1940s, when he returned to this most traditional medium. Gabo no longer strove to be an innovator at all costs and no longer let materials dictate to him. To remain true to the form in which his creative imagination represented new images, Gabo needed stone. Thus, from a symbiosis of light plastic and solid limestone came *Construction in Space: Stone with a Collar* 1933–7. The streamlined, sensual forms of

[106] Letter from Thomas P. Whitney to Gabo with the summary of Gabo's War Diary, 25 October 1970, TGA.

Photograph of Naum Gabo and Miriam
in London, c.1937

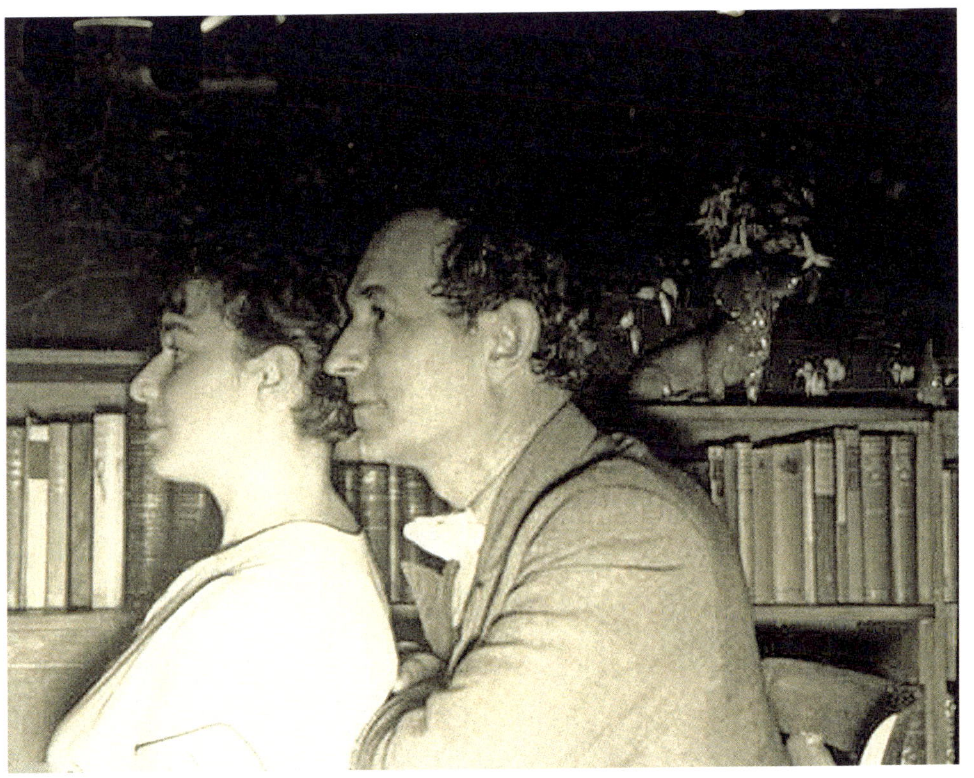

Cover of *Book No.1* of Gabo's war diaries,
1939–41

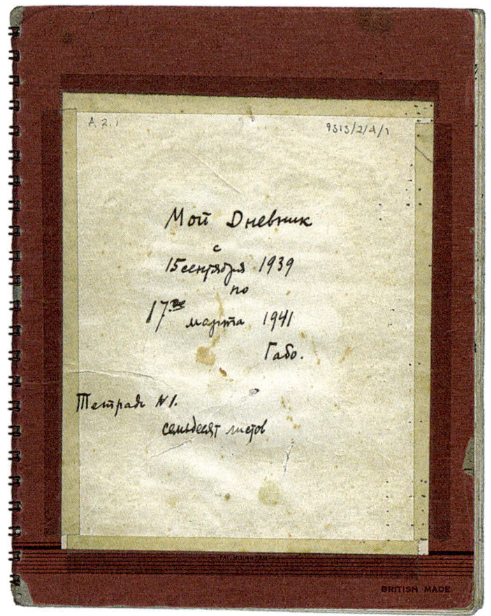

Kinetic Stone Carving 1936–44, one of Gabo's most emotional
works, were inspired by his wife, and the piece was to be a present
for her. In 1944, he completed the work in Portland stone – a local
limestone favoured by British sculptors. In his 1948 exhibition catalogue, Gabo included photographs of this work, taken from four different angles so as to demonstrate the dynamic, or kinetic, properties
of the sculpture.[107] As usual, Gabo dated the work not with its year
of completion, but with the year 1936, when he had developed a
mental image of the new work. ■ Although his
earlier ideas of using stone forms in conjunc-
tion with plastic elements date from the Paris

107 *Naum Gabo – Antoine Pevsner*, exh. cat.,
Museum of Modern Art, New York 1948,
pp.32–3

→ (p.146–7)
Notes and press cutting related to the
January 1941 events, Gabo's war diaries

Book No.2 of Gabo's war diaries, 1941–2

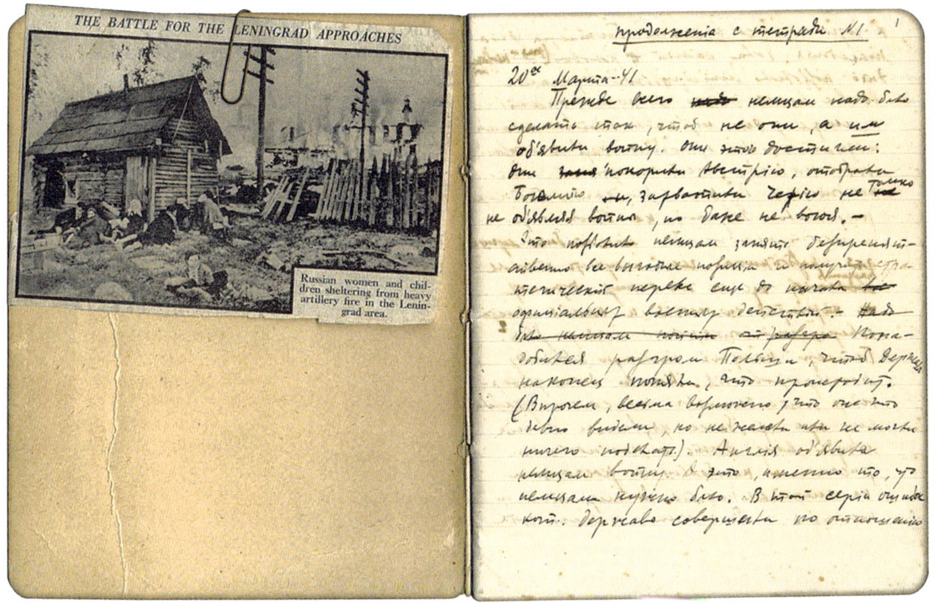

period, Gabo's true, profound interest in stone as a material arose
from his acquaintance with British modernist sculptors. The technique of direct carving, when a form grows out of a block of stone
or a piece of wood without a preliminary plaster or clay model, was
developed by European sculptors such as Constantin Brancusi and
later perfected by British sculptors Jacob Epstein and Eric Gill. The
next generation of sculptors, such as Hepworth and Moore, continued to profess their respect for the material and carved direct, a
technique that had previously been considered suitable for a stone
carver, but not a sculptor. Their approach was of great interest to
Gabo, who planned a whole row of sculptures carved from stones

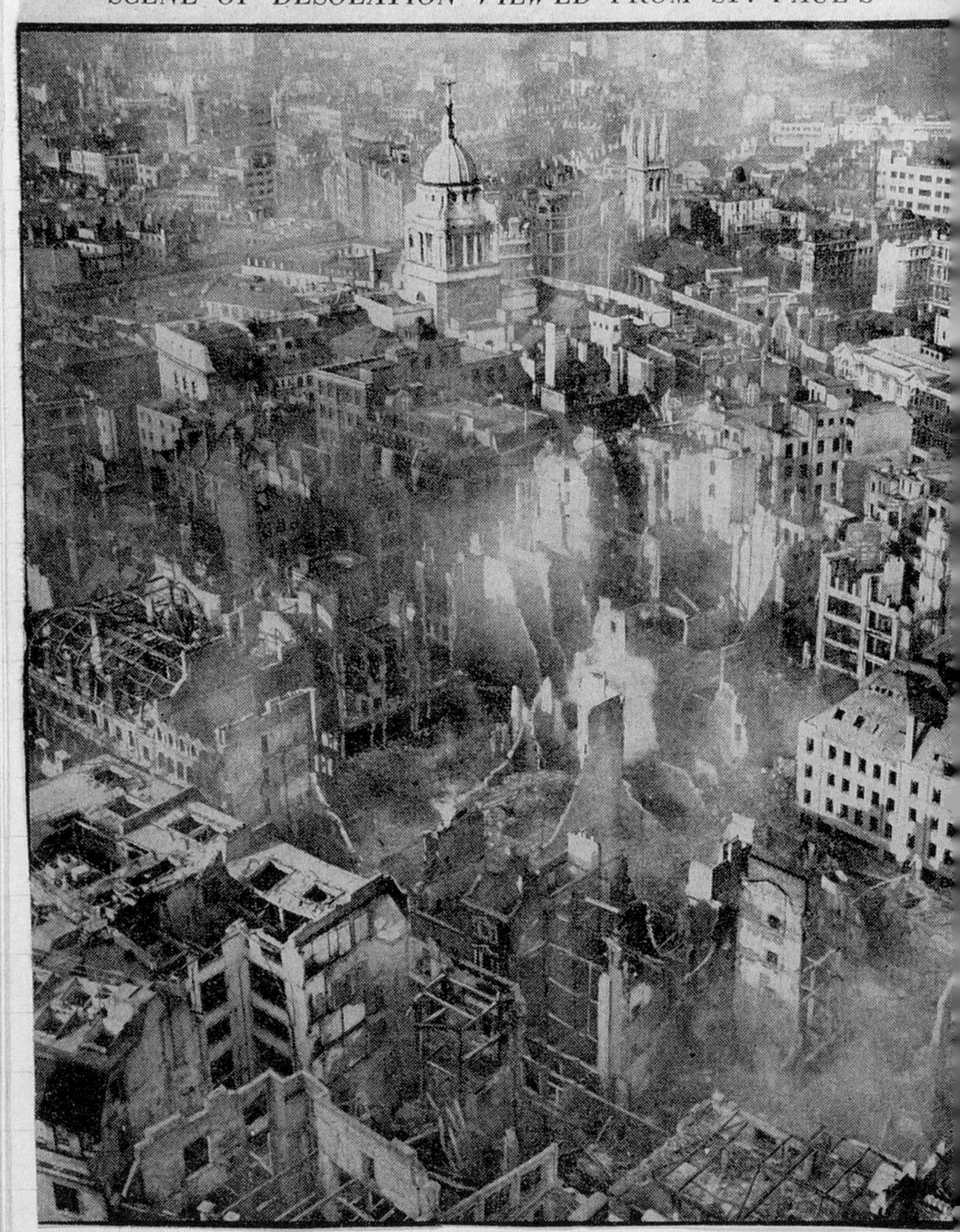

SCENE OF DESOLATION VIEWED FROM ST. PAUL'S

59.

The miraculous escape of St. Paul's Cathedral when bombers were scattering incendiaries all around it. on Sunday night is revealed by this remarkable picture. The photograph was taken, looking westwards, from the Golden Gallery surmounting the dome of the cathedral. The conspicuous building in the background is the Central Criminal Court. The devastated area of burnt and broken buildings, virtually in the shadow of the cathedral, is mainly the famous booksellers' quarter bounded by Ave Maria-lane and Paternoster-row. Hardly one structure has escaped.

Так / закончился 1940-ой год.
Не могу - и не хочу - стеснить
моего восхищения перед этой страной
и этим народом не повторив заме-
чательных слов первого из англи-
чан - Черчиля :
„Они зажгли в нашем сердце
пламя, которое будет гореть
и печь и не погаснет до тех
пор, покуда последний след
нацизма не исчезнет."

Эти слова - великие в своей простоте
и правде заслуживают того,
чтоб быть эпитафом на 1940 год.

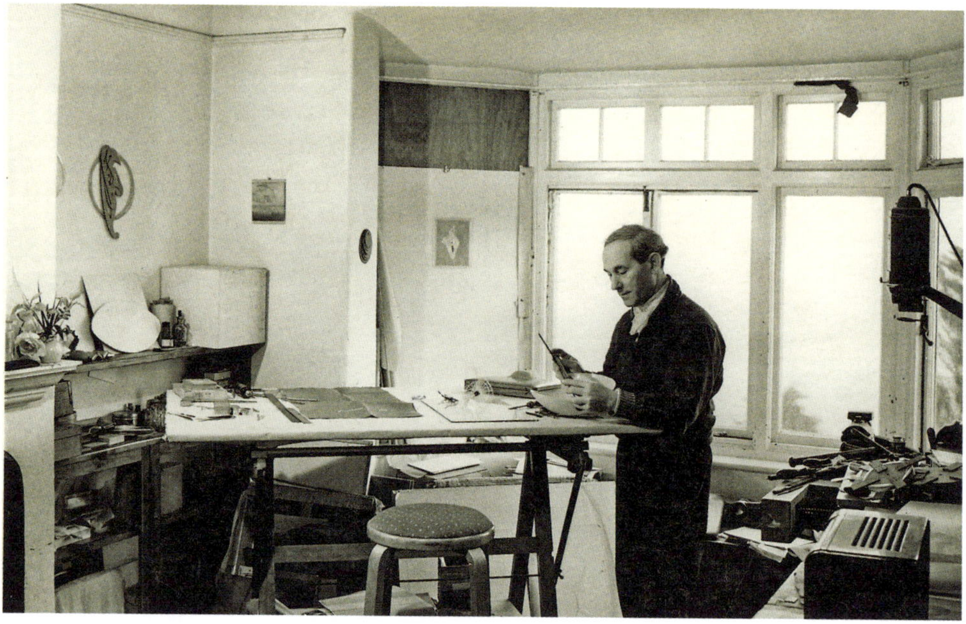

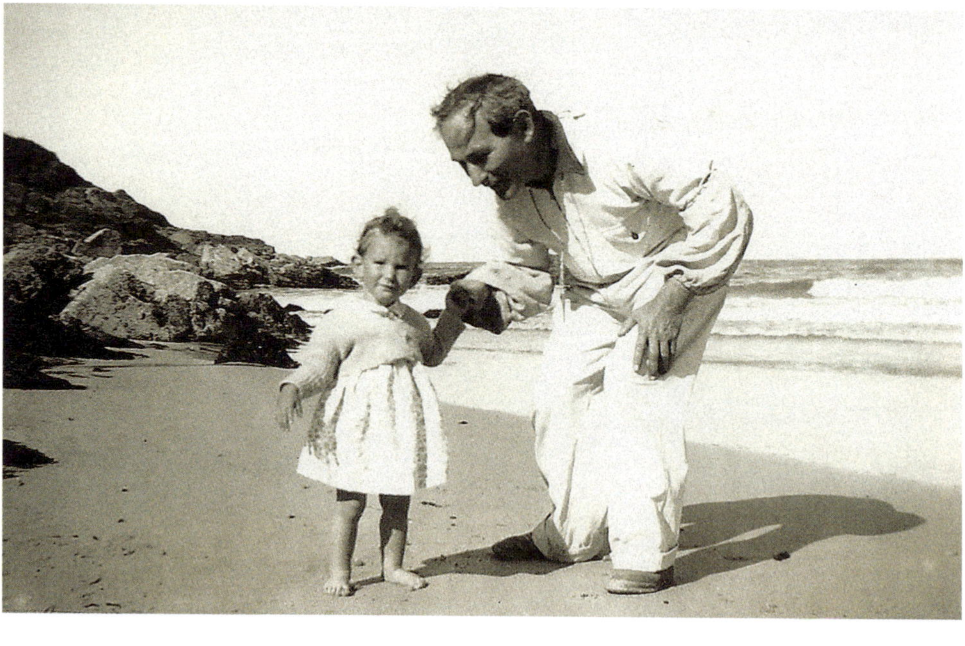

←
Photograph of Gabo in his studio
in Carbis Bay, Cornwall, c.1945

Photograph of Gabo and Nina on
the beach in Carbis Bay, c.1943

notable for their different pliable properties.  It was during this period that, for the first time since his youthful experiments, he returned to painting. This body of works was executed using a bright palette of shades and pigments of the same colour, one for each painting, where the abstract fluid forms fill the entire canvas with a certain 'kinetic' rhythm, as in *Kinetic Oil Painting in Four Movements* 1943, *Turquoise, Kinetic Oil Painting* 1945 and *Strontium* 1945. They are evocative of various three-dimensional works created at the same time. One of the distinctive traits of Gabo's works was its universal aspect. It would seem that forms born from his imagination were able to exist in both two- and three-dimensional space, as transparent constructions or as a flow of streamlined forms, as monochrome engravings and tonally developed paintings, small models and monumental sculptures. The paintings were often shown mounted on a wall panel that could rotate on its axis, either manually or by being connected to a motor. Francisco Infante-Arana, one of the pioneers of kinetic movement in Soviet art, recalls that Alexei Pevsner, in demonstrating the illustrations of the sculptor's works to young non-conformist artists in Moscow in the 1960s, similarly stuck Gabo's paintings, as illustrations cut from exhibition catalogues, on a rotating panel.[108] The profound belief, rooted in the very source of Russian constructivism, that the visual environment could exert a decisive impact on society, never ceased to motivate Gabo. In the pre-war years, he happily accepted commissions for design projects – from coat hangers and a cigarette box to a whole range of cabin fittings for an ocean liner (1937). Gabo adopted his favourite medium of plastic

[108] From a conversation with the author, State Tretyakov Gallery, Moscow 2005.

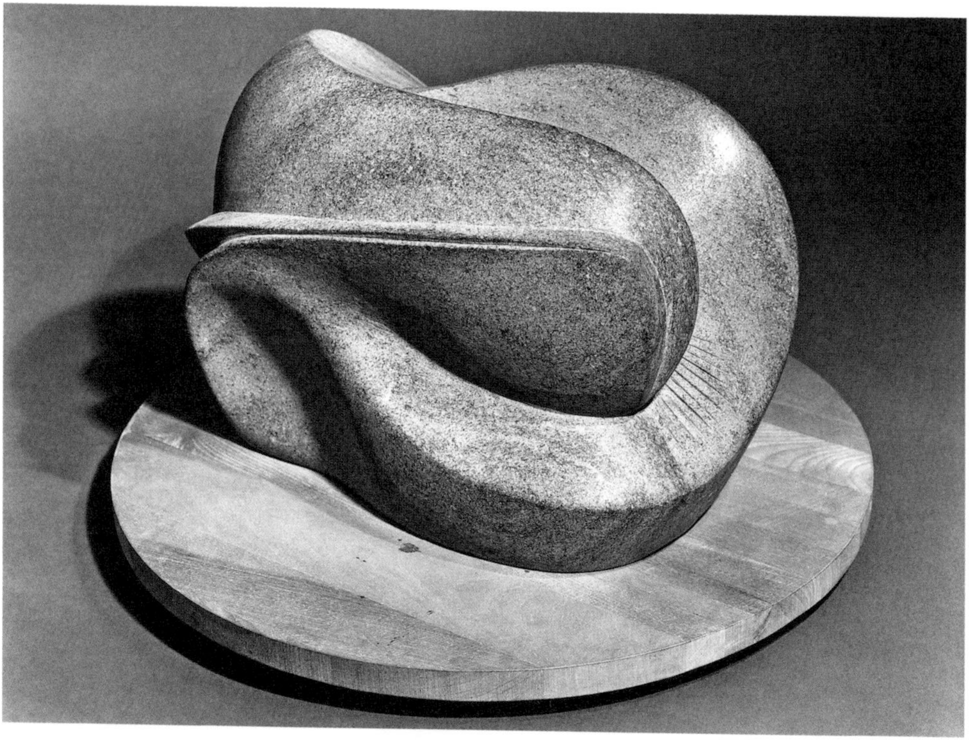

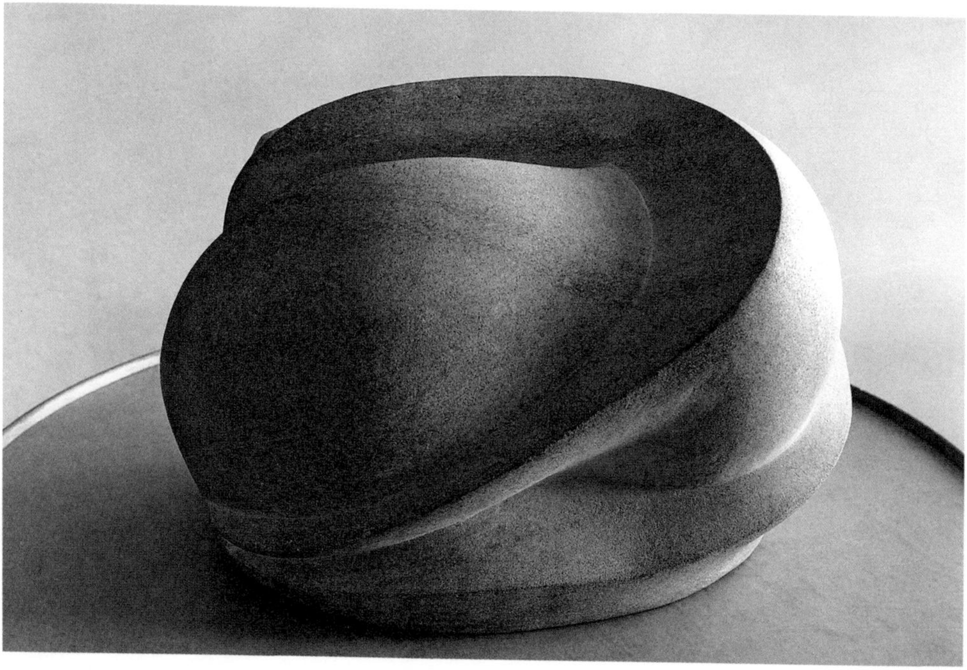

←

Kinetic Stone Carving 1936–44
Portland stone, 25.5 x 36.5 x 25.5

for the designs. In 1941, he used a bright red and yellow plastic to create the *Perpetual Calendar.* In spring 1943, he was invited by Read, then director of the Design Research Unit, to produce a model of the new generation automobile. Gabo finished the design in 1944 and presented the model to the commissioner – the Jowett motor car manufacturer. His car design was very original, but did not find its way to the production line as Jowett doubted that it met all necessary practical requirements.[109] One of the most distinctive features of Gabo's work was his possession of universal qualities as a master designer-artist, possibly acquired through his encounters with the Vkhutemas and the Bauhaus schools of design. He found solutions easily to both purely artistic and technical problems if these were an outlet for his creative ideas. Although the majority of his design projects never got to the production stage, Gabo accepted new commissions with great enthusiasm.

[109] *Constructing Modernity* 2000, p.295.

Strontium 1945
Oil on cardboard, 22.5 x 29.5

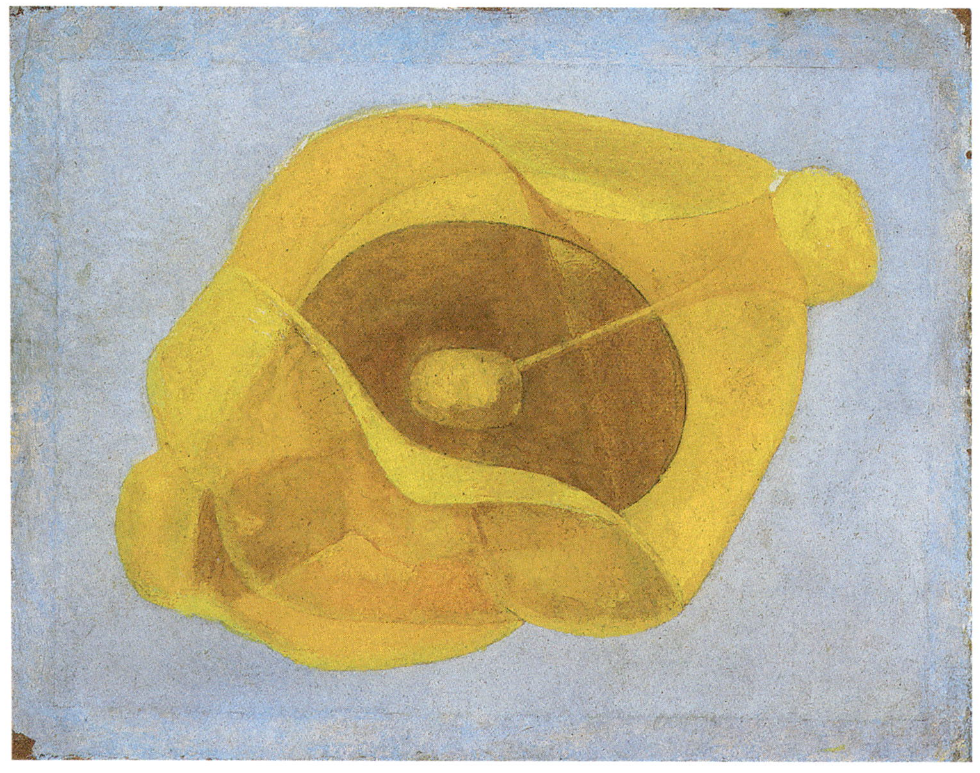

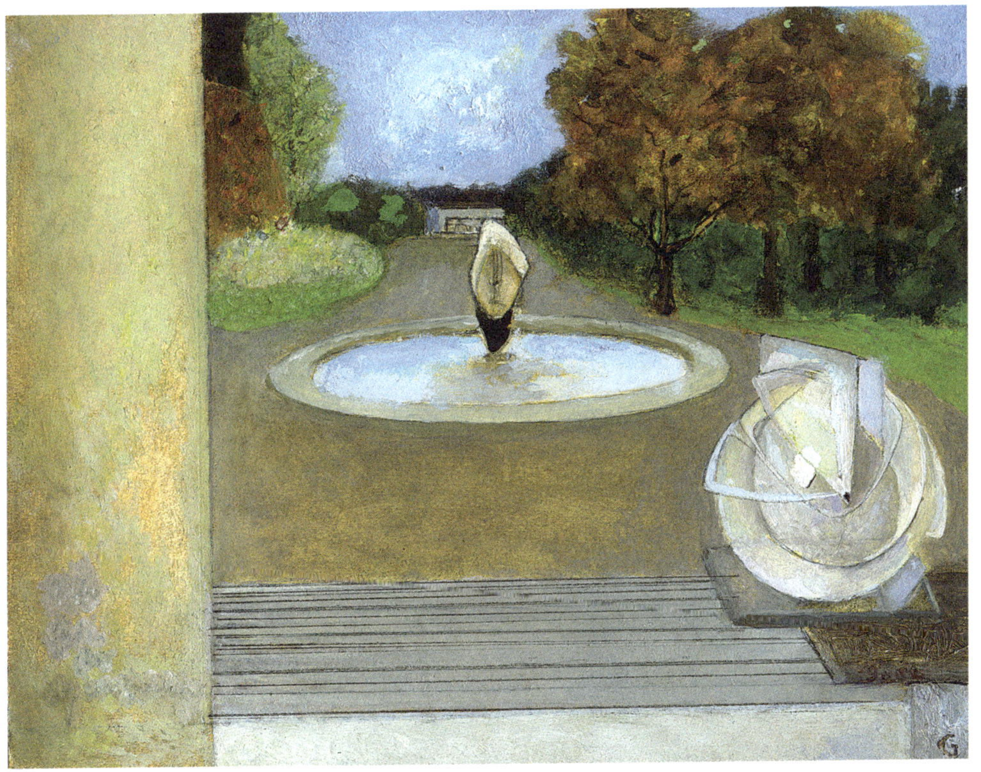

Landscape Garden View with Sculpture
c.1938
Pencil and oil on cardboard, 19 x 24

Photograph of the *Jowett Car Model* 1944,
1944

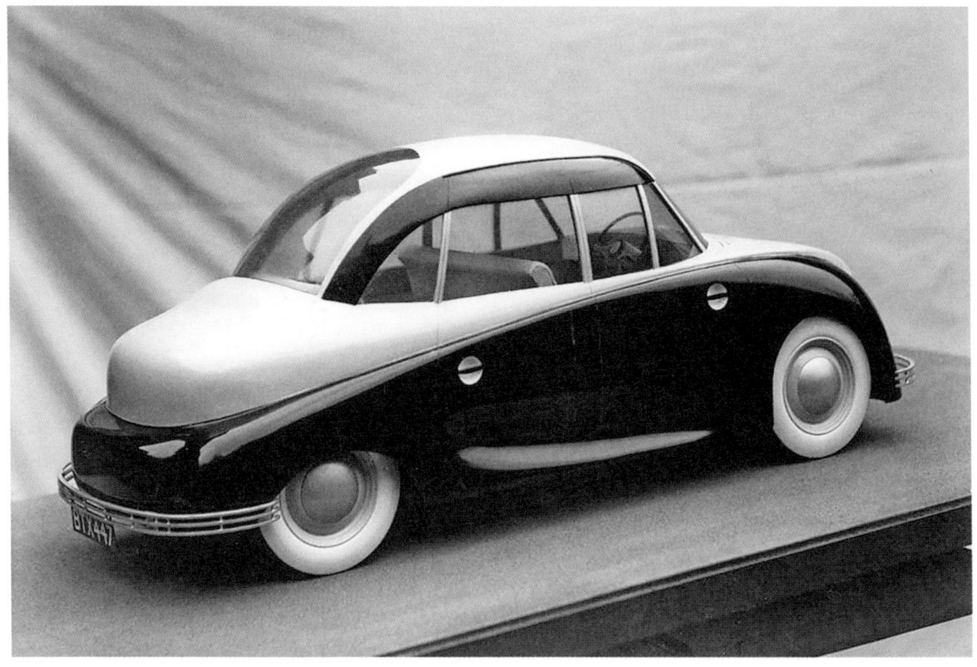

Photographs of designs for a coat hanger,
1937

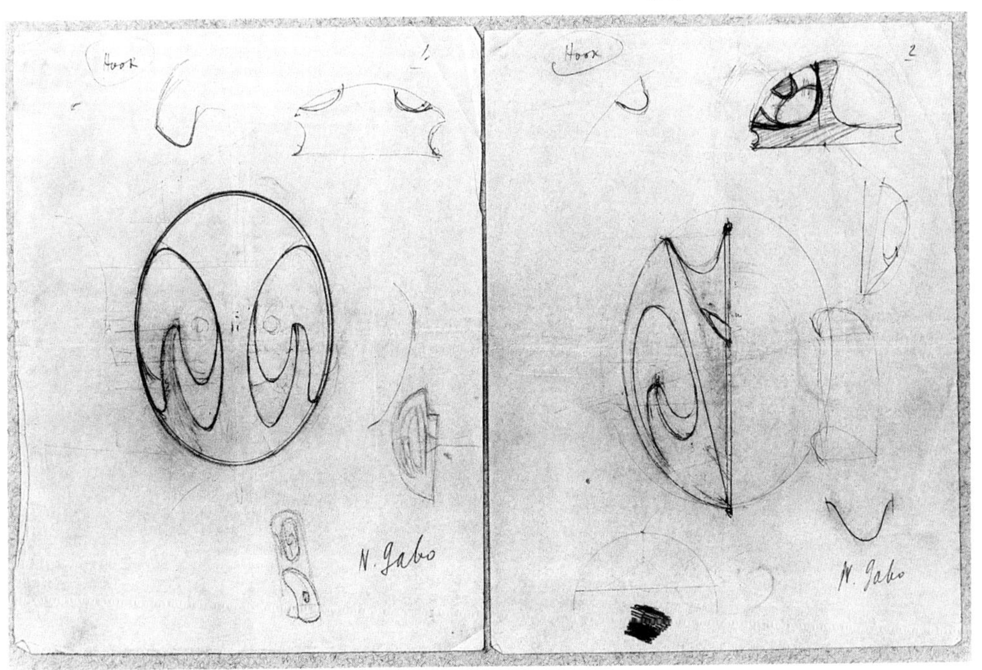

'HEAVENLY INSTRUMENTS': THE TECHNIQUE OF LINEAR STRINGING

Gabo, his wife Miriam and their baby daughter Nina, born in 1941, lived in Cornwall until 1946. It was extremely difficult for Gabo to obtain the materials for his constructions during the war. Perspex was produced only for military requirements. Forced to compromise and make do with off-cuts, the sculptor completed several complex spatial constructions such as the previously mentioned *Spiral Theme*. Experiments with pieces of plastic of various shapes and sizes formed the basis of a new method, which soon would become the sculptor's signature technique – stringing. Here the volume is created by a simple framework, coiled with various kinds of threads or strings in such a way that they visually differentiate the basic shape of the frame. ■ The principal volume of *Linear Construction in Space No.1* 1942–3 is created by nylon filament woven around a plastic frame. It was the first of a whole series of works using the method of stringing. ■ On 18 January 1943, Gabo noted in his diary: 'Leningrad has been freed! I cannot find the words to express my joy, pride and admiration of my people and this city. I only regret one thing, that I personally did nothing, and physically am incapable of doing anything, to earn the right to consider myself a part of the great feat. The next work, which I have already begun, I dedicate

Linear Construction in Space No.1 1942–3
Acrylic and nylon, 34.9 x 34.9 x 8.9

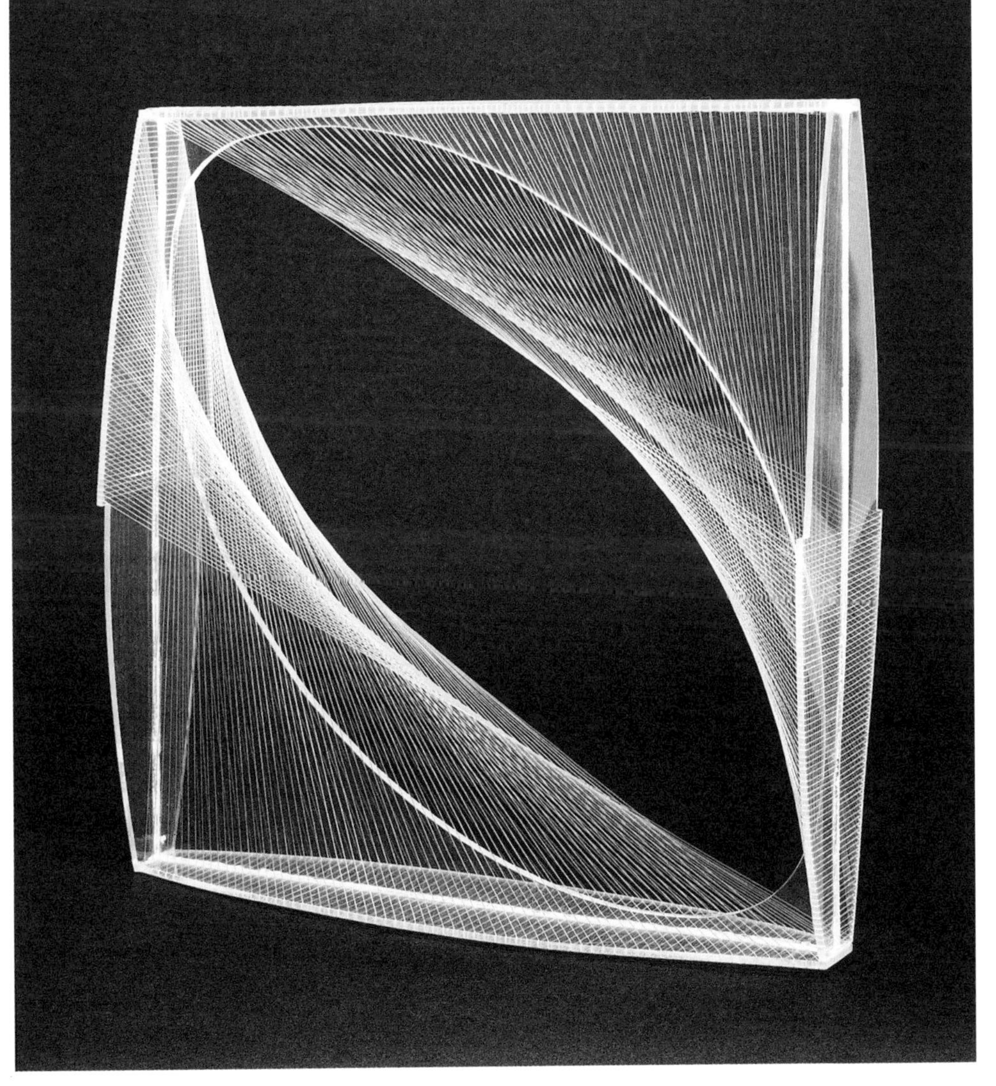

to Leningrad. I do this not out of a feeling of duty, but as an expression of my deep, sincere feelings of admiration for my homeland, the humble feelings of a refractory son to a grieving and ardently loving mother from whom fate has separated me. I will try with all my might to make this work the best of my best, or I will not allow it to see the light of day.'[110] ■ Judging by his diary, Gabo worked on the construction dedicated to Leningrad for an entire year. On 27 January 1944, he noted: 'It was a year and a week ago that I celebrated the liberation of Leningrad. I rejoiced too soon. Another whole year of suffering, hunger, siege and devastation was needed for my wishes to be realised … My construction commemorating that day has also been completed. One collector called it a heavenly instrument. Of course, I didn't let him in on the secret of its meaning.'[111] ■ Thus, Gabo dedicated his first *Linear Construction in Space* to the liberation of Leningrad from its two-and-a-half-year-long siege in the hope that the sculptural form he had produced would one day grow to be a monument commemorating the event. This was not meant to be, although the majority of monumental works envisaged and completed by him from the 1950s to the 1970s did contain a stringed element. ■ Gabo did not invent the method. Miriam Gabo recalled: 'The first strings I saw was one [sic] … at Henry [Moore]'s studio here in London before the war. When we came back to [our flat at] Cholmley Gardens I guess Gabo said: "Strings, I'll show them what to do with strings!". So I guess he hadn't used them then.'[112] The appearance of the new technique is generally related to the interest

110 Naum Gabo, Diary, 18 January 1943, TGA.

111 Ibid., 27 January 1944, TGA.

112 Transcript of an audio record, 'Miriam Gabo interviewed by David Lewis and Sarah Fox-Pitt', 28 May 1981, p.43, TGA.

many artists had in the collections of science museums and, in particular, in mathematical models. According to the technique's pioneer, Henry Moore: 'Undoubtedly the source of my stringed figures was the Science Museum … I was fascinated by the mathematical models I saw there, which had been made to illustrate the difference of the form that is halfway between a square and a circle … It wasn't the scientific study of those models but the ability to look through the strings as through a bird cage, and to see one form within another, which excited me.'[113] ■ In the world of science, interest in such models was dormant by the 1920s. They gathered dust in the glass cabinets of schools and institutes, where they were discovered by artists. From the same period are both Man Ray's series of photographs *Mathematical Objects*,[114] published in 1936, and the first sculptural works using the stringing method – Moore's *Stringed Relief* and *Stringed Figure*, both 1937. Moore used the stringing technique for three years, from the earliest composition, *Stringed Relief*, in which he included only a few strings, to *The Bride* 1939–40, in which thin wire is used to model half the scope of the entire volume. In his sculptures, strings complement the form while at the same time resisting it: symmetry versus a free flow of curves, solid volume versus space, mass versus a vectored dynamism. Moore, having been the first to use strings in his sculptural forms, very soon found the method exhausted: 'they were fun, but … ingenuity rather than fundamental human experience'.[115] However, Hepworth and Gabo continued to employ the stringing

113 Henry Moore and John Hedgecoe (eds.), *Henry Spencer Moore*, Thomas Nelson, London 1968, p.105.

114 Neil Baldwin, *Man Ray, American Artist*, C.N. Potter, New York 1988, p.199.

115 Sally Festing, *Barbara Hepworth. A Life of Forms*, Viking, London 1995, p.136.

→

Barbara Hepworth 1903–75
*Sculpture with Colour
(Deep Blue and Red)* 1940
Cast material and mixed media,
10.5 x 14.9 x 10.5

Henry Moore 1898–1986
Stringed Figure 1938/60
Bronze and elastic string,
27.3 x 34.4 x 19.7

method throughout their creative careers. ■ Hepworth, having until 1939 worked predominantly with the texture of the surface in her basic solid forms, entered a new creative phase soon after the outbreak of the war. The volume of her sculptures opened up, was differentiated by colour and complemented with a new element – strings. Many experts identify the influence of Gabo as a leading factor in prompting Hepworth to use the stringing method in her works. This kind of conclusion was drawn on the basis that Gabo's first stringed work *Linear Construction in Space No.1* was pre-dated: in one list of the sculptor's works, the first model for this construction was dated 1938, although in 1996 Martin Hammer and Christina Lodder proved that there was insufficient justification for such a dating and confirmed that it was indeed early 1942 when the first model was devised.[116] The recollections of Miriam Gabo confirm the existence of an earlier model of the *Linear Construction in Space No.1*, now lost, in which red threads were used for stringing. By this time, Hepworth had already created her first stringed sculptures, using coloured threads, in, for example, her 1940 piece *Sculpture with Colour (Deep Blue and Red)*, which indicates the profound influence on Gabo of her experiments. ■ Thus, Gabo had not drawn inspiration directly from the mathematical models, but from the new sculptural method of differentiation of space in sculpture, which had previously been used by his contemporaries. From the very begin-ning, employing colourless, transparent material for his constructions, the sculptor searched for ways of achieving an even

[116] Martin Hammer and Christina Lodder, 'Hepworth and Gabo: a Constructive Dialogue', in David Thistlewood (ed.), *Barbara Hepworth: Reconsidered*, Tate Gallery, London 1996, pp.121–2.

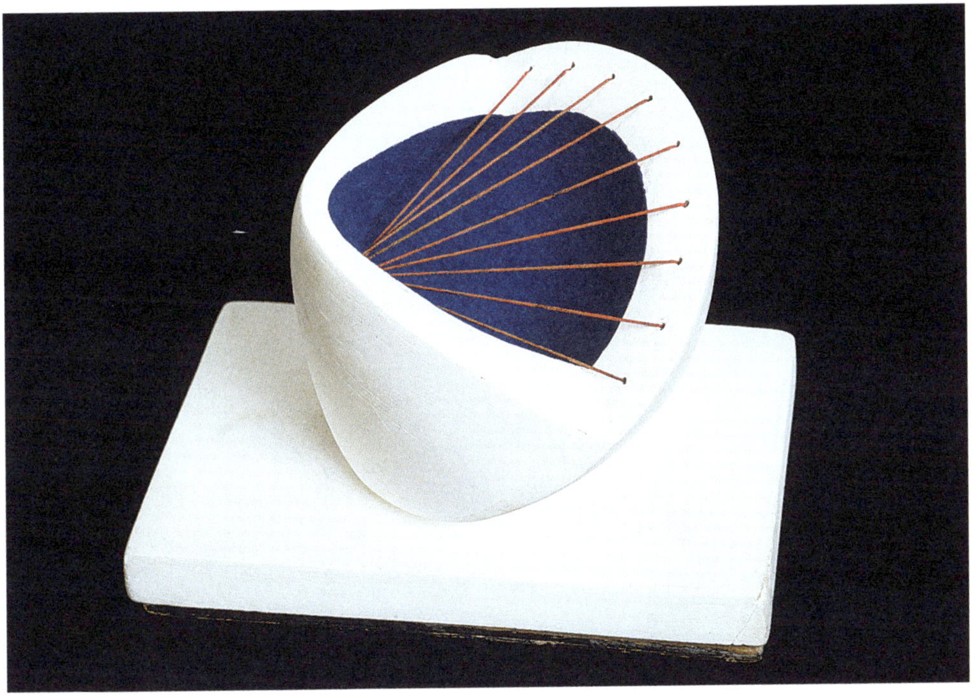

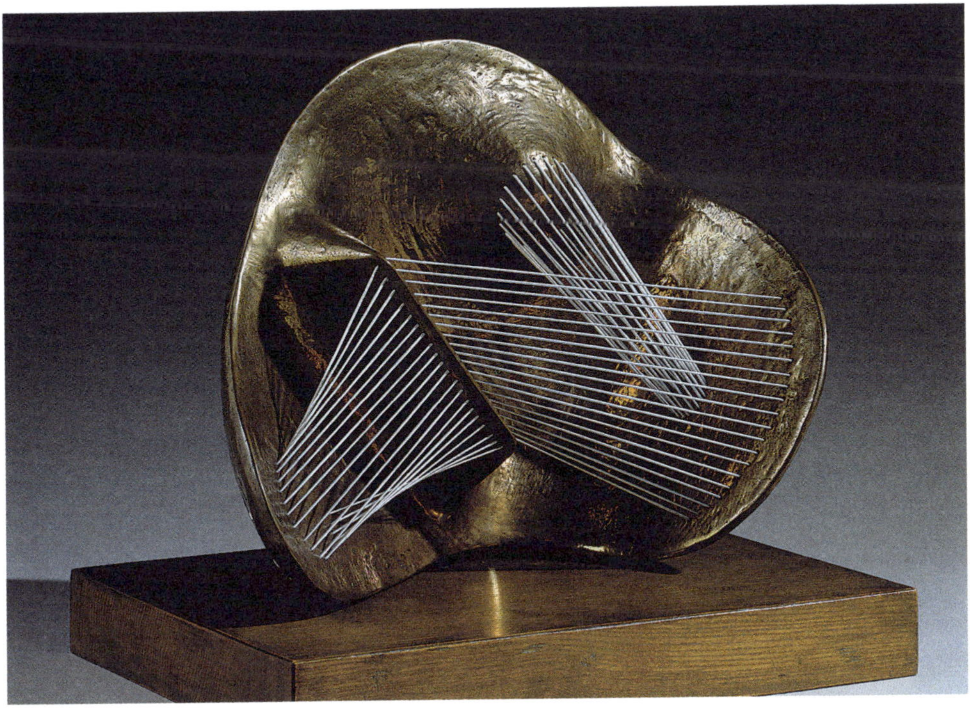

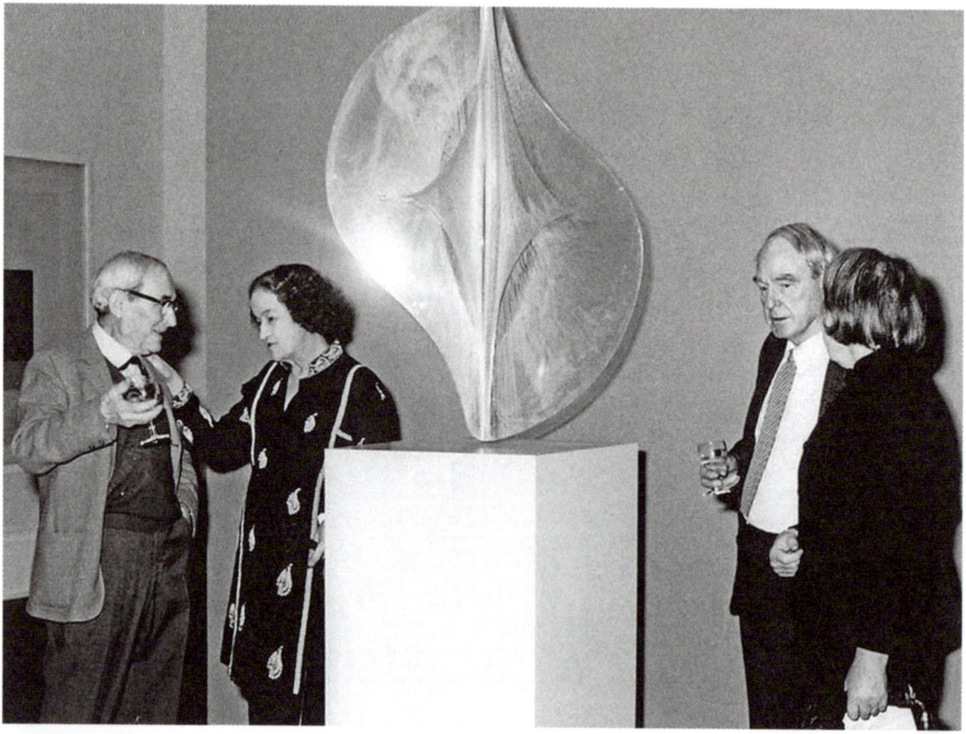

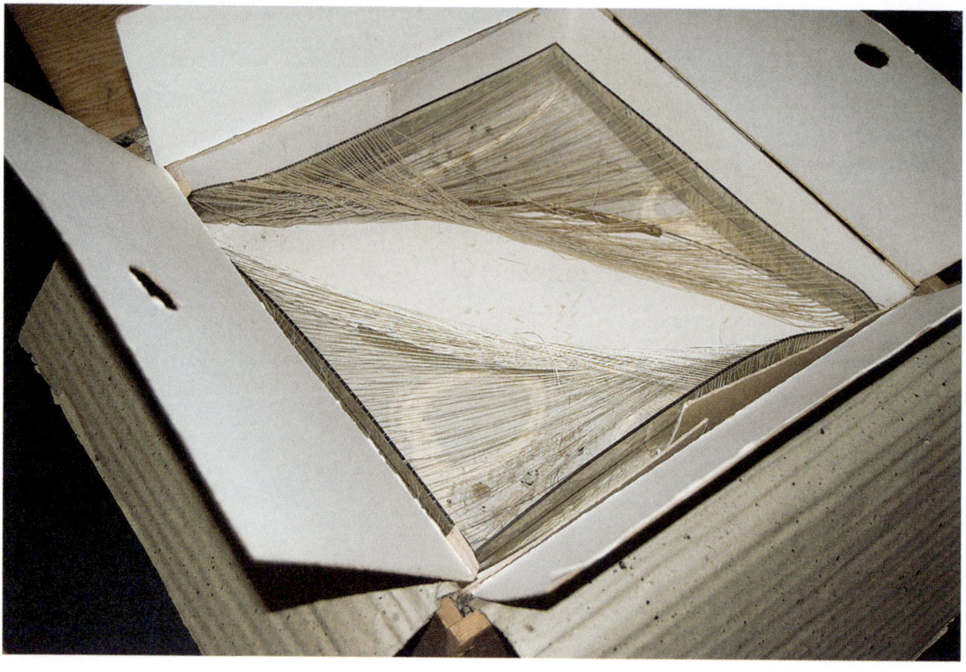

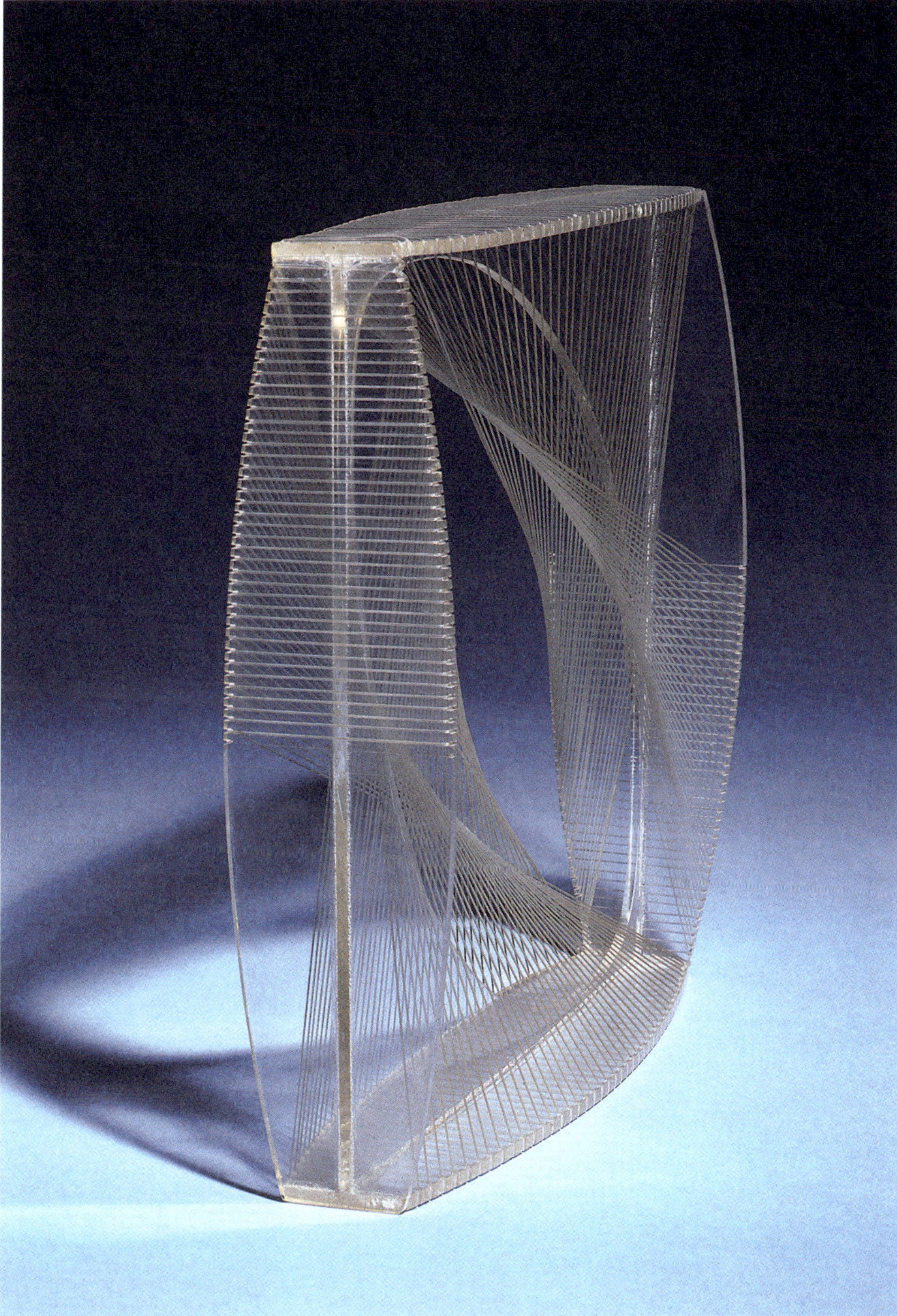

← (p.162)
Photograph of Gabo, Barbara Hepworth and
Henry Moore at Herbert Read's memorial
display at the Tate Gallery, 1970

Prototype of *Linear Construction in Space
No.1* 1942
Plastic, silk and cotton threads,
28 x 28 x 5

← (p.163)
Linear Construction in Space No.1 1942,
this version c.1952
Perspex and nylon, 21 x 21 x 5.5

greater effect of dematerialisation, when space permeates form. He was eager to achieve the inner shimmering of transparent forms, drawing attention to their dynamic interior. His *Spiral Theme* already exploited that effect by employing surface incisions. Abandoning the illusory approach, Gabo was able to perfect it only by employing the stringing method in the first work of his *Linear Constructions* series. The new technique, grasped through the works of Moore and Hepworth, allowed Gabo to achieve the same effect as by working directly with space. ■ *Linear Construction in Space No.1* is distinctive for its geometric symmetry of form, which is specific to Gabo's early works of the *Column* series. In his new work, thanks to the latest inventions of the chemical industry, he was able to transform a relatively simple volume with a rectangular plane into a complex construction, illuminated from within. Gabo's favourite stringing medium, nylon, was invented in the USA in the 1930s. The threads made out of this synthetic, colourless material are characterised by a heightened elasticity and durability and, most importantly, are endowed with the property of being able to be stretched considerably and later contracted to their initial length. Nylon thread was produced in the UK at the beginning of the 1940s by Imperial Chemical Industries Ltd (ICI).[117] Before the war, Gabo had become friends with Dr John Sisson, a chemist at ICI specialising in plastics. Through this friendship, Gabo found out very early on about the new type of plastic, Plexiglas, marketed in the UK under the brand name Perspex. ■ It was only at the end of 1944 that Gabo obtained both the materials from which he was able to cre-

[117] Penelope Curtis, *Modern British Sculpture from the Collection*, Tate Gallery, Liverpool 1988, p.56.

→ (p.166)
Photograph of *Linear Construction in Space No.2* 1942, this version 1970

→ (p.167)
Linear Construction in Space No.2
1970–1
Acrylic and nylon, 113 x 60 x 59

ate his *Linear Constructions* – Perspex and nylon. Before he began to use nylon filaments, Gabo tried silk and elasticated thread for stringing. It proved to be insufficiently tensile, as evident from the example of the first completed version of the construction, sold by Gabo to a private collector in March 1943. Its Perspex frame was wound with elastic threads, which, although they were highly flexible, became loose, ragged and collected dust, depriving the construction of its key characteristic – transparency. In 1945, these elastic threads were replaced with nylon ones.[118] ■ *Linear Construction in Space No.1* consists of a rectangular transparent framework with an elliptical void in its centre, around which nylon threads are wound and set close together. Each thread represents a line, delineating a plane, hence the name of the series *Linear Constructions*. The strings are wound through the elliptical opening and around the frame, so that they intersect in the space, and then are placed in shallow notches cut into the lateral sections of the construction. The two synthetic materials, Perspex and nylon, have very specific physical properties: the former collects pockets of light like a prism, while the latter absorbs it evenly along the whole length of its threads, thus employing the light to develop a new way of defining form in sculpture. Here the surface itself plays a secondary role: it is only space and light that allow the viewer to see *Linear Construction No.1*. The Perspex is transparent and light reflects off the cut surface of the edges while, at the same time, the matt nylon extinguishes the light, to produce a shimmering effect overall. This construction marks a new phase in Gabo's creative output. The works that appeared after

[118] *Constructing Modernity* 2000, p.290.

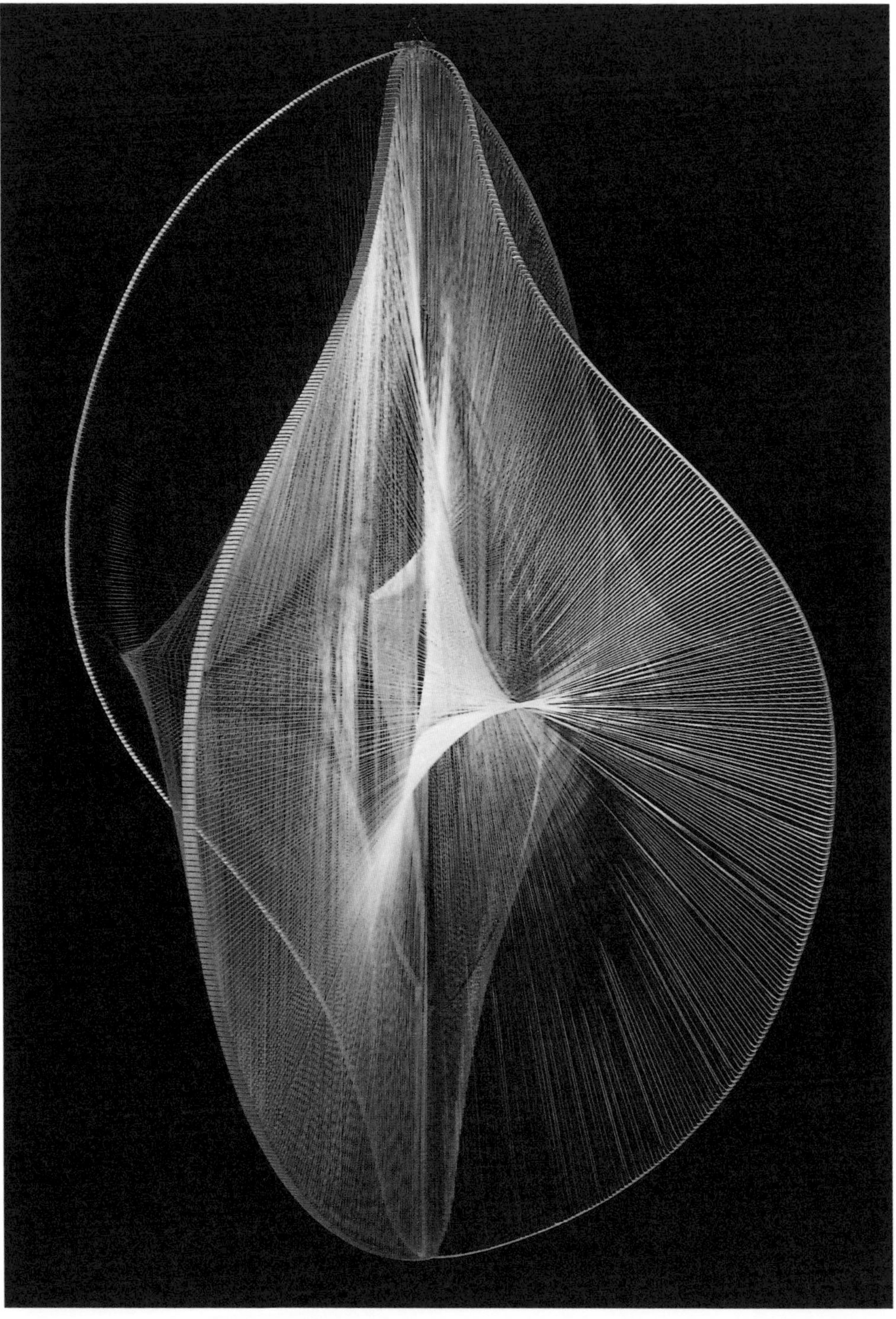

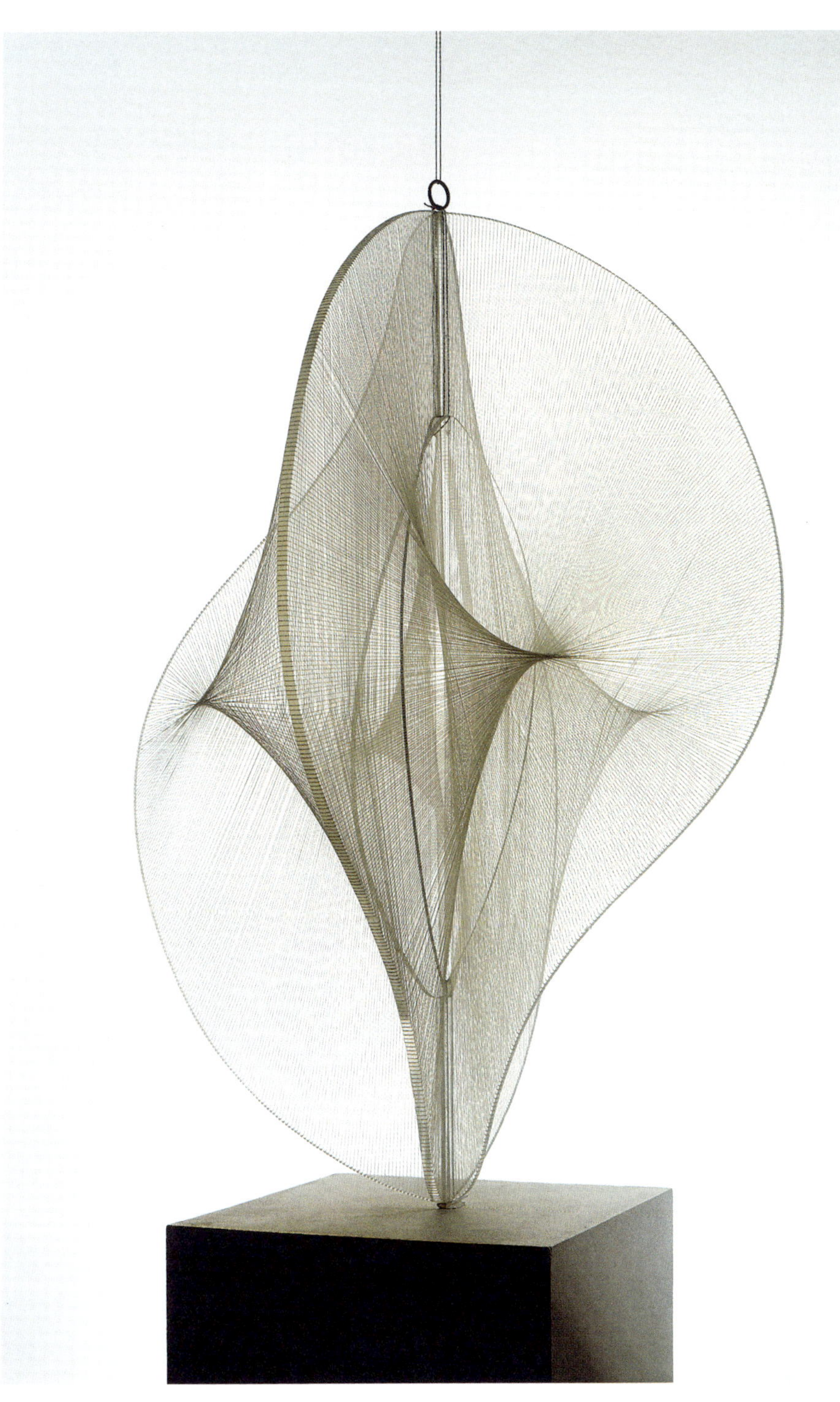

Conservation photograph of a fragment
for *Linear Construction in Space No.2*

Photograph of Gabo in his studio with the
frame for *Linear Construction in Space No.2*,
late 1950s

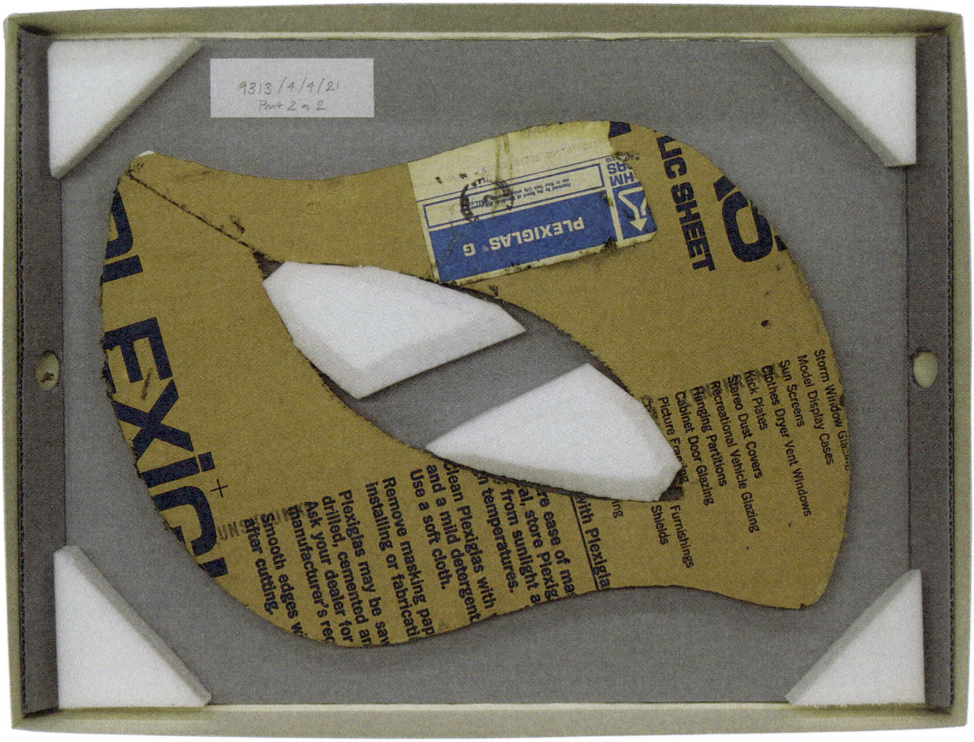

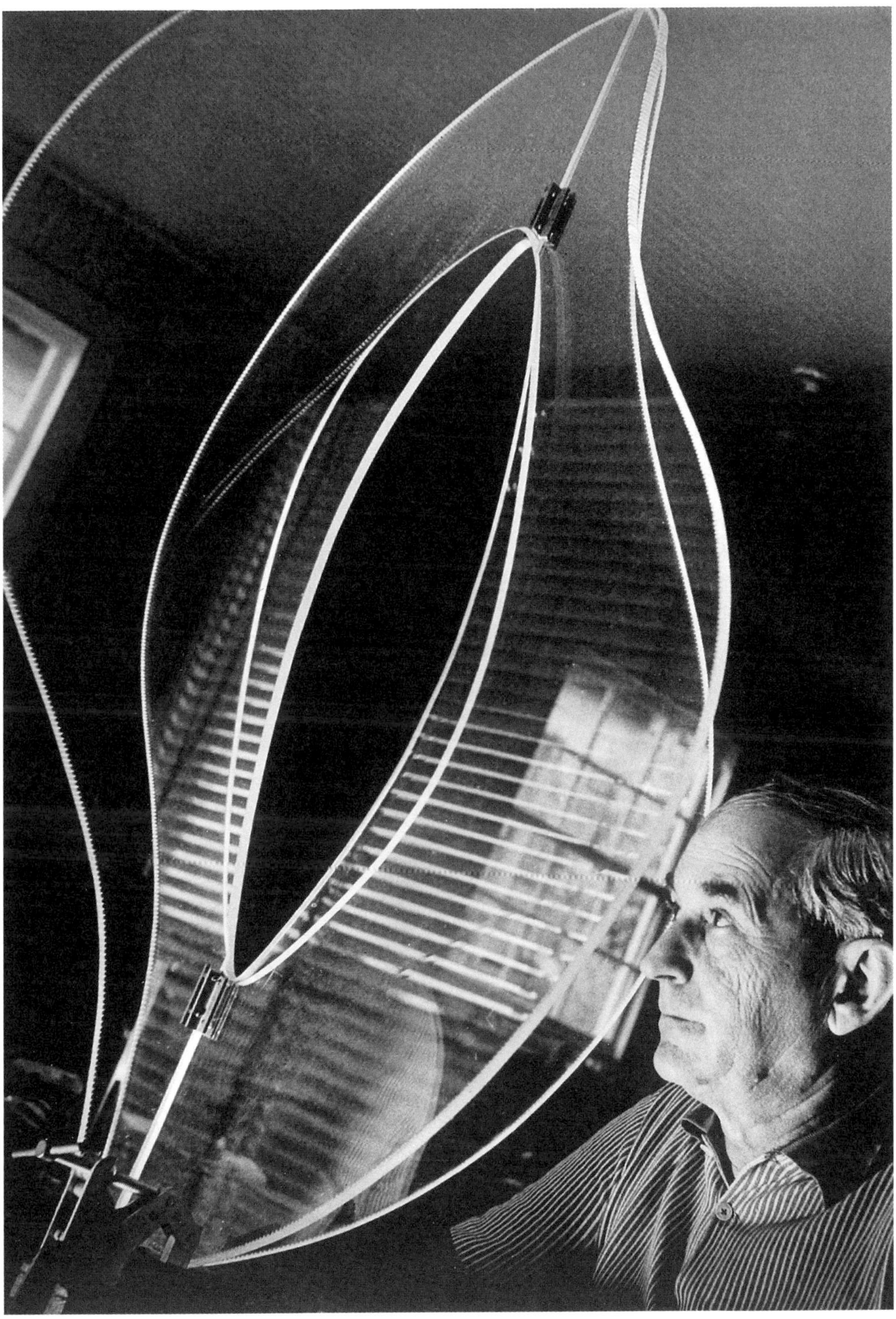

Linear Construction No.1 are radically different from all previous series. Gabo created seventeen versions of varying sizes of this construction and eleven variations where the lateral walls of the frame have 'steps', although the proportion, outer appearance and effect of light and vibrancy remain unchanged in each work. ■ The theme of *Linear Constructions* was continued by the sculptor with *Linear Construction in Space No.2* 1949, as soon as he moved to the USA in 1946. Apparently, this was Gabo's favourite work.[119] Its general structure consists of two identical curvilinear planes of transparent Perspex, with a small ellipse cut out at the centre, intersecting at right angles. The framework is extended with transparent nylon stringing, which is set into shallow notches on the curved ribs of the intersecting planes. The stringing is circular, beginning at the upper section of one plane; it crosses to the lower section of the perpendicular verge, then to the upper section of the next, and so on. The threads intersect, giving the appearance of curvilinear, inter-penetrating surfaces. Certain versions of the construction were intended to be displayed suspended. They hover over their bases, the gentle swaying and rotation provoking an expressive play of light on the threads and ribs of the construction. Each thread is a vector along which light glides, giving the construction dynamism. Since all its components are transparent and are not defined by colour or volume, the distinction between inner and outer space and between the material and immaterial is eliminated. ■ Gradually, Gabo introduced an element of stringing to the majority of his works, using both synthetic threads and metal

119 Steven A. Nash, 'Naum Gabo: Sculptures of Purity and Possibility', in *Sixty Years of Constructivism* 1985, p.41.

strings as in *Construction in Space: Arch No.2* c.1958, rods as in *Construction for the Bijenkorf Building Rotterdam* 1956–7, and jets of water for the *Revolving Torsion: Fountain* 1972–3 in London. The stringing technique was either the main medium for defining the shape of works, as in *Vertical Construction No.2* 1965–6 or was used as an additional element, as in *Bronze Spheric Theme* c.1960. It was used in sculptures such as *Construction in Space: Suspended* c.1957 and monumental projects such as *Spheric Theme* 1969–70 in Oslo. Once Gabo had started employing the stringing method, he used it in the majority of his constructions and projects. Several of his earlier works were reinterpreted with the introduction of a string element. ■ For Gabo, stringing was a natural continuation of the theme of transparent form that he had been developing from 1937, endeavouring to create a 'living surface'. For Hepworth, who worked with closed forms until the end of the 1930s, the addition of strings accompanied the introduction of colour in her new works, which unfolded in space. The surrealist Moore ceased to use the stringing method precisely because its origins lay in mathematical models and not organic forms. Gabo took an important step forward; he gave the string element an independent, leading role, to form the very volume that visually differed from the framework, thus allowing space and light to permeate, glide along the surface and be reflected in the borders, complicating and filling the composition with 'kinetic rhythms'. ■ Gabo lived in Cornwall until the end of the war, leaving Britain in 1946 to make the USA his permanent home. His wife, herself an American, assisted him in obtaining the necessary documents.

Aged fifty-six, he no longer had the strength to remain in Europe, where wars, revolutions and pogroms had driven him from one country to another, and where in his own country he was considered a traitor and in all others an outsider. The family moved to New York in November and soon settled in Connecticut, first in Woodbury and then in Middlebury, where the sculptor was to spend the rest of his life.

→ (p.174)

Photograph of *Revolving Torsion: Fountain*
1972–3, outside St Thomas's Hospital,
London

Vertical Construction No.2 1965–6
Stainless steel and stainless steel spring
wire, 292 high

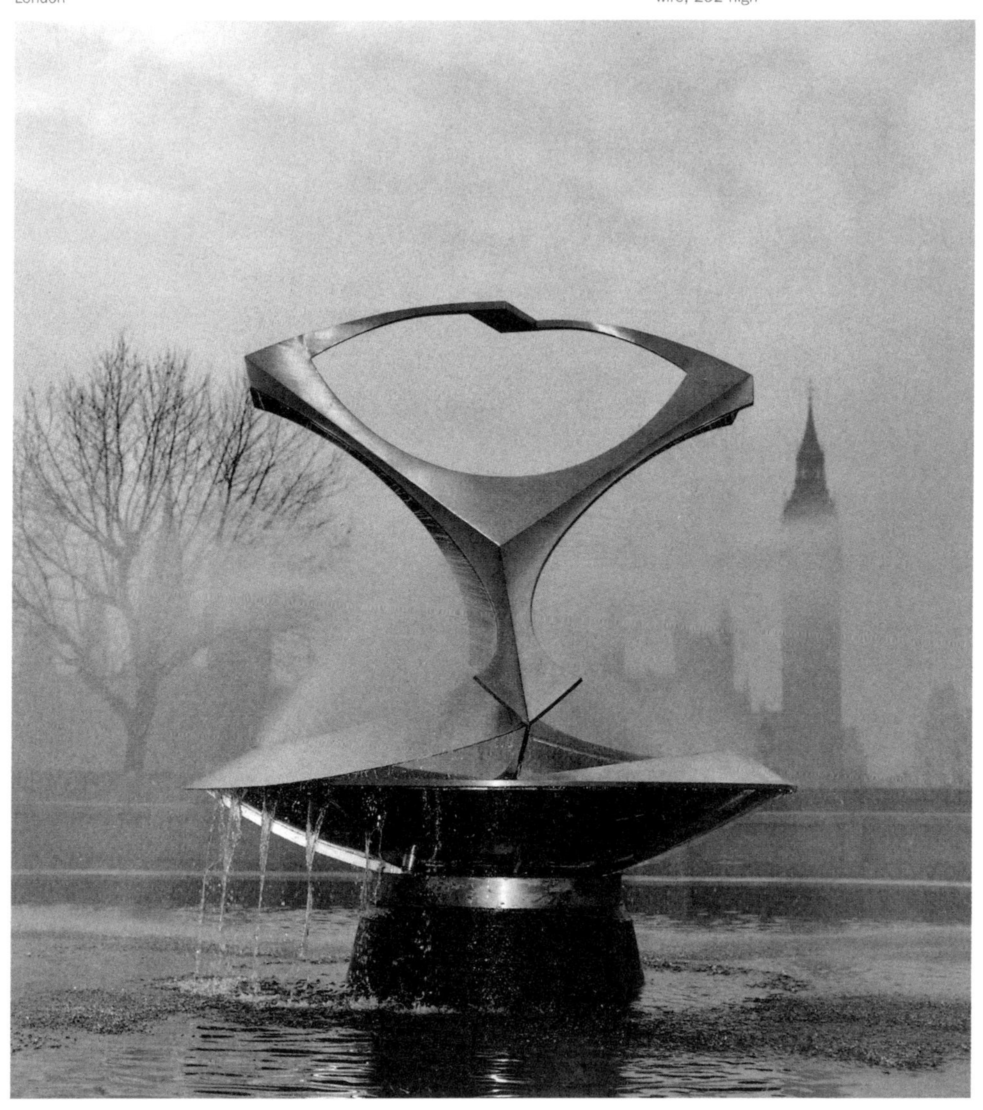

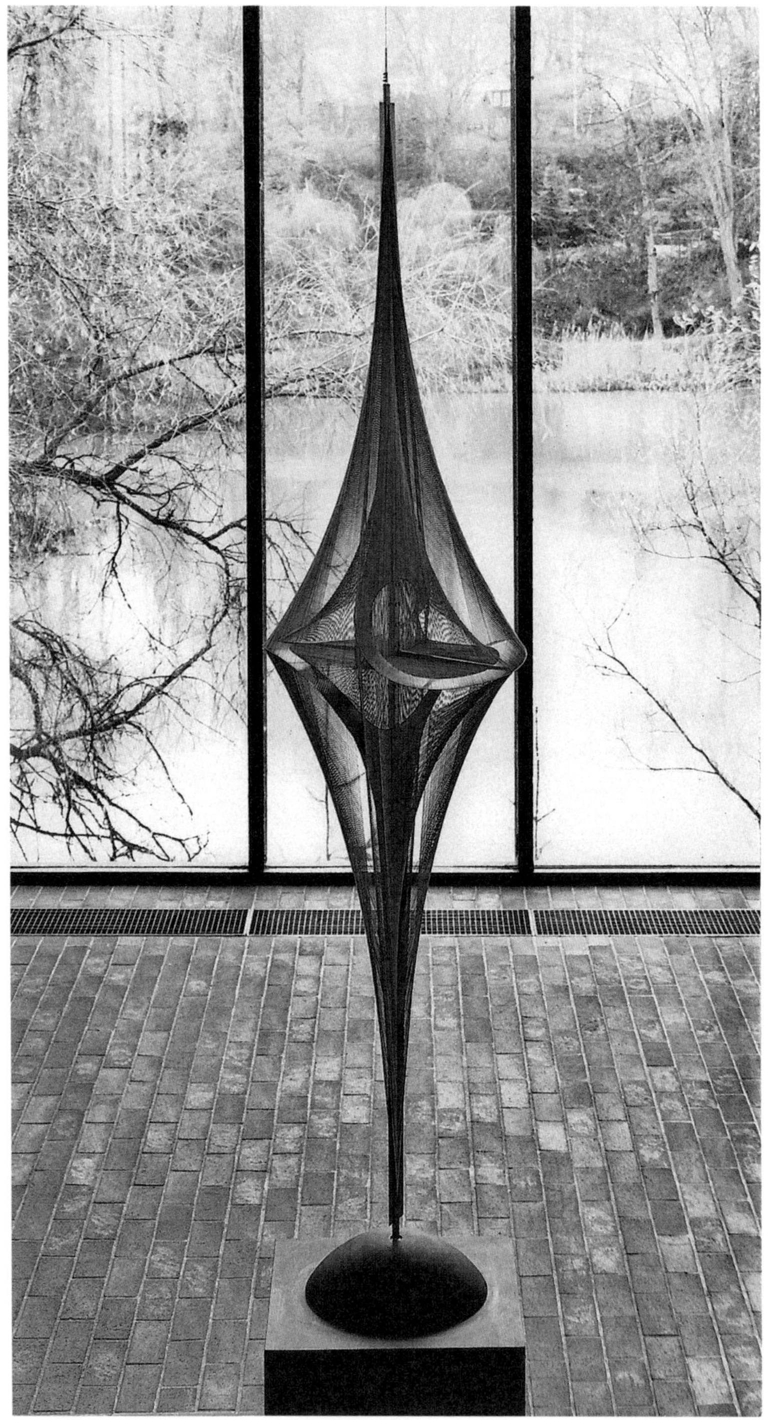

Construction in Space:
Suspended (Variation)
1957, this version 1971
Perspex, nylon, phosphor-bronze
on aluminium and Perspex base,
53 x 61.9 x 55.9

Bronze Spheric Theme c.1960
Phosphor-bronze on wooden base,
92.1 x 66.7 x 72.4

Photograph of *Spheric Theme* 1969–70
outside the Munch Museum, Oslo

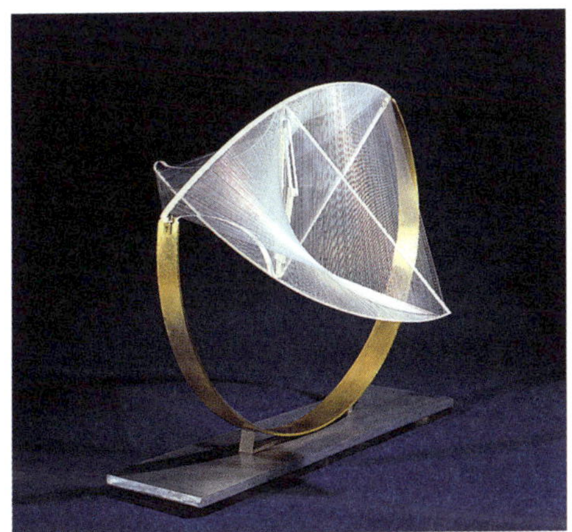

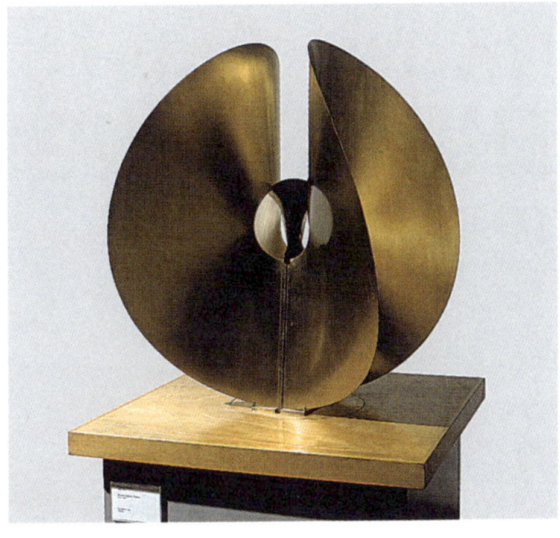

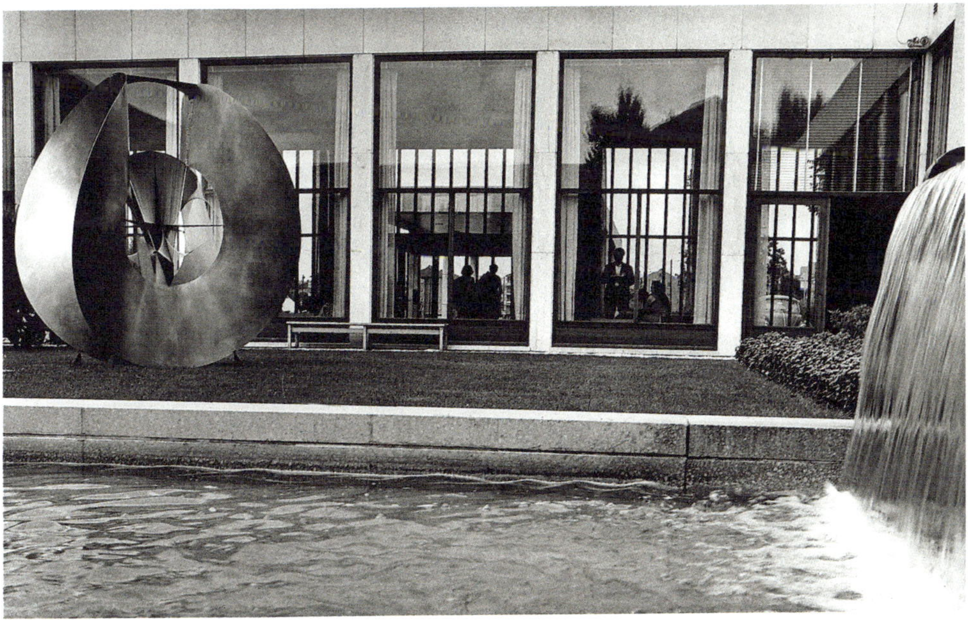

MONUMENTS FOR THE NEW WORLD (1946–77)

Almost as soon as he arrived in the United States, Gabo undertook to organise a combined retrospective exhibition of his works along with those of Antoine Pevsner, who had miraculously survived the Nazi occupation of France. The exhibition was held in the most prominent venue for modern art at the time – the Museum of Modern Art (MoMA), New York. The introductory article for the exhibition catalogue, written by Herbert Read, ranked Gabo and Pevsner alongside Malevich and Tatlin, thus consolidating for many years to come their reputation as leaders of the Russian avant-garde. 'The art of Antoine Pevsner and Naum Gabo is positive and prophetic, and it looks beyond the immediate convulsions of our epoch to a time when a new culture based on an affirmative vision of life will need and will call into being an art commensurate with its grandeur.'[120] This exhibition underpinned the key role of Gabo as a pioneer in abstract sculpture and a leader of the constructivist movement in art. ■ The years spent in America can be considered the most calm and productive of the sculptor's life. It was during this period that he truly gained worldwide acclaim and, with it, received international commissions, exhibition opportunities, popularity among public and private

120 Herbert Read, 'Constructivism: the art of Naum Gabo and Antoine Pevsner', in *Naum Gabo – Antoine Pevsner*, exh. cat., Museum of Modern Art, New York 1948, p.13.

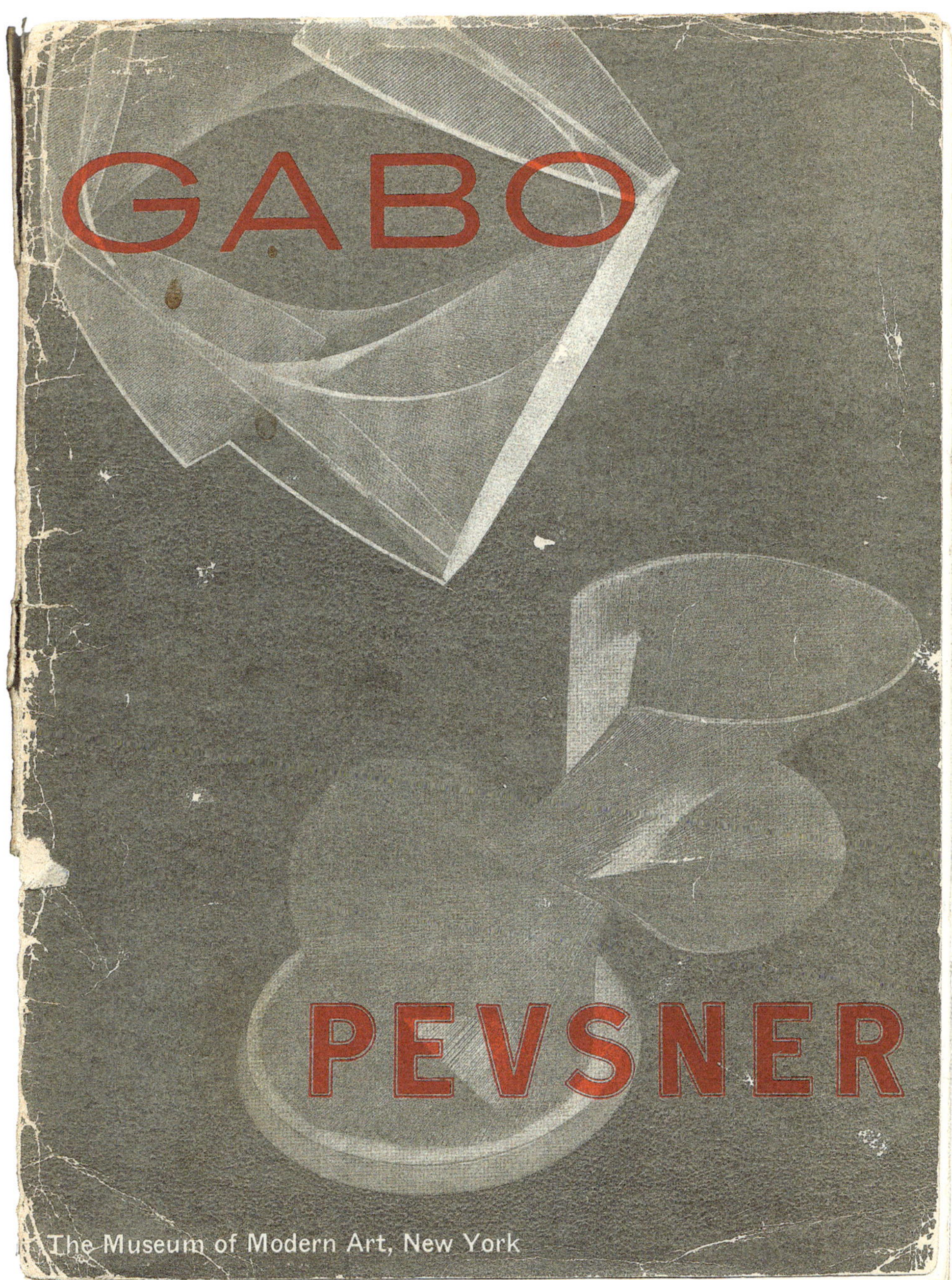
GABO
PEVSNER
The Museum of Modern Art, New York

art collectors, and invitations to lecture and publish his aesthetic thoughts. Gabo's first monograph came out in 1957 under the title *Gabo: Constructions, Sculpture, Paintings, Drawings and Engravings*,[121] followed a few years later by the publication of a collection of his lecture series, delivered in 1959 at the National Gallery of Washington.[122] He was finally able to realise many of his previously conceived constructions as monumental sculptures. His earlier works, such as *Constructed Head No.2*, *Column* and *Spheric Theme* were erected in the grounds of Britain's Tate Gallery, the Louisiana Museum of Modern Art in Denmark, and Princeton University, USA. During these years, Gabo completed a large number of commissioned works, among which were several public monuments. ■ The stringing method, which became Gabo's signature technique during the American period, was now being used for site-specific monuments. Examples of large-scale constructions, consisting of open, metal, linear structures, were there for Gabo to see: the Eiffel Tower resembles a light wire structure; the same can be said of Vladimir Shukhov's Shabolovka Radio Tower in Moscow. Similarly, Tatlin's *Model for a Monument to the Third International* was a construction formed of thin vertical and spiral beams, permeable, woven from space. It was with great enthusiasm that Gabo, who had already tried to apply the stringing method in his sculptural design for the lobby of the Esso building (1949) and the suspended *Construction for the Baltimore Museum of Art* 1950–1, accepted the offer to execute a monumental construction for the exterior of the Bijenkorf (Beehive) commercial centre in

[121] Published by Lund Humphries, London and Harvard University Press, Cambridge, MA.

[122] The A.W. Mellon Lectures in Fine Arts published as *Of Divers Arts* in 1962.

Rotterdam. ■ Rotterdam was gradually being reconstructed from the ruins left by the Second World War. The appearance of the new city was shaped not only by architects but also by sculptors. Ossip Zadkine's *The Destroyed City* (*De Verwoeste Stad* 1952–3) became a symbol of grief for those lost, whereas the symbol of hope and vitality was Gabo's construction for the city centre. The story of the emergence of this work speaks of Gabo's profound desire to create a constructive monument in Europe. Prepared to make compromises in order to fulfil his dream, he discarded his first project (1954), a monumental wall relief, the central section of which elaborated the form of the beehive and three-dimensional elements, which echoed the *Linear Constructions.* The city planning commission turned the project down, stating a preference for a free-standing monument. 'I was called upon as an artist to make a sculpture to fill out a space 60 feet high, 45 wide and 12 feet deep, which the Town Planner demanded to be filled out with a bulge to follow a certain building-line along a street …' Gabo wrote to Read.[123]
■ Using another work that had never been built as a basis, his *Model for a Monument to the Unknown Political Prisoner*, Gabo developed its open linear forms with an expressive stringed core. The Rotterdam monument, twenty-five metres high, is constructed from concrete, steel, bronze wire and marble. An elongated steel form, based on the same principle as the *Spheric Theme*, grows upwards from the pavement. Its wings are twisted on the axis, slightly diverging along the sides of the arch before joining at the vertex. In the centre stands a bronze structure, made of rods developed further with wire stringing,

[123] Letter from Naum Gabo to Herbert Read, 19 November 1954, Yale.

Photograph of the model of the Bijenkorf
building in Rotterdam with Gabo's *Model of
the Relief Construction* 1954, 1954

→

Photograph of *Construction for the Bijenkorf
Building Rotterdam* 1956–7

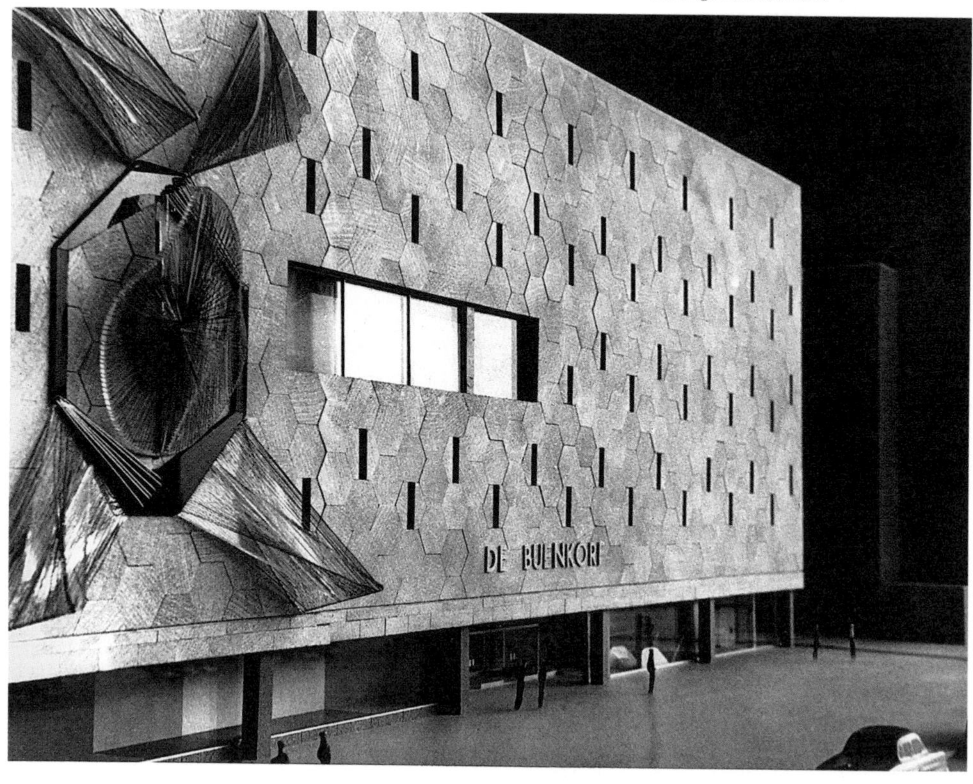

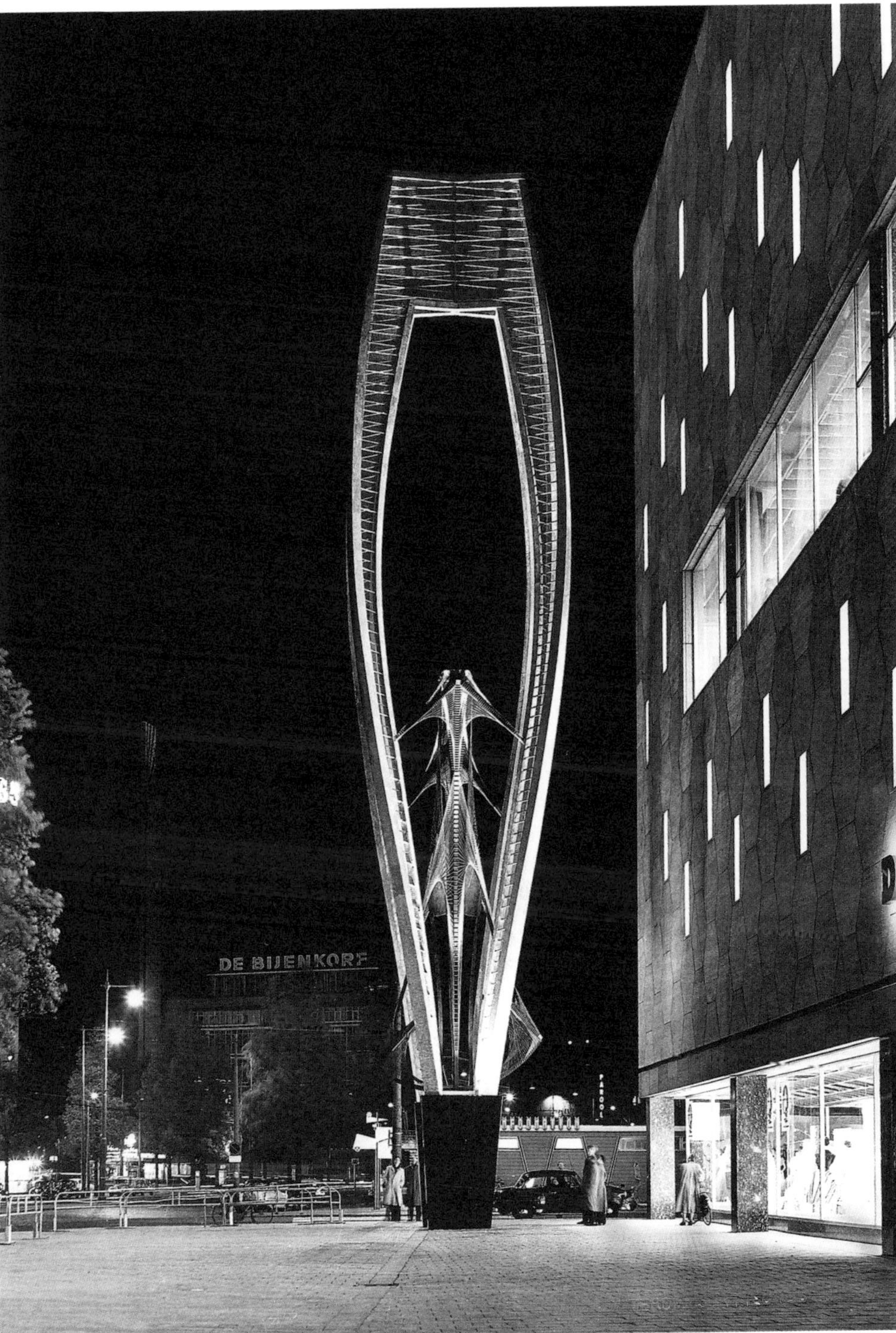

DE BIJENKORF

Photograph of the *Architectural Model for the Esso Building: 52nd Street Entrance* 1949 (detail), 1949

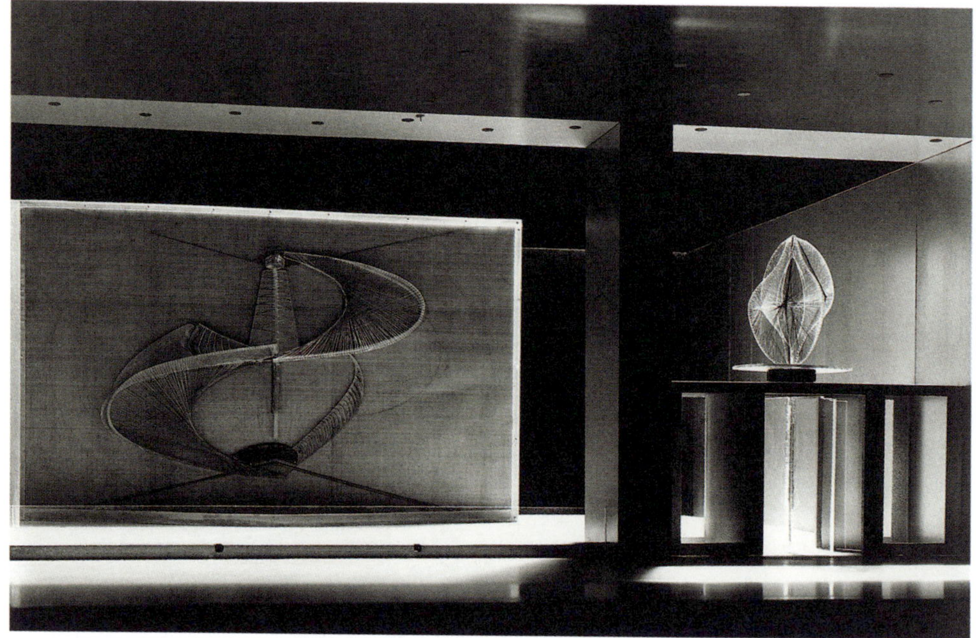

which bind the framework of the inner structure. From the front, the construction appears to be something of a symmetrical arc, whereas seen from the sides it resembles the tongue of a flame or a cathedral spire. In this work, Gabo succeeded in creating a symbiosis of rational construction, to which he was devoted in his early works, and more organic forms, characteristic of his works created from the 1940s onwards. ■ Gabo soon conceived an image of the construction and explained the idea in a letter to Read: 'I don't remember whether I have ever told you that I was building my construction on the principle of a tree, the image of which, above the

→ (p.184)
Photograph of Naum Gabo, Nina, Miriam,
Katherine Dreier and Nellie Van Doesburg
in Dreier's house, c.1947–8

Photograph of *Spheric Theme* 1972–4,
Princeton University

→ (p.185)
Photograph of Gabo by the monumental
version of *Constructed Head No.2* 1966
installed outside the Tate Gallery, 1969

roots, is the trunk and its branching limbs, in space – those were the main elements of my construction.'[124] The sculptor supervised the construction of the monument from beginning to end, altering the degree of twist in the principal beams and the angle of their slope, which speaks for his astounding intuition as an engineer. The open and penetrable structure of the sculpture, its curved and slightly twisted forms and the use of the stringing element all lend a particular harmony to the work. The monument is at the same time grand and light, tectonic and rhythmical, containing both symmetrical and asymmetrical shapes. ■ The sculptor was now working with both different coloured plastics and more traditional materials such as metal and stone. When his health did not allow him to employ his usual materials, Gabo turned to engravings and created a whole body of graphic works.[125] The *Opus* series of monoprints, intended as a collection of twelve engravings, was never completed in an album. The title recalls Gabo's long-standing interest in music as an art form with the strongest potential as constructive art. ■ Monochrome forms, floating in space, were printed on thin paper. According to Nina Williams, Gabo's first experiments were on toilet paper, after which he worked with different kinds of medium, preferring thin, semi-transparent sheets that were better viewed through a shaft of light. The laconic compositions of the monoprints are directly linked to the sculptures that Gabo was working on at the time. For example, *Opus 5* 1950 is based on a variation of those very forms that were used in the design of the unrealised project for the lobby of the Esso building in

[124] Letter from Naum Gabo to Herbert Read, 23 September 1955, Yale.

[125] Graham Williams, *Naum Gabo. Monoprints from Engraved Wood Blocks and Stencils*, The Florin Press, Kent 1987.

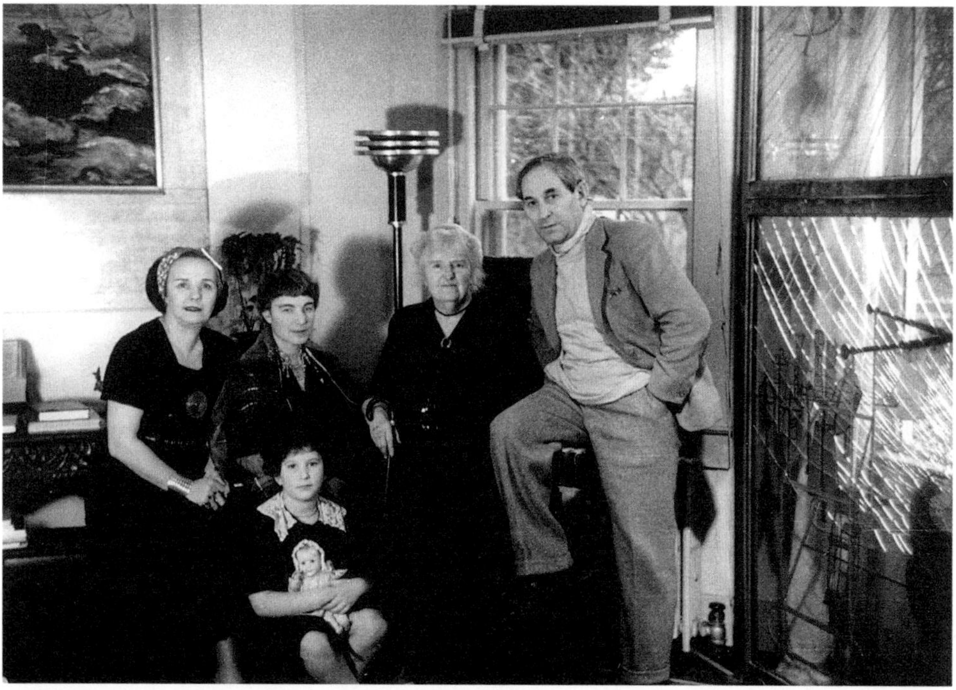

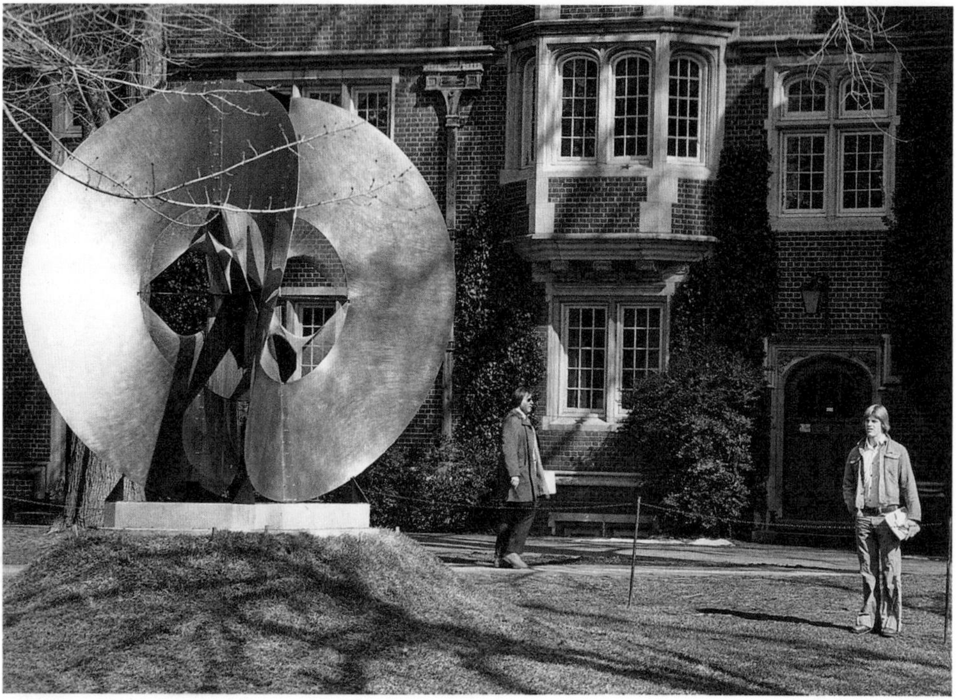

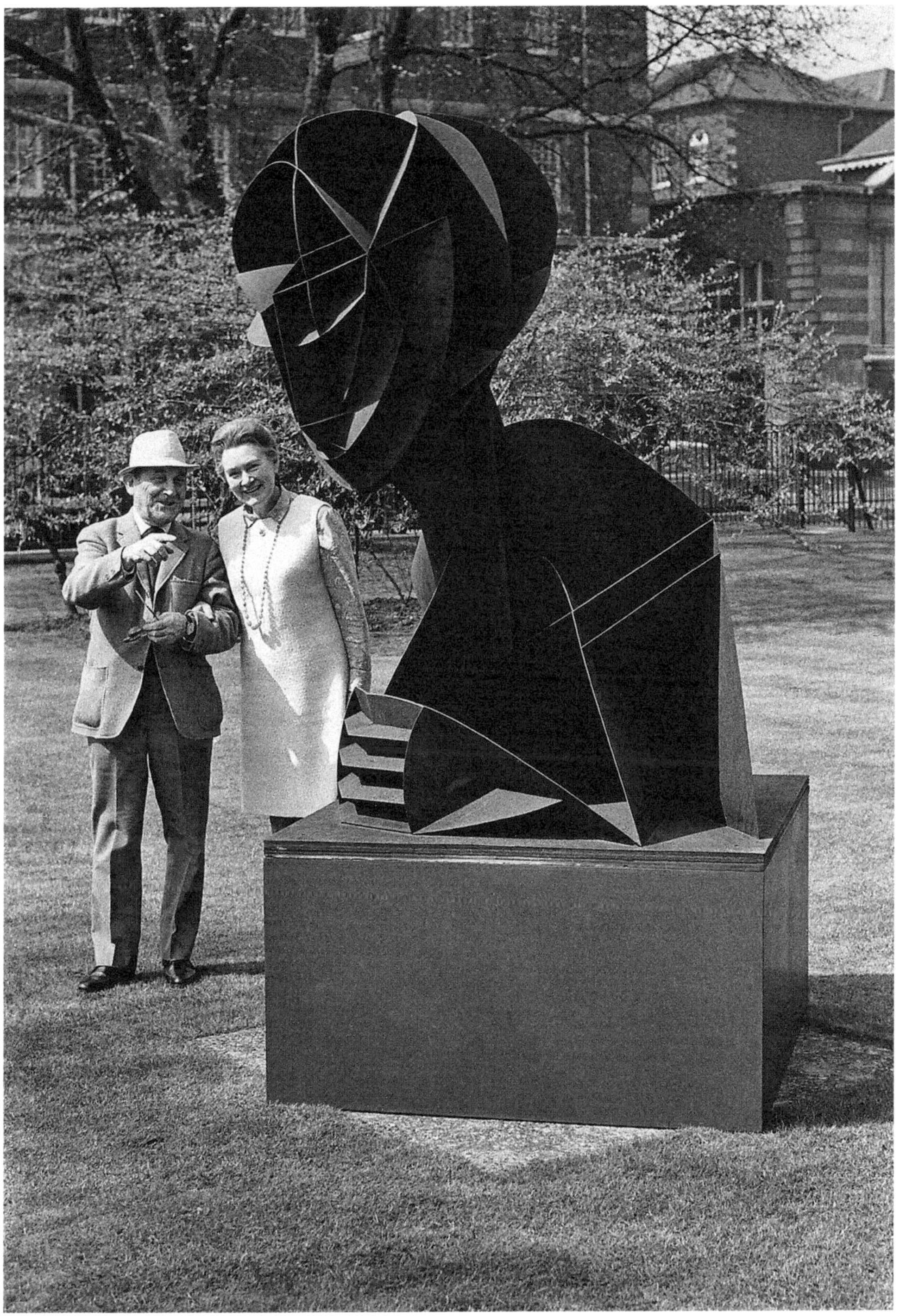

Photograph of *Relief Construction for the US Rubber Company Building* 1956, Rockefeller Centre, New York

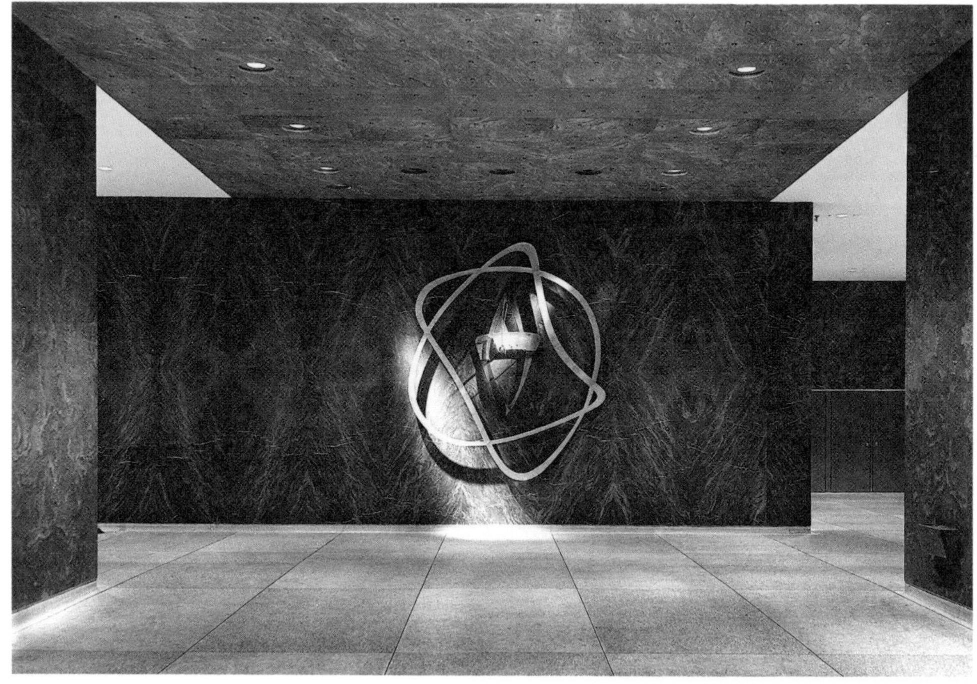

New York in 1949. The smooth transformation of three-dimensional structures into two-dimensional shapes, monumental works into engravings and vice versa is evident in *Opus 6* 1953 and *Relief Construction for the US Rubber Company Building* 1956. The Gabo archive contains a plastic prototype transformed by Gabo into an engraving, which also served as a template for the model of *Relief Construction.* Two streamlined forms, intersecting on the surface of the stone wall, frame a flame-like shape in its centre. If the three-dimensional *Relief Construction* is seen as dynamised by rotating

Opus 3 1950
Relief print on paper, 20.3 x 14.4

Opus 5 1950
Relief print on paper, 24.3 x 30.2

→ (p.188)
Opus 6 1955–6
Relief print on paper, 38.5 x 33.4

→ (p.189)
Cover Design for a Portfolio of Prints c.1975
Wax crayon and printer's ink with roller on
paper, 51.1 x 43.2

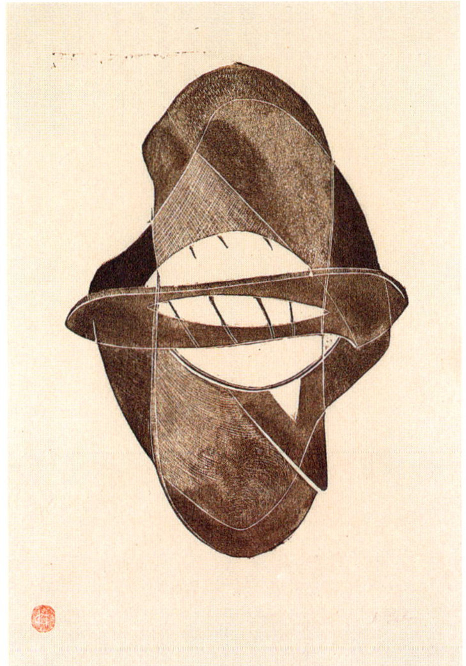

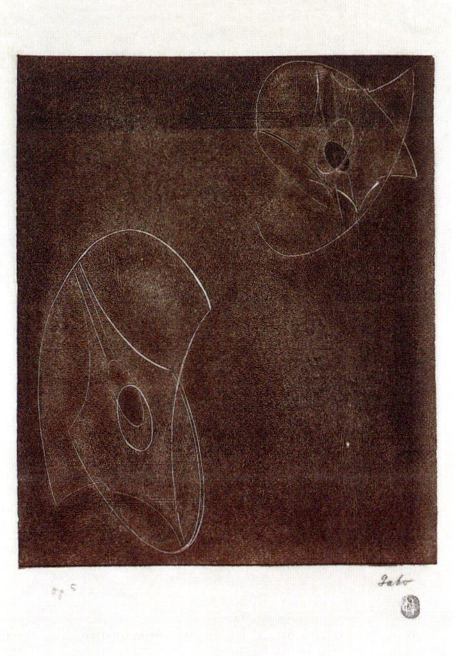

motion, the same form in the flat engraving possesses the dynamics of a three-dimensional object, as if free-falling in space. ■ At the very end of the 1950s, Gabo's family life was about to take an unforeseen but happy turn. In 1959, Gabo received an unexpected letter from the director of the Whitney Museum informing him that a letter addressed to him had been sent by someone in the USSR who had apparently known Gabo during childhood and had preserved the sculptor's letters and documents. On opening the enclosed letter, Gabo recognised the handwriting of his younger brother, Alexei.

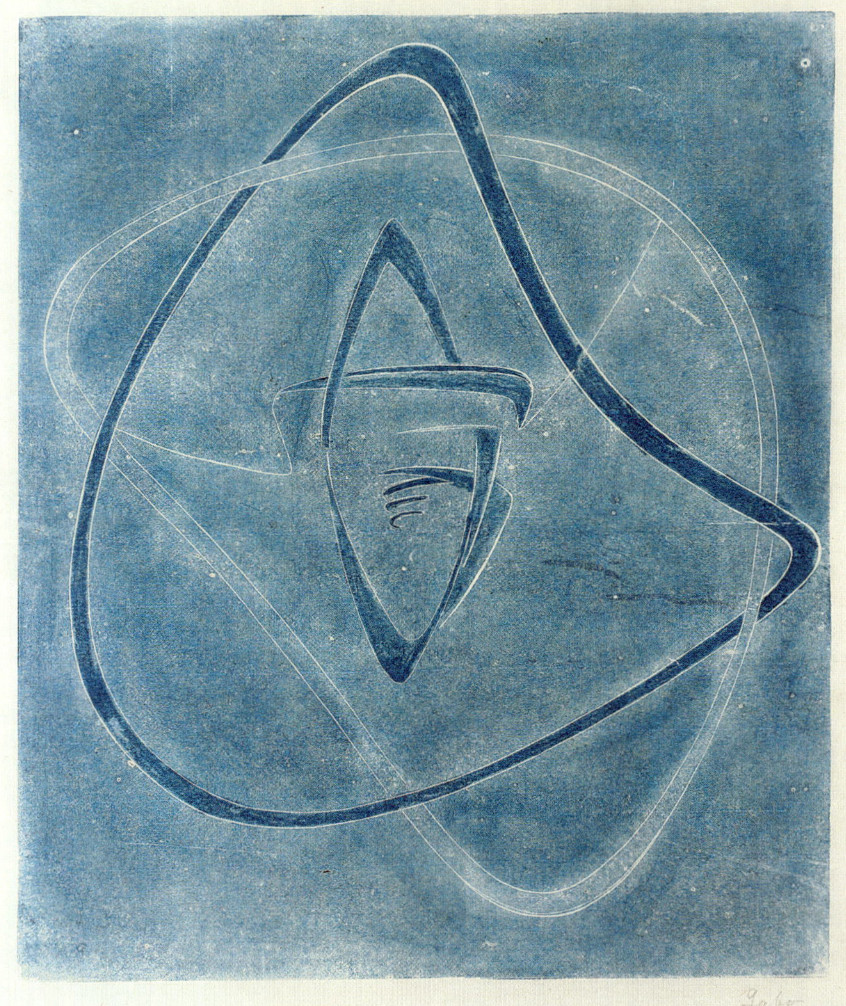

Opus 6
Gabo

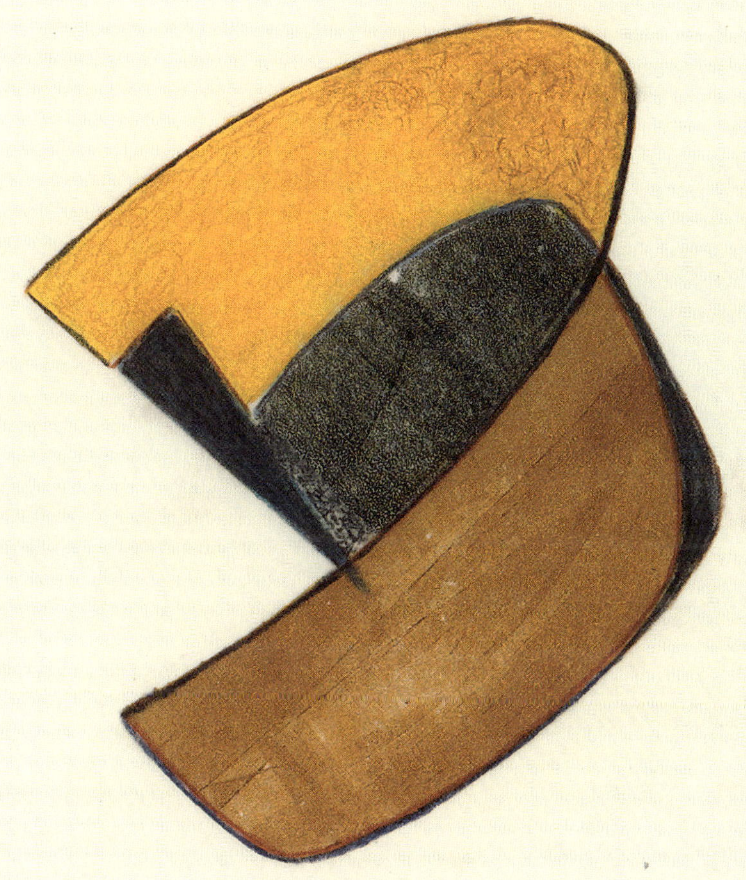

Сентябрь 24. 1959

Дорогой мой, любимый мой, брат мой
Нехем!

Неужели я нашел тебя? Ты жив!

Я ищу тебя уже много лет! Я пишу тебе в радости, но глаза мои полны слез. Почему ты ни разу не попытался дать о себе знать? Ведь так много перемен произошло! Или ты еще и сейчас не намерен выйти на свет из тени прошлого?

Сегодня я получил ответ из Нью-Йорка от мистера Lloyd Goodrich'a; он любезно сообщил мне твой адрес. Копию моего письма к нему он переслал тебе. Не удивляйся его содержанию. Что еще я мог придумать, чтобы оправдать мое обращение к нему?

На Американской выставке в Москве я осматривал

*Kinetic Spheric Theme (Monument
to the Astronauts)* 1966, unfinished
Muntz-metal, plastic and stainless steel
gauze, 54.3 x 54.7

Model for Monument to the Astronauts
c.1966–8
Plastic, plastic-coated paper and pencil,
8.9 x 7.6 x 5.7

←
Letter from Alexei Pevsner to Gabo,
24 September 1959

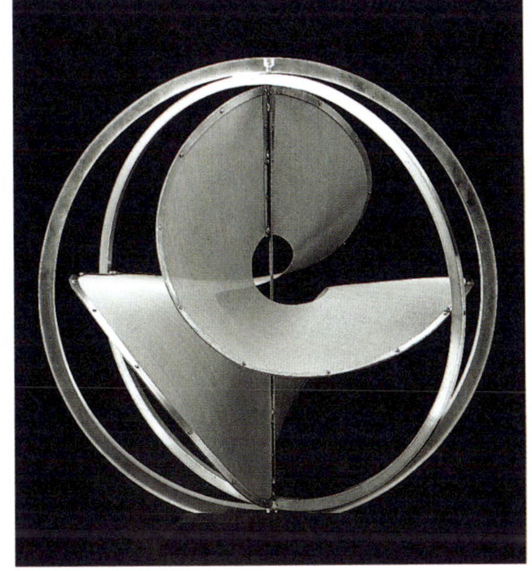

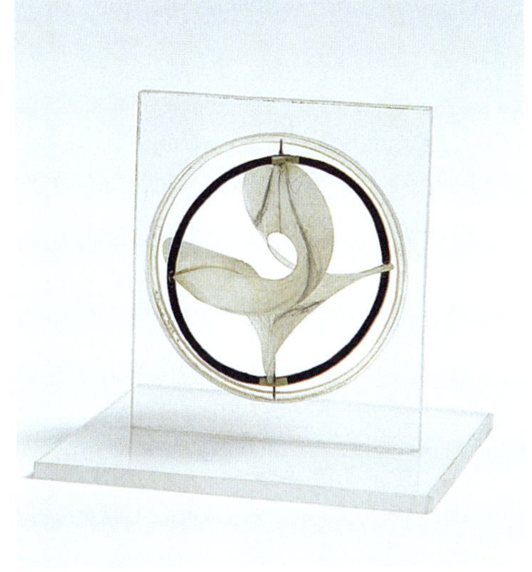

The sculptor's daughter recalls this being the first time that she saw her father cry. Gabo regained a family that, for the last twenty-five years, he had considered lost forever, as contact with his relatives in the USSR had been cut off since 1936. The brothers began a lively correspondence. Gabo told his brother about his success as an artist and his happiness as a family man. Alexei wrote to Gabo about their parents, who had passed away, and about brothers, sisters and nephews who were all in good health. Alexei had for many years kept works and documents from Gabo's first years as an artist including watercolours from the 1910s, photographs of his student years and the period of the First World War and the 1917 Revolution, a copy of *The Realistic Manifesto* and early drawings. Alexei threw all his energy into searching for works by Gabo and Antoine Pevsner

$\rightarrow$

Photograph of Gabo working on *Linear Construction in Space No.4*, 1957

in the holdings of Soviet museums, resulting in his discovery of a number of paintings by Pevsner and Gabo's *Project for the Palace of Soviets.* In addition to bringing his brother up to date with the latest trends in Soviet art, Alexei introduced young, innovative Soviet artists to Gabo's works. He served similarly as a link between his brother and the first soviet researchers of prohibited avant-garde art. The touching correspondence between the brothers is preserved in the Tate Archive and consists of hundreds of letters sent between them from 1959 to 1977. ■ In 1962, forty years after leaving his native country, Gabo was able to return to the USSR. As a tourist, he visited Leningrad, Moscow and Sochi, saw his siblings and was introduced to his nephews. This was Gabo's last trip to his homeland. Alexei, having acquired all the necessary export documents, sent Gabo his early studies and drawings in America; other photographs and documents he took himself when he went to visit the Gabo family in Connecticut in 1968. Alexei's recollections of Gabo's and Antoine's youth and the early years of Gabo's creative career were published in Amsterdam in 1964, illustrated by original photographs and correspondence from his collection.[126] ■ At this last stage of his creative career, Gabo showed particular interest in metal as a medium for small and large-scale projects alike. He reinterpreted some of his earlier works, such as *Constructed Head No.2* and *Constructed Head No.3*, *Torsion* and *Spheric Theme*, now using phosphor-bronze or stainless steel. The shining metal frameworks of the constructions are embellished with metal stringing. The dynamic element of the compositions is sometimes achieved by technical means, as

[126] *Biographical Sketch* 1964.

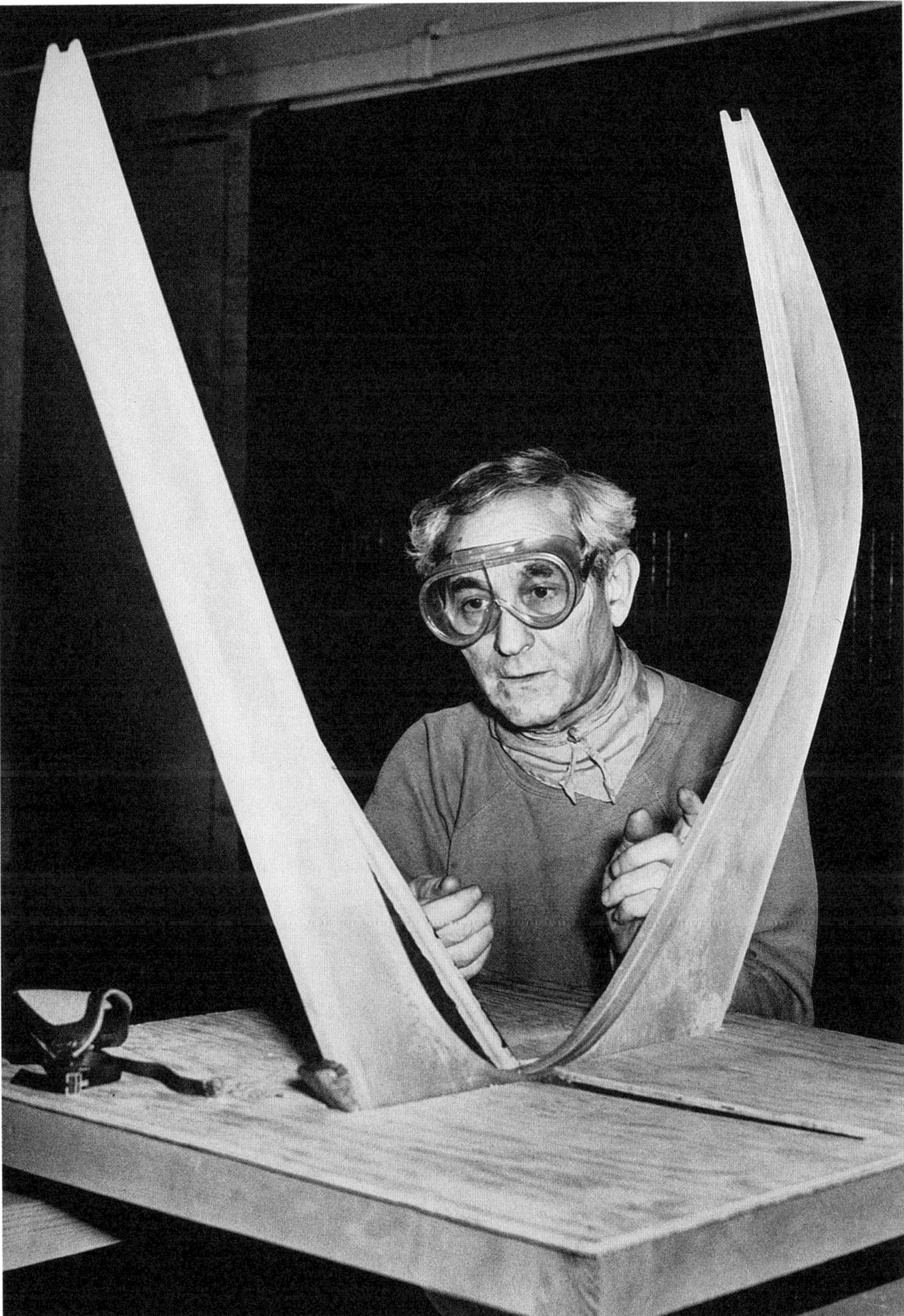

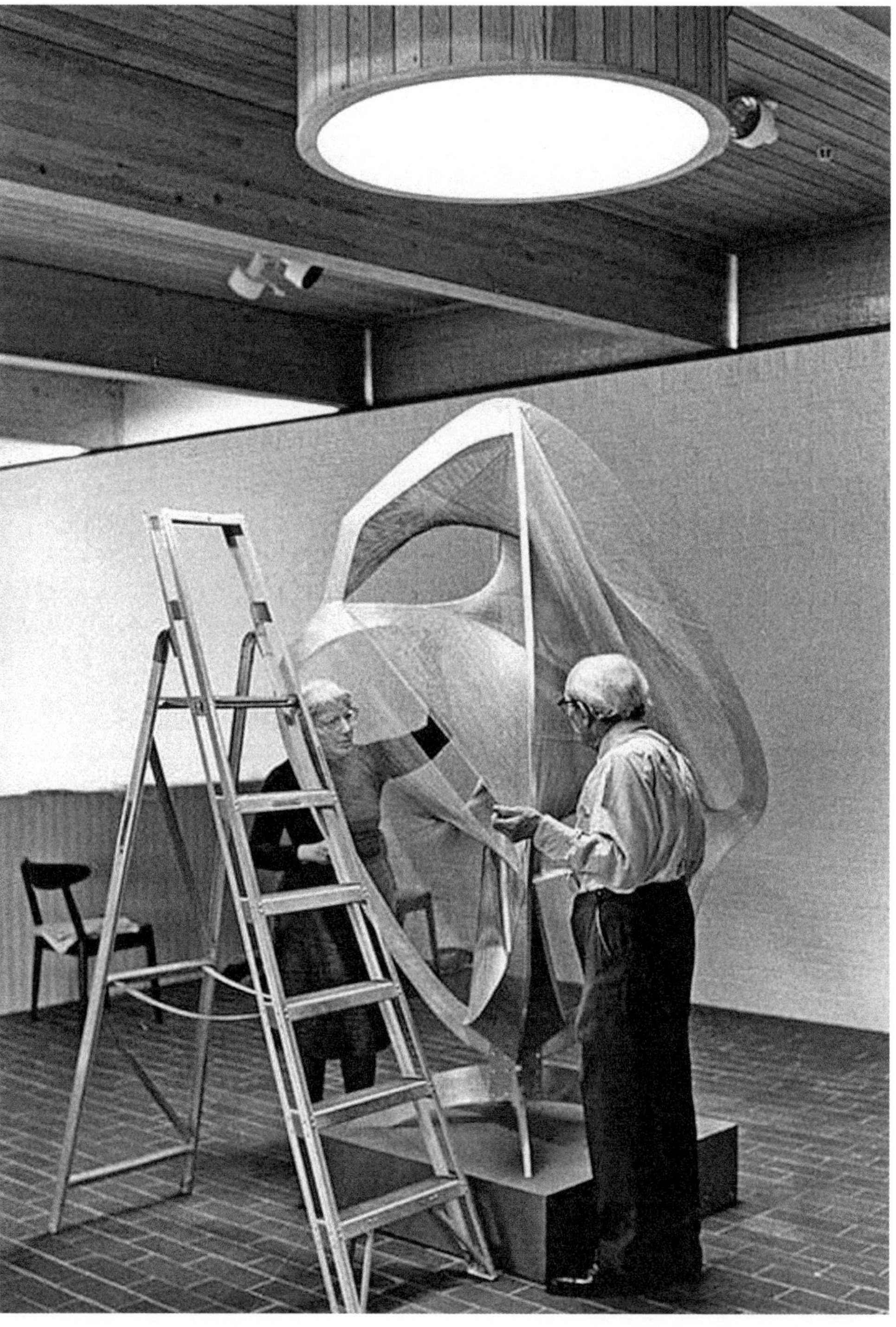

←

Photograph of Naum and Miriam Gabo at
the installation of *Linear Construction in
Space No.4* 1970, Louisiana Museum
of Modern Art, Denmark, 1970

in *Vertical Construction No.2* 1965–6, which rotates around its axis thanks to a motorised device hidden in its base. Whereas in the 1950s Gabo received commissions for site-specific monumental projects, in the 1960s he aimed to fulfil his long-standing dream of seeing his earlier works in the form of public monuments – the embodiment of his constructive idea. It was for this reason that he switched from Perspex to more stable materials. It also became increasingly difficult for him to work on his own and, from the 1960s, he was aided by an assistant, Charles Wilson, a sculptor who specialised in welding metalwork. The majority of sculptures of this late period were created with Wilson's help, as were the attempts to restore and reconstruct earlier works of Gabo's Berlin period. ■ The 1960s were a time of real triumph for Gabo. His book *Of Divers Arts* was published in 1962 and its emergence marked the definitive recognition of the sculptor as a classic master of modernism. The text is different from all his previous writings, as Gabo included narratives of various stories and recollections mixed up with biographical facts, presenting his life as a kind of quest for the 'constructive idea'. In his practical work, Gabo was taken by the intention of creating a monument to man – conqueror of the cosmos. He started to work on a model of *Kinetic Spheric Theme (Monument to the Astronauts)* in 1966, but it was never completed. His favourite theme was reinterpreted again as a core element of the composition set on a metallic rod so that it rotated around its axis inside a spherical space defined by two circular orbits. ■ During this period, Gabo made frequent trips to Europe, where he was busy with the organisation and installation of retrospective exhibitions, which toured Amsterdam and Duisburg, Zurich and London, Berlin, Grenoble and Lisbon in 1965–6 and 1971–2. Gabo continued to work throughout his last years. He was able to see his most treasured ideas come to life, while his sculptures became classic examples of twentieth-century art and his more audacious projects were realised as monuments, embellishing public spaces, buildings and museums. During these years, succumbing to pressure from friends and family, he set about writing his memoirs. His notes and recollections include detailed images of a distant past – his childhood in the countryside, school years in Bryansk and Tomsk, the return to his homeland engulfed by the outbreak of revolution in 1917. All his last memories are connected with Russia, from which he had been estranged for most of his life: 'Well, it will soon be 85 years since the day of my birth and, despite the long path my life has taken and when I scrutinise everything I have been through, I see only my own image which stands out brighter than the rest – the image of myself as a young boy, saturated to the core by Russia, its people, its nature, its songs, language, its land and sky … '[127] ■ Gabo passed away in hospital on 23 August 1977 after many years of fighting old age and illness. His daughter Nina recalls: 'He died considering himself a Russian artist. Papa's last words were in Russian.'[128]

[127] Naum Gabo, *K portretam*, p.148, TGA.

[128] From a conversation with the author, Kent, 2011

BG – Gabo-Archiv, Künstler-Archive, Berlinische Galerie, Berlin.

Biographical Sketch 1964 – Alexei Pevsner, *A Biographical Sketch of my Brothers, Naum Gabo and Antoine Pevsner*, Augustin and Schoonman, Amsterdam 1964.

Catalogue Raisonné 1985 – Colin Sanderson and Christina Lodder, 'Catalogue Raisonné of the Constructions and Sculptures of Naum Gabo', in S. Nash and J. Merkert (eds.), *Naum Gabo: Sixty Years of Constructivism*, Prestel Verlag, Munich 1985, pp.193–272.

Circle 1937 – J.L. Martin, Ben Nicholson, N. Gabo (eds.), *Circle: International Survey of Constructive Art*, Faber and Faber, London 1937.

Competition for the Palace of Soviets 1993 – *Naum Gabo and the Competition for the Palace of Soviets Moscow 1931–1933*, Berlinische Galerie, Berlin 1993.

Constructing Modernity 2000 – Martin Hammer and Christina Lodder, *Constructing Modernity: The Art and Career of Naum Gabo*, Yale University Press, New Haven, CT 2000.

Gabo 1957 – Naum Gabo, *Gabo: Constructions, Sculpture, Paintings, Drawings and Engravings*, Lund Humphries, London and Harvard University Press, Cambridge, MA 1957.

Gabo on Gabo 2000 – M. Hammer and C. Lodder, *Gabo on Gabo. Texts and Interviews*. Forest Row, East Sussex, Artists Bookworks 2000.

Of Divers Arts 1962 – Naum Gabo, *Of Divers Arts*, Bollingen Series XXXV, Bollingen Foundation 1962.

Sixty Years of Constructivism 1985 – S. Nash and J. Merkert (eds.), *Naum Gabo: Sixty Years of Constructivism*, Prestel Verlag, Munich 1985.

TGA – TGA9313, Tate Archive, London.

Yale – Naum Gabo Papers, Yale Collection of American Literature, Beinecke Rare Book and Manuscript Library, Yale University, New Haven, CT.

Naum Gabo's original works, writings and archival materials
© Nina and Graham Williams
Photographic reproductions of all works and archival materials from
Tate Collection and Archive © Tate, 2012

Photograph of Naum Gabo c.1933
Tate Archive
p.1

Photograph of Naum Gabo in his studio with *Torsion: Project for a Fountain* 1970–3
Tate Archive
p.2

INTRODUCTION
Self-Portrait 1912
Oil on canvas
56 x 47.5
Private collection
p.8

CHILDHOOD AND STUDENT YEARS (1890–1914)
Antoine Pevsner
1884–1962
Portrait of Mother 1911
Oil on canvas
38 x 36 (oval)
Photograph: Graham Williams
Tate Archive
© Association 'Les Amis d'Antoine

Pevsner', Paris/DACS, London 2012
p.13

Map of town of Bryansk with Railway Station suburb, 1906 (detail)
The State Archive of the Bryansk Region
p.14

View of Railway Station suburb, town of Bryansk, 1900s
Postcard
p.15

Photograph of Boris Pevsner, c.1912
Tate Archive
p.15

Photograph of Naum Gabo aged about fourteen, c.1905
Tate Archive
p.15

Photograph of Mark and Eremei Pevsner on horseback, 1920–30
Tate Archive
p.17

Photograph of Naum Gabo in front of Munich University, c.1913
Tate Archive
p.21

Photograph of Pevsner family picnic in Russia, c.1910
Tate Archive
p.21

Christmas c.1912
Pastel on paper
36.3 x 45
Private collection
p.23

First page of the
manuscript *Concerning
my Brothers Naum
Gabo and Antoine
Pevsner. Biographical
Sketch of Alexei
Pevsner*, 1960
Tate Archive
p.24

GABO'S
CONSTRUCTIONS
AND RUSSIAN
CONSTRUCTIVISM
(1914–22)
A page with Norway
period photographs,
from the manuscript
*Naum Gabo.
Biographical Sketch of
Alexei Pevsner*, 1960
Tate Archive
p.29

Photograph of
Constructed Head No.1
c.1915
Tate Archive
p.31

*Two Cubes
(Demonstrating the
Stereometric Method)*
1930
Painted plywood,
two objects, each
30.5 x 30.5 x 30.5
Tate
p.31

*Studies of Mother
and Child* c.1916–17
Pencil on card
30 x 26
Private collection
p.32

*Study of Female
Torso* c.1916
Pencil on paper
48 x 35
Collection: Naum Gabo
Archives, Berlinische
Galerie, Landesmuseum
für Moderne Kunst,
Fotografie und
Architektur, Berlin
p.33

*Study for Constructed
Head No.2* c.1916
Blue pencil on paper
18 x 11
Collection of Nina
and Graham Williams
p.33

*Model for Constructed
Head No.3
(Head in
a Corner Niche)*
1916–17
Cardboard
61 x 48.5 x 34.5
Private collection
p.34

Constructed Head No.1
c.1915
Plywood
53.5 high
Städel Museum,
Frankfurt am Main
p.35

Photograph of
Constructed Head No.2
c.1916, 1924
Tate Archive
p.37

*Constructed Head
No.3 (Head in a Corner
Niche)* 1964
Bronze
62.2 x 70 x 35
Collection: Naum Gabo
Archives, Berlinische
Galerie, Landesmuseum
für Moderne Kunst,
Fotografie und
Architektur, Berlin
p.38

Photograph of Gabo and
Snezhka by *Constructed
Head No.2* 1966,
Middlebury,
Connecticut, 1967
Collection of Nina
and Graham Williams
p.39

Constructed Head No.2
c.1916
Galvanised iron
45 x 43.2 x 43.2
Private collection
p.40

Photograph of templates
for *Constructed
Head No.2* prior to
conservation, 1995
Tate Sculpture
Conservation
Department files
p.43

*Model for Constructed
Torso* c.1917,
reassembled 1981
Cardboard
39.5 x 29 x 16
Tate
p.44

*Study for Constructed
Torso* 1916
Pencil on paper
42.2 x 33
Collection: Naum Gabo
Archives, Berlinische
Galerie, Landesmuseum
für Moderne Kunst,
Fotografie und
Architektur, Berlin
p.45

Naum Gabo's
photographic
identification
document, c.1917
Tate Archive
p.49

Photograph of
Constructed Torso
1917 at the *First
Russian Art Exhibition*,
Berlin, 1922
Collection of Nina
and Graham Williams
p.49

*Kinetic Construction
(Standing Wave)*
1919–20, replica 1985
Metal, painted
wood and electrical
mechanism
61.6 x 24.1 x 19
Tate
p.53

Cover and list of
Gabo sculptures in
the *Constructivistes
russes: Gabo et
Pevsner – Peintures,
Constructions*
catalogue, Galerie
Percier, Paris, 1924
Collection of Nina
and Graham Williams
p.85

Photograph of Gabo
in his studio, Berlin,
1920–30
Tate Archive
p.87

*Construction in Space:
Diagonal* c.1925,
reassembled 1986
Glass, metal and
celluloid
61 x 16.3 x 16
Tate
p.88

*Monument for an
Airdrome (Variant of
1924)* c.1933, this
version 1948
Perspex and brass
41.6 x 108 x 57.7
Tate
p.89

*Monument for an
Institute of Physics
and Mathematics*
c.1924, reassembled
1990
Brass, plastic and
crystal, 44 high
Collection of
Gareth Williams

© Gareth Williams
p.90

Rotating Fountain
c.1925, reassembled
1986
Metal and plastic
44 x 40 x 40
Tate
p.91

Circular Relief c.1926
Plastic on wood
49.8 x 49.8 x 22.9
Tate
p.94

Torsion c.1929,
this version 1937
Perspex
35.2 x 41 x 40
Tate
p.95

Photograph of *Revolving
Torsion: Fountain*
1972–3 outside
St Thomas's Hospital,
London
Collection of Nina
and Graham Williams
p.97

Production photograph
of *La Chatte* 1927,
1927
Tate Archive
p.99

Photograph of stage
set for *La Chatte* 1927,
1927
Tate Archive
p.99

Antoine Pevsner
1884–1962
*Model for the Statue of
Aphrodite in the Ballet
La Chatte* 1927
Plastic
14.9 x 4.4 x 5.1
Tate
© Association 'Les Amis
d'Antoine Pevsner',
Paris/DACS, London
2012
p.100

Photograph of Alice
Nikitina in her
La Chatte costume,
dedicated to Gabo,
1928
Tate Archive
p.101

*Drawing of the Stage
Design for* La Chatte
1927
Tate Archive
p.102

Photograph of Alicia
Markova with the *Model
for the Set of* La Chatte
1927 at the Tate
Sculpture Conservation
Department, 1988
Tate Archive
p.102

Photograph of Gabo,
Antoine and Virginie
Pevsner in Berlin,
1920–30
Tate Archive
p.104

Costume Sketch for
La Chatte 1927
Graph paper, pencil
and pastel
25.5 x 19
Private collection
p.104

Costume Sketch for
La Chatte 1927
Paper, pencil and pastel
26.7 x 21
Private collection
p.105

*Design for Palace of
Soviets: Plan of First
Level and Foundations*
1931
Pencil and india ink
on paper
99 x 86
Photograph: courtesy of
the A.V. Shchusev State
Research Museum of
Architecture, Moscow
p.110

*Design for Palace of
Soviets: Plan of Main
Hall and Section* 1931
Pencil and india
ink on paper
98.3 x 85.5
Photograph: courtesy of
the A.V. Shchusev State
Research Museum of
Architecture, Moscow
p.111

*Design for Palace of
Soviets: Two Elevations
and Section* 1931
Pencil and india
ink on paper

98 x 145.3
Photograph: courtesy of
the A.V. Shchusev State
Research Museum of
Architecture, Moscow
p.113

*Design for Palace
of Soviets, Façade of
the Small Hall* 1931
Pencil on graph paper
23.2 x 26
Collection: Naum Gabo
Archives, Berlinische
Galerie, Landesmuseum
für Moderne Kunst,
Fotografie und
Architektur, Berlin
p.113

**CREATIVITY AND THE
WAR: THE BRITISH
PERIOD (1936–46)**
Photograph of Gabo
and Ben Nicholson on
the beach, Cornwall,
c.1942
Tate Archive
p.118

Photograph of Gabo
and Miriam in London,
c.1936
Tate Archive
p.123

*Spheric Theme:
Transparent Variation*
c.1937
Celluloid and Perspex
21.5 diameter
Private collection
p.127

*Construction in Space:
Stone with a Collar*
c.1933, this version
c.1936–7
Stone, cellulose acetate,
slate and brass
37 x 72 x 55
Tate
p.127

Photograph of
*Construction in Space:
Crystal* 1937
Collection of Nina
and Graham Williams
p.129

Study for *Construction
in Space: Crystal* c.1937
Pencil on paper
24 x 20.5
Collection: Naum Gabo
Archives, Berlinische
Galerie, Landesmuseum
für Moderne Kunst,
Fotografie und
Architektur, Berlin
p.130

Photograph of
*Construction in Space:
Crystal* exhibited in
Chicago in April 1953
Collection of Nina
and Graham Williams
p.131

Press cutting regarding
Gabo's *Construction in
Space: Crystal* 1938–9
at the *Decorative
Arts exhibition,*
San Francisco, 1939
Tate Archive
p.131

Photograph of *Model for
Spheric Construction:
Fountain* 1938 and
*Model for Spheric
Theme* 1937
Collection of Nina
and Graham Williams
p.132

*Card Model for Spheric
Theme* [1936–51]
Tate Archive
p.132

Ernst Haeckel
1834–1919
Legion Nassellaria,
an illustration from the
*Report on the Scientific
Results of the Voyage
of* HMS Challenger
*during the Years
1873–1876*
p.132

*Model for a Monument
to the Unknown
Political Prisoner* 1952
Plastic and wire mesh
38.1 x 8.9 x 9.5
Tate
p.134

*Construction in Space:
Arch No.2* c.1958,
this version 1963
Phosphor-bronze,
copper and stainless
steel spring wire
82.6 high
Private collection
p.135

Conservation
photograph of
a fragment for
*Construction in Space:
Arch No.2*
Tate Archive
p.135

*Sketch for Spheric
Theme* 1937
Blue pencil on paper
19.7 x 32.1
Tate
p.136

Spiral Theme 1941
Cellulose acetate
and Perspex
14 x 24.4 x 24.4
Tate
p.141

Spiral Theme 1941
Cellulose acetate
and Perspex
14 x 24.4 x 24.4
Tate
p.141

*Sketch for Spiral
Theme* c.1941 (detail)
Pencil on paper
12.4 x 24.1
Tate
p.141

Photograph of Naum
Gabo and Miriam in
London, c.1937
Tate Archive
p.143

Cover of *Book No.1*
of Gabo's war diaries,
1939–41
Tate Archive
p.144

Book No.2 of Gabo's war
diaries, 1941–2
Tate Archive
p.145

Notes and press cutting
related to the January
1941 events,
Gabo's war diaries
Tate Archive
p.146–7

Photograph of Gabo in
his studio in Carbis Bay,
Cornwall, c.1945
Photograph: Studio
St Ives
Tate Archive
p.148

Photograph of Gabo
and Nina on the beach
in Carbis Bay, c.1943
Collection of Nina
and Graham Williams
p.148

Kinetic Stone Carving
1936–44
Portland stone
25.5 x 36.5 x 25.5
Tate
p.150

Strontium 1945
Oil on cardboard
22.5 x 29.5
Private collection
p.152

*Landscape Garden View
with Sculpture* c.1938
Pencil and oil on
cardboard
19 x 24
Tate Archive
p.153

Photograph of the
*Jowett Car Model
1944,* 1944
Tate Archive
p.154

Photographs of designs
for a coat hanger, 1937
Tate Archive
p.155

'HEAVENLY
INSTRUMENTS':
THE TECHNIQUE OF
LINEAR STRINGING
*Linear Construction in
Space No.1* 1942–3
Acrylic and nylon
34.9 x 34.9 x 8.9
Tate
p.157

Barbara Hepworth
1903–75
*Sculpture with Colour
(Deep Blue and Red)*
1940
Cast material and
mixed media
10.5 x 14.9 x 10.5
Tate
© Bowness,
Hepworth Estate
p.161

Henry Moore
1898–1986
Stringed Figure 1938/60
Bronze and elastic string
27.3 x 34.4 x 19.7
Tate
Photograph: Reproduced
by permission of The
Henry Moore Foundation
p.161

Photograph of Gabo,
Barbara Hepworth and
Henry Moore at Herbert
Read's memorial display
at the Tate Gallery, 1970
Tate Archive
p.162

Prototype of *Linear
Construction in
Space No.1* 1942
Plastic, silk and cotton
threads 28 x 28 x 5
Tate Archive
p.162

*Linear Construction
in Space No.1* 1942,
this version c.1952
Perspex and nylon
21 x 21 x 5.5
Private collection
p.163

Photograph of *Linear
Construction in
Space No.2* 1942,
this version 1970
Collection of Nina
and Graham Williams
p.166

*Linear Construction in
Space No.2* 1970–1
Acrylic and nylon
113 x 60 x 59
Tate
p.167

Conservation photograph
of a fragment for *Linear
Construction
in Space No.2*
Tate Archive
p.168

Photograph of Gabo
in his studio with
the frame for *Linear
Construction in
Space No.2,*
late 1950s
Tate Archive
p.169

Photograph of
*Revolving Torsion:
Fountain* 1972–3
outside St Thomas's
Hospital, London
Tate Archive
p.173

*Vertical
Construction No.2*
1965–6
Stainless steel
and stainless
steel spring wire
292 high
Private collection
p.174

*Construction in
Space: Suspended
(Variation)* 1957,
this version 1971

Perspex, nylon,
phosphor-bronze
on aluminium
and Perspex base
53 x 61.9 x 55.9
Private collection
p.175

Bronze Spheric Theme
c.1960
Phosphor-bronze on
wooden base
92.1 x 66.7 x 72.4
Tate
p.175

Photograph of
Spheric Theme
1969–70 outside
the Munch Museum,
Oslo
Collection of Nina
and Graham Williams
p.175

MONUMENTS FOR
THE NEW WORLD
(1946–77)
Cover of *Naum Gabo
– Antoine Pevsner*
exhibition catalogue,
MoMA, New York, 1948
p.177

Photograph of
the model of the
Bijenkorf building in
Rotterdam with Gabo's
*Model of the Relief
Construction* 1954,
1954
Collection of Nina
and Graham Williams
p.180

Photograph of
*Construction for
the Bijenkorf Building
Rotterdam* 1956–7
Collection of Nina
and Graham Williams
p.181

Photograph of the
*Architectural Model
for the Esso Building:
52nd Street Entrance*
1949 (detail), 1949
Collection of Nina
and Graham Williams
p.182

Photograph of Naum
Gabo, Nina, Miriam,
Katherine Dreier and
Nellie Van Doesburg
in Dreier's house,
c.1947–8
Tate Archive
p.184

Photograph of *Spheric
Theme* 1972–4,
Princeton University
Collection of Nina
and Graham Williams
p.184

Photograph of Gabo
by the monumental
version of *Constructed
Head No.2* 1966
installed outside
the Tate
Gallery, 1969
Collection of Nina
and Graham Williams
p.185

Photograph of *Relief
Construction for the
US Rubber Company
Building* 1956,
Rockefeller Centre,
New York
Collection of Nina
and Graham Williams
p.186

Opus 3 1950
Relief print on paper
20.3 x 14.4
Tate
p.187

Opus 5 1950
Relief print on paper
24.3 x 30.2
Tate
p.187

Opus 6 1955–6
Relief print on paper
38.5 x 33.4
Tate
p.188

*Cover Design for
a Portfolio of Prints*
c.1975
Wax crayon and
printer's ink with roller
on paper
51.1 x 43.2
Tate
p.189

Letter from Alexei
Pevsner to Gabo,
24 September 1959
Tate Archive
p.190

*Kinetic Spheric Theme
(Monument to the
Astronauts)* 1966,
unfinished
Muntz-metal,
plastic and stainless
steel gauze
54.3 x 54.7
Private collection
p.191

*Model for Monument
to the Astronauts*
c.1966–8
Plastic, plastic-coated
paper and pencil
8.9 x 7.6 x 5.7
Tate
p.191

Photograph of Gabo
working on *Linear
Construction in
Space No.4*, 1957
Photograph:
Don A. Coviello
Tate Archive
p.193

Photograph of Naum
and Miriam Gabo at
the installation of *Linear
Construction in Space
No.4* 1970, Louisiana
Museum of Modern Art,
Denmark, 1970
Tate Archive
p.194